WARBIRD FACTORY

NORTH AMERICAN AVIATION IN WORLD WAR II

WARBIRD FACTORY

John Fredrickson

ZENITH
PRESS

This book is dedicated to the memory of 1st Lt. Winton R. Wey, a twenty-four-year-old flight-test engineer who perished in the wreck of an experimental B-25 Mitchell attack bomber, known as NA-98X, at the Inglewood warbird factory on the evening of April 24, 1944.

Quarto is the authority on a wide range of topics.

Quarto educates, entertains and enriches the lives of our readers—enthusiasts and lovers of hands-on living.

www.quartoknows.com

© 2015 Quarto Publishing Group USA Inc.
Text © 2015 John Frederickson

First published in 2015 by Zenith Press, an imprint of Quarto Publishing Group USA Inc., 400 First Avenue North, Suite 400, Minneapolis, MN 55401 USA. Telephone: (612) 344-8100 Fax: (612) 344-8692

quartoknows.com
Visit our blogs at quartoknows.com

Zenith Press titles are also available at discounts in bulk quantity for industrial or sales-promotional use. For details contact the Special Sales Manager at Quarto Publishing Group USA Inc., 400 First Avenue North, Suite 400, Minneapolis, MN 55401 USA.

10 9 8 7 6 5 4 3 2 1

ISBN: 978-0-7603-4816-1

Library of Congress Cataloging-in-Publication Data

Fredrickson, John.
  Warbird factory : North American Aviation in World War II / John Fredrickson.
    pages cm
  Includes bibliographical references and index.
  ISBN 978-0-7603-4816-1 (hbk.)
  1. North American Aviation–History. 2. Airplane factories–California–Inglewood–History–20th century. 3. Kindelberger, James Howard, 1895-1962. 4. Mitchell (Bomber)–Design and construction–History. 5. Aircraft industry–California–Inglewood–History–20th century. 6. Aircraft industry–United States–History–20th century. 7. World War, 1939-1945–Economic aspects–United States. 8. World War, 1939-1945–California–Inglewood. 9. Inglewood (Calif.)–Economic conditions. I. Title. II. Title: North American Aviation in World War II.
  UG1242.B6F726 2015
  338.7ʹ623746097309044–dc23
                    2015018018

Acquiring Editor: Dennis Pernu
Project Manager: Madeleine Vasaly
Art Director: James Kegley
Layout: Diana Boger

Printed in China

Front cover: B-25 Mitchells move along the final assembly line at a North American Aviation's massive plant in the Fairfax industrial district of Kansas City. This plant first augmented the original Inglewood production line before becoming the world's sole source of the iconic medium bombers in the summer of 1944. Production continued for another year at the dizzying but sustained pace of about three hundred airplanes per month.

Title pages: A B-25 in navy or marine service was designated PBJ-1 (for Patrol Bomber, with the letter "J" being assigned to North American Aviation). This PBJ-1H at Inglewood was built with an optional 75mm cannon in the nose.

Back cover: A young woman perches precariously on the top of a stepladder as she polishes the four-bladed propeller of this Mustang.

Back flap: The 1934 vintage design of the North American trainer was durable, and after considerable updating, was still viable a decade later.

CONTENTS

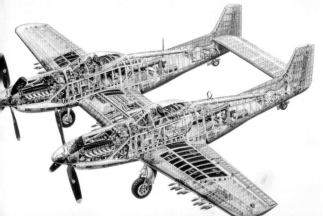

ACKNOWLEDGMENTS

The kind, sustained, and generous assistance of Michael Lombardi and Thomas Lubbesmeyer of the Boeing Historical Archives in Bellevue, Washington, was invaluable to the creation of this book. The first bits of North American history began to arrive at the Boeing Archives shortly after the aerospace units of Rockwell International were purchased in December 1996. Michael Lombardi is the senior corporate historian for the Boeing Company who had the wisdom and foresight to seek out, organize, and preserve the massive remaining collection of source documents and photographs that chronicle the history of North American Aviation Inc. from predecessor companies, the war years, the Cold War era, and the several space programs.

I was granted unrestricted access over the past three and a half years to this vast collection. We believe fresh new information and insights have been discovered despite the many well-researched previous books that have probed the fascinating history of North American Aviation and its products.

Rocky Ruckdaschel was the historian during the era of Rockwell International (circa 1965 to 1996) who assisted past authors with their research into the Mustang and other North American Aviation related topics. Rocky was very active with the group of North American retirees who called themselves the "Bald Eagles." With the implementation of Social Security in the 1930s, most workers in the United States were required to retire on their sixty-fifth birthday. Some of the "Bald Eagles" may have felt they were pushed out of their beloved jobs prematurely. Mandatory retirement at age sixty-five was not mitigated until the presidency of Ronald Reagan in the 1980s. Some of the "Eagles" remained intellectually active by seeking out and preserving the anecdotes and recollections from the early years at Dundalk, thus creating the oral legacy that enriches this book. Past issues of the retiree quarterly newsletter were an additional source of historic information.

Norm Avery was hired by North American in 1940 and started his career as a draftsman on the B-25 project at Inglewood. He devoted his life to documenting the history of North American aircraft. His 1993 book, *B-25 Mitchell: The Magnificent Medium*, is considered by many historians to be the primary authority on that model. His notes and working papers are an invaluable research tool. Robert Hutton of Madison, Wisconsin, generously shared his personal experiences as a World War II instructor pilot and P-51 combat pilot during the Korean War.

The Eisenhower Presidential Library and Museum of Abilene, Kansas, pointed the way to the wartime history of the General Eisenhower's Fairfax-built B-25J transport that was assigned for his exclusive use from May 1944 to May 1945 and provided essential photographic documentation. The Truman Presidential Library and Museum of Independence, Missouri, assisted with the research of Truman's visit to Inglewood in August 1941.

The Dayton, Ohio, public library provided newspaper clippings dated 1944, which detailed the life of Maj. Perry J. Ritchie. The National Museum of the US Air Force at Wright-Patterson AFB was the source for the photographs of Major Ritchie. The historians at Maxwell AFB, Alabama, provided copies of the four accident reports that involved him plus the routing between Inglewood and Eighth Air Force in England for Eisenhower's B-25 on its delivery flight in May 1944.

The descendants of the Wey family were very supportive in seeking to preserve the memory of their uncle, Winton R. Wey. They knew he died in service to his country in a 1944 airplane crash, but were uninformed as to the circumstances. Jim Graham, grandson of Dutch Kindelberger, assisted with fact checking while generously sharing family recollections.

Other manuscript proofreaders included Michael Alexander, a Seattle-based aviation consultant with over forty years' experience in airline training and commercial aircraft

marketing; and Carl Fredrickson, a stress engineer who specializes in the design of engine pylons for forthcoming transport jets. Both men, as lifelong students of aviation history, pointed out not only my many errors of usage but also offered invaluable guidance regarding optimum portrayal of factual events as they intermix with human attitudes.

The leaders of North American were extremely proud of their creations and consummate marketers. Many of the documents in the North American historical files ooze with praise of their own products and some of that perpetual salesmanship has, no doubt, found its way into this text.

—John Fredrickson, 2015

Wartime Inglewood worker Ben Chang seems to be happy with his task—installing cockpit window panes on a Mitchell B-25.

PREFACE

The North American Aviation Inc. (NAA) campus at Inglewood, California, was a beehive of activity during the most challenging time in United States history: the war years from 1938 to 1945 when aircraft assembly lines hummed with activity as engineers, hunched over their drafting tables, conceived lethal new designs and made improvements to existing models. The company was home to the warbirds that helped seal the most crushing dual victories in the history of warfare: the stunning defeats of 1945 when the German government, followed by the Japanese Empire, capitulated in unconditional surrender.

The AT-6 trainers, B-25 medium bombers, and P-51 fighters that helped win the war are at the crux of the NAA legacy and mystique. NAA's legendary airplanes resulted from the genius, labor, and tenacity of its people. The star performers in this story include James Howard "Dutch" Kindelberger and other executives who organized the business; engineers who had a passion for aviation and who envisioned and designed the aircraft; factory workers who fabricated then assembled the parts; managers who organized the workers; and brave airmen who took the airplanes into battle. The supporting cast includes field-service representatives, procurement specialists, service workers, mechanics, union organizers, and an occasional politician. When feasible, the story is told in the actual words of the protagonists. The upbeat central themes of engineering brilliance and manufacturing acumen are offset by occasional instances of tragedy, missed opportunities, and personal conflicts.

The sudden collapse of airplane production at the end of the war was unsettling. Employees were laid off by the tens of thousands as major plants were quickly cleared out and abandoned. Within weeks, previously invaluable combat airplanes, spare parts, and tooling were consigned to the scrap heap. Life in postwar America also included the assimilation of returning veterans, who were focused on establishing families and fulfilling the pent-up demand for material things that had been deferred, first by the Great Depression and then by war. Suburbs sprouted as new homes were erected on former open spaces.

Most families initially set aside their memories of war in the headlong quest for marriage, children, and a new home, automobile, and television set.

A trickle of peacetime movies, magazine articles, and books celebrating the war began to appear. These tales often focused on the main battles without emphasis on how the industrial bounty was utilized to achieve victory.

More recently, curiosity has shifted to the sources of the abundance resulting from President Franklin Roosevelt's 1940 visionary appeal for the full-throttle production of war materiel. How did so much of everything needed for war get made? Our goal is to explore the genesis of the forty-thousand-plus airplanes that were the legacy of NAA between 1938 and 1945 and the resolve of the dedicated people who transformed industrial America from the doldrums of the Great Depression into sustained levels of aircraft production never previously envisioned.

A goat nibbling on a Nazi flag spilling out of a garbage can is a great way to symbolize disrespect for the fascist regimes that made a mess of Europe starting in the mid-1930s.

The dual accomplishments of military mobilization concurrent with a surge in industrial production were facilitated by the arrival of large numbers of women and minorities into the workplace. The result was a permanent societal shift that slowly, but ultimately, yielded expanded career opportunities for all Americans. These changes transformed the national perspective regarding diversity and the roles of women in the job market as the nation advanced from an agrarian, to an industrial, and finally, to a service economy.

During World War II, Americans of all ages committed themselves to the war effort in a manner seldom seen before or since.

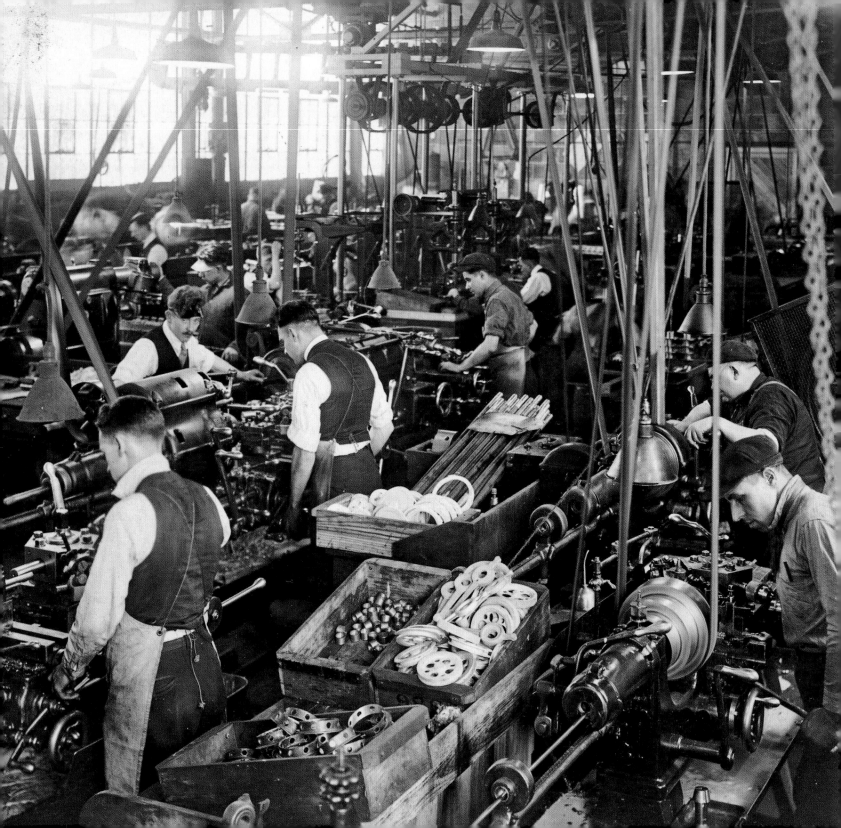

THE GENESIS OF NORTH AMERICAN AVIATION

What happened many years ago in the automobile industry is now happening in the aviation world. . . . North American is striving to build a self-contained economically sound organization backed up by the strong support of General Motors Corporation.

—Chairman Ernest R. Breech, General Aviation
Division of General Motors, July 1933

Workers inside Berliner & Joyce Aircraft's Dundalk, Maryland, factory when times were still prosperous.

In the years following the Wright Brothers' first flight in 1903, entrepreneurs were already starting to cobble together interlocking business consortiums consisting of air carriers, airframe builders, and aircraft engine manufacturers. Early aviation demanded many specialized instruments and a long list of component parts. The challenges were many, the pace of change was quick, and the rate of business failure was high.

Bi-wing cloth-covered flying machines and the pilots who flew them grabbed the popular imagination. Aviation became more than just an adventure. Entrepreneurs with the right mix of intuition, luck, skill, and tenacity could make money building airplanes for the military and civil markets.

North American Aviation began life as an American branch of a Dutch company started by Anthony Fokker. Fokker was born in 1890 and, while lacking in formal education, was the designer and builder of World War I combat airplanes for the Germans. Following the war, Fokker adroitly departed for his home country and founded a new business, Nederlandse Vliegtuigenfabriek (Dutch Aircraft Factory).

In 1922, Fokker moved to the United States. The North American branch of his company was named Atlantic Aircraft Corporation, and multiple factories were established in the eastern United States. The products and business were often referred to as Fokker-America, Fokker-Atlantic, or simply Fokker. The Model F.10A Super Trimotor, powered by three Pratt & Whitney Wasp engines of 400 horsepower each, was a signature product. The fuselage structure was supported by welded steel tubing while the wings, with a span of seventy-five feet, were framed of wood and covered with a thin plywood sheet.

Anthony Fokker, in the lower left, admires a montage of his airplane designs.

A self-promoting showman, Anthony Fokker was a skilled aviator and a popular and charismatic character with pilots as well as the decision makers appointed over them. His designs were notable for their inherent aerodynamic stability. In a speech to the Historical Branch of the Los Angeles Section of the Institute of Aeronautical Sciences on November 28, 1952, John J. Sloan stated:

Fokker designs came in all sizes and shapes. Production runs were often small as compared to modern practice.

> The Fokker tri-motors were marvelously easy to fly, being very light for their gross dimensions. One of Tony's favorite tricks was to leave the controls in flight [in the days before autopilot], walk back among the passengers in the cabin. The tri-motor's nose would fall and the craft would glide down a bit until the additional speed brought the nose up, then it would repeat the maneuver without falling off to one side or the other.

The decade of the Roaring '20s was wild and crazy, reflecting the uninhibited exuberance of the prosperous years following World War I. Out of this cauldron emerged monumental transportation, technological, and communication innovations. It also was a time of business expansion and great prosperity as speculation in securities ran rampant. Public interest in aviation was galvanized by the historic transatlantic flight of Charles Lindbergh in May 1927. Lindbergh's accomplishment fueled even more unmerited investment, this time in aviation-related securities. As airline traffic grew, the number of airline passengers and pounds of air cargo soared by a factor of three between 1927 and 1928.

Unfortunately, much of the public investments were mismanaged, stolen, or otherwise squandered. The resulting inevitable crash of the stock market came in October 1929. While average investors were devastated, business continued pretty much as normal for the top echelon of industrialists.

Amid this chaos, North American Aviation (NAA) was incorporated under the laws of the State of Delaware on December 6, 1928, by Clement Melville Keys. A Canadian immigrant who managed Curtiss-Wright and founded a number of other aviation-oriented businesses, Keys, unlike other pioneers of aviation, was indifferent to the romance of flight. He was, instead, a promoter who had studied the railroad barons of the 1800s as the railroad editor for the *Wall Street Journal* in 1901. He hoped to emulate their financial success, but the railroad business had matured and was no longer yielding big returns. NAA was created to be a holding company with financial interest in airlines and companies manufacturing airframes, aircraft engines, propellers, and other components. NAA was intended, by the icy calculus of Keys and his associates, to make money by investing in a fresh and still-evolving technology.

The period between the wars was not only an era of complicated and dynamic business relationships but also a period of rapid innovation in the still adolescent business of aviation. Improved technology made its way back and forth between civil and military designs. Airframe materials shifted from wood and cloth to metal. A single cantilevered wing replaced bi-wings, wires, and braces. Engines became more powerful and their reliability improved. Airborne navigation evolved. Civil air transportation grew beyond mail and parcels into ever-increasing passenger payloads, as engineers struggled with the vexing problem of two-way "wireless" radio communication.

Under the direction of the legendary business magnate Alfred P. Sloan, General Motors Corporation (GM) mastered mass production and the marketing of motor vehicles during the 1920s and 1930s. GM was flush with cash in 1929 as Sloan and Charles F. Kettering, the company's iconic head of research, grappled with options for expanding in new and profitable directions. As a board member at United Air Lines, Kettering already had an insider's view into the lucrative world of the early commercial air transport.

But the barriers to becoming an airplane manufacturer were significant. Such a venture required facilities, specialized equipment, intellectual property, and human capital. Even for a megacorporation with the resources of GM, it was more expedient to acquire a going concern rather than build from scratch. The pair cast a shrewd eye toward aviation-oriented businesses as they pondered the feasibility of emulating the Boeing-led consortium. GM took the plunge in 1929 with the outright purchase of Allison Engineering, an aircraft engine builder. GM paid more dearly that year when it purchased a 40 percent share of Fokker-America and a 24 percent stake in parts manufacturer Bendix Corporation for a combined total of $23 million. GM also took what subsequently became a controlling interest in the then-separate holding company called North American Aviation, which owned Eastern Airlines and Western Air Transport plus other aviation-oriented businesses. The airlines would be divested as a result of the Air Mail Act of 1934, though divestiture of Eastern would not occur until 1938.

Meanwhile, things were not going well for Anthony Fokker. His business relationships were tainted by his claims of credit for the accomplishments of colleagues and other unethical behavior. Further, Fokker embraced wood as a critical component in an era when the industry was rapidly shifting to metal. This lapse of judgment caused a serious fatal accident that destroyed his reputation and brand name.

On March 31, 1931, a Model F.10, operated as Transcontinental and Western Air (later to become TWA) flight 599 from Kansas City to Los Angeles (with a stop scheduled in Wichita), crashed on the Kansas prairie, taking the lives of legendary Notre Dame collegiate football coach Knute Rockne and seven others. The investigation determined that the wing broke

Alfred P. Sloan, a leading industrialist of the twentieth century who steered General Motors Corporation to greatness and made significant investments in North American and predecessor companies, is seen here visiting Inglewood on August 21, 1941.

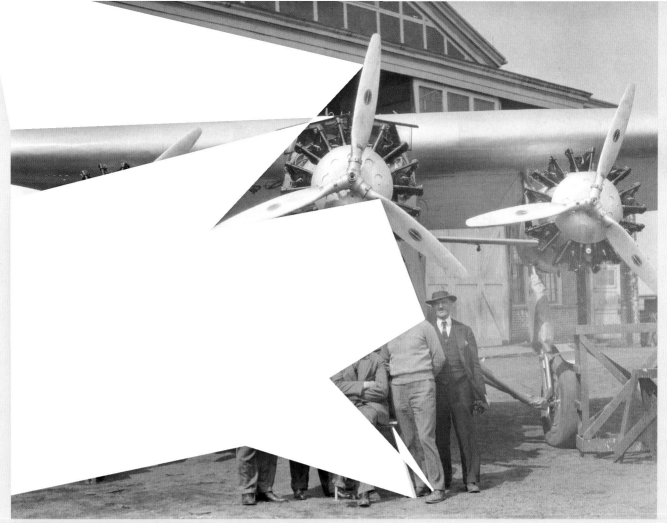

Anthony Fokker (seated) poses with employees in front of a Ford Trimotor airliner. The Ford Trimotor was fabricated of metal, which earned it the nickname of "The Tin Goose." A total of 199 were fabricated between 1925 and 1933.

TRI-MOTOR AIRLINERS

The limited power of early aircraft engines made the tri-motor configuration popular for transport designs of the late 1920s (both terms, tri-motor and trimotor, are found in various source documents). Engines were attached to the nose as well as each wing. Builders experimented with a variety of aircraft engines in search of the optimum power, performance, cost, and reliability. A multitude of designs, permutations, and designations were separately promulgated by at least four different American airframe builders:

THE FORD MOTOR COMPANY was already building airplanes when General Motors decided to enter the aviation business in 1929, and had assembled 199 all-metal tri-motor transport airplanes (a model sometimes called "The Tin Goose") from 1925 to 1933, when the product line was discontinued.

THE FOKKER F.VII evolved into the F.9 when manufactured by Atlantic Aircraft Corporation in the United States. It was superseded by the Fokker F.10 when passenger seating was increased from eight to twelve.

THE BOEING Model 80 was built to haul both passengers and mail. The bi-wing design made it distinctive.

STINSON built two versions of a wooden-winged tri-motor. Model SM-6000 had high wings with external braces. Model A was an externally braced low-wing monoplane.

It is easy to confuse the early tri-motor aircraft because of their similar appearance. The critical difference resides with the construction of the wings. The entire Ford-built airframe was fabricated of metal while the Fokker F.10 wings comprised a thin veneer of plywood covering wooden spars.

The three-engine configuration disappeared from American-built airliners for thirty years until the Boeing 727 entered service in 1964. The Douglas DC-10 and the Lockheed L-1011 followed in 1971 and 1972 as wide-bodied tri-motor jets that saw both civilian and military service.

in flight because prolonged exposure to rainwater had caused a wooden spar to delaminate and weaken to the point of structural failure. All Fokker Trimotors were grounded and then could fly only after frequent inspections. Fokker airplanes were shunned—nobody wanted to fly aboard the same type of airplane that had killed Knute Rockne. Airliners fabricated of wood and cloth were destined to be replaced with those of metal.

Fokker sold his remaining holdings in Atlantic Aircraft to GM, which renamed the holdings the General Aviation division of General Motors. Though he retained his Dutch aviation interests, Fokker's departure from the American market was permanent. He died in New York in 1939 at the age of forty-nine of pneumococcal meningitis.

GM needed one more company before General Aviation could be fully assembled. In 1929, Henry Berliner had merged with Temple Nach Joyce to establish Berliner & Joyce Aircraft in a 58,000-square-foot factory in Dundalk, Maryland, near Baltimore. As the Great Depression eroded the market for civil aircraft, Berliner & Joyce switched focus on low-production small aircraft for the US Army and Navy. In 1930, General Aviation acquired Berliner & Joyce in 1930.

Ernest R. Breech was GM's top executive in charge of General Aviation. The son of an Ozark blacksmith, Breech was a brilliant accountant blessed with formidable gifts for financial management, strategic thinking, and self-marketing. While still in his mid-thirties, Breech had advanced from chief accountant for the Yellow Truck & Coach Manufacturing Company of Chicago to the top rung of General Motors as the point man for all GM aviation enterprises.

GM now controlled General Aviation, had acquired Berliner & Joyce, and owned substantial stakes in four other companies: Douglas Aircraft Corporation of Santa Monica, California; Transcontinental and Western Air (T&WA, later TWA); Eastern Air Transport; and Western Air Express. It was all very complicated, and powerful Washington, DC, politicians who had grown suspicious of financiers and their consortiums were beginning to take note.

A year later, the aviation industry's paradigm was changed. Senator Hugo Black of Alabama, the future US Supreme Court justice, enlisted a cadre of politically motivated and like-minded anti-big business colleagues to help investigate the recent awarding of airmail contracts as terms like "collusion" and "fraud" were bandied about the great halls of power. The search for scapegoats while delving into the alleged causes of the current economic malaise would make for great political theater.

Black's technique was to persuade witnesses that he already had the facts and merely wanted confirmation for the record. Senate investigator A. B. Patterson prepared a three-page typed interrogatory for North American Aviation—a holding company with an ownership interest in various airlines—containing thirty-eight wide-ranging questions that broadly probed into all aspects of the businesses. Seattle-based industrialist William Boeing and his companies received an equivalent list of questions. Courteous, smiling, puffing gravely on his cigar, Black, a savvy and experienced prosecuting attorney, set about to refresh the aviation executives' memories during the hearings, leading them to admissions that enabled him to conclude with damaging summations of their testimony.

The Berliner & Joyce plant at Dundalk in August 1929. Nearby Helen's Bar was a popular afterhours watering hole for the workers (later called the Dundalk gang) after prohibition ended in 1933.

The US Navy was the major customer for Berliner & Joyce aircraft, including planes like this XFJ-2.

Boeing's staff did their best on short notice to gather responses to the sometimes ambiguous questions. Boeing's testimony began at 10:30 a.m. on February 6, 1934, and went on for hours as he squirmed uncomfortably in his seat. Unfamiliar with the minor nuances of the written answers prepared by others, Boeing stumbled frequently. Black led a tag team of questioners with Senators Wallace White Jr. and Patrick McCarran sometimes chiming in. The investigative process, which resembled a prosecution, did not provide for a defense attorney to run interference for the witness by interjecting objections. William Boeing seldom volunteered anything during his testimony except for one brief insight offered as he was badgered about the increase in value of his investment:

BLACK: Now, the salaries and dividends—I will ask you if it is not true that the salaries and dividends far more than paid for the $487,000 that you state was [invested] in cash and property?

BOEING: Mr. Chairman, you must remember that this aircraft thing is a life work with me, it has gone over the whole of my life. I went through all the hazards, periods when everyone thought I was a fool.

BLACK: They don't think that now, do they?

BOEING: Well, I don't know. I risked a good, big part of my personal fortune at that time and I stayed with it. This may be a reward for a life's work—I don't know.

The result of the hearings was the Air Mail Act of 1934, whereby airframe builders were banned from hauling US Mail. A further outcome was the breakup of the Boeing-led consortium into three separate companies. A fiasco arose when all post office contracts with airline companies were abrogated for two months and the army temporarily took over flying the airmail. A spate of military airplane crashes and twelve dead army pilots were the tragic result. The New Deal suffered its first serious embarrassment as bitter public criticism ensued.

THE SEEDS OF A JUGGERNAUT

William E. Boeing was born in 1881. His father was a self-made German immigrant, Wilhelm, who earned his wealth in the iron ore and timber businesses but died of influenza when young William was a mere eight years old. A generous inheritance ensured Wilhelm's only son would receive the best education, which included a stint at Yale.

The self-motivated William Boeing, driven to achieve success on the scale of his father, relocated from Virginia to rain-soaked western Washington State while still in his twenties in search of his own fortune as a timber baron. A nationwide construction boom stimulated the demand for lumber and Bill Boeing prospered, but life in the small coastal logging town of Hoquiam soon became mundane. The search for excitement triggered a move to the nearby city of Seattle where Boeing became smitten with airplanes and flying.

In 1916, Boeing established an airplane company in the former Heath shipyard, snugly situated on waterfront a short distance upstream from the confluence of the Duwamish Waterway and the tidewater of Seattle's Elliot Bay. He hired a diverse crew: men with woodworking skills, women who were experts at sewing fabric, and an American-educated Chinese aeronautical engineer named Wong Tsoo.

The fledgling Boeing Airplane Company was soon building airplanes for early mail routes. Starting in March 1919, he teamed with Eddie Hubbard to establish the international airmail link between Seattle and Victoria, British Columbia. Boeing occasionally piloted the route himself. The web of airmail routes grew over the following years until the main corridor extended from New York to San Francisco with ever-expanding branches reaching many locales.

Early airmail pilots observed with curiosity that individuals sometimes presented themselves at the airfields, seeking transportation. When circumstances permitted, and in exchange for fare, an occasional passenger would sit amid the sacks of mail. The spaces allocated for passengers in airplane designs were expanded.

Bill Boeing was the founder and mastermind behind the biggest and most formidable of the aviation consortiums. He had a sharp eye for sizing up people and businesses. When he encountered exceptional men of vision and organizational ability, he recruited them either as partners or employees. The business expanded into other aviation endeavors far from Seattle, as gifted managers with entrepreneurial skills were placed into emerging business opportunities.

The capstone of the Boeing corporate pyramid was United Aircraft and Transport Corporation (UATC), an empire created in 1929 when the Boeing firms teamed up with Frederick Rentschler of Pratt & Whitney. Bill Boeing liked doing business with the ebullient Rentschler. The resulting portfolio of companies touched all aspects of commercial and military aviation, including engines, airframes, propellers, and air transport. The list of brand names included Boeing Airplane Company, Stearman, Sikorsky, Hamilton, Chance Vought, and United Air Lines. The Boeing-organized consortium became an economic juggernaut but in 1934 was pilloried by politicians and broken up by antitrust legislation.

In March 1919 Bill Boeing and Eddie Hubbard won their first air mail contract between Seattle and Victoria, the provincial capital of British Columbia. The distance was only 72 miles but saltwater (Puget Sound and the Strait of Juan de Fuca) prevented the construction of a highway or railroad. Boeing sometimes piloted the airplane himself. *Boeing Archives*

William Boeing's pride was wounded beyond repair by the tawdry, humiliating experience of the Senate hearings and the resulting legislation. He sold all of his interests in disgust and resigned from the aviation world at the age of fifty-three to redirect his energies toward real-estate development, horse breeding, and other leisure activities. It remains unknown if he harbored plans for early retirement before the hearings.

There would be no more Boeing family ownership or involvement in the companies he founded. The capable associates whom he had handpicked and mentored took charge of the three now-independent companies: United Air Lines, United Aircraft Corporation (i.e., Pratt & Whitney engines), and the Boeing Airplane Company. Infused with fresh blood, each business not only survived but went on to greater prosperity, dominating their respective markets in the coming decades.

As for General Aviation, it initially floundered under GM ownership. A leadership vacuum emerged in the wake of Anthony Fokker's departure. Engineers ceased designing innovative products, salesmen were not aggressive, and manufacturing lagged. The business operated at a loss and finger-pointing ensued. GM was discovering that building airplanes was a world apart from building automobiles.

Ernest Breech, GM's man in charge of North American holdings, went on an executive talent search in 1934 with two important positions to fill: leaders for both General Aviation and T&WA who would be consistent with the management attributes of GM under Sloan's leadership. GM made rational decisions in areas of planning and strategy, stabilization, financial growth, and leadership. Robust aviation engineering credentials, extraordinary drive and communication skills, and a magnetic personality were sought to augment Breech's own considerable financial acumen.

The new leader of T&WA would need to rebuild the airline after the Rockne tri-motor crash. Jack Frye, already T&WA's director of operations, won the position. Meanwhile, the president and managing director of General Aviation was expected to jump-start the sleepy enterprise that was mired in obsolete technology but holding vital human capital in the form of a great brain trust of German and Dutch aviation talent—the most valuable and enduring legacy of Anthony Fokker's leadership. Eastern Air Transport remained under the capable leadership of Capt. Eddie Rickenbacker (the World War I hero was normally referred to as "Captain" in all correspondence).

Airlines like T&WA urgently sought modern replacements for the wooden planes of the past. Frye approached the Boeing Airplane Company looking to acquire a quantity of the new Model 247. He was refused because production was already committed to a Boeing affiliate: United Air Lines. Frye next appealed to Donald Douglas of Douglas Aircraft, who responded with a bigger and better transport airplane design that soon vanquished the Boeing Model 247. The early model was the DC-2 which, with improvements, evolved into the legendary DC-3 and the C-47 for army air corps service ("DC" is an abbreviation for "Douglas Commercial"). It was the first design that did not become obsolete within a very few years and it became the foundation upon which modern airlines flourished. The DC-3 was well suited for not only the transport of mail and parcels, but also up to twenty-six passengers.

As at Boeing, the Air Mail Act of 1934 also redirected the trajectory of North American Aviation. The legislatively ordered breakup of the Boeing holdings dashed any aspiration General Motors may have harbored to build a competing aviation empire. The legacy of Senator Hugo Black and the airmail hearings of 1934 was to cause American airframe builders, engine manufacturers, and airline companies to be independent from each other. As its other holdings were divested, the scope of business at NAA was narrowed to the design, manufacture, and sale of military airplanes, airplane parts, and related services.

Sloan would continue to look after General Motors' shrinking financial investment in NAA, nurturing and helping when he could. The remaining stake in Eastern Airlines, the last vestige of the holding company, was sold outright in 1938.

The North American logo adorned not only plant facades but also the rudder pedals on most of the forty thousand-plus airplanes assembled between 1938 and 1945, which was more than any other US airframe builder.

CHAPTER 2

DUTCH

Dutch Kindelberger was an extremely capable engineer and demonstrated great technical competence in aircraft design and manufacturing. He developed into a fine administrator, came to be recognized as a man who could produce outstanding military airplanes at low cost.

—Alfred P. Sloan, writing in his autobiography

"Dutch" Kindelberger at the controls of an early airplane in 1918. Starting in mid-1934, he would remain in firm control of North American Aviation Inc. for the balance of his lifetime.

James Howard "Dutch" Kindelberger's legacy is inextricably intertwined with North American Aviation history. Like the Wright Brothers, Glenn Martin, William Boeing, Donald Douglas, Jack Northrop, and James McDonnell, he is considered one of the pioneers of aviation, though he receives less recognition than the others because NAA did not bear his surname.

Kindelberger was a self-made man who, through hard work, good luck, and tenacity, arose from humble beginnings to become a titan of American business. He was a skillful storyteller and extrovert who relished opportunities to spin tales for any audience. Stories often featured within company publications recounted his own life history, development of the early airplanes, and the company's move from Dundalk, Maryland, to Inglewood, California. Despite occasional divisive strikes by organized labor, the workforce most often held their leader in high esteem. They thrived on tales of his exploits and their shared corporate history during his entire tenure, which spanned nearly three decades, from 1934 until his death in 1962.

Kindelberger was born in Wheeling, West Virginia, to German immigrant parents in 1895 and manifested the stereotypical German traits of punctuality, hard work, and competitiveness. He stumbled in his youth by dropping out of high school at age sixteen to become an apprentice steelworker but quickly realized his error. To escape the foundry and the bleak future of "throwing pig iron around from seven in the morning 'till 5:30 at night," young Kindelberger redirected his energies toward achieving the best technical education possible. His early misstep was corrected by devoting long hours to obtaining high-school equivalency. Acceptance at the Carnegie Institute of Technology resulted in an opportunity to earn a top-tier technical education, of which he made the most. Election to president of his freshman class rewarded his formidable budding interpersonal skills.

Kindelberger's lifelong nickname was awarded during his collegiate days at Carnegie. Years later, he reminisced about it with a reporter from the company newspaper:

"I just fell heir to it," he said. "There was another man in college whose name was Kindl. The other students called him Dutch and when he left they just had to have another to hang it on. Due, I think, to the similarity of our last names they hung it on me. The strange thing about it is that while the name stuck to me afterward, he lost it entirely. I see him occasionally. He is now general manager of the Delco plant in Dayton, Ohio." When asked "How many of your employees call you Dutch?" he replied "Everyone, I think. The office boy does not call me that to my face but from a portion of his conversation which I once overheard, I am sure that he does when my back is turned."

During World War I several nations, in their quest for military supremacy, adopted the then-infant technology of powered flight as weaponry. The entry of the United States into the war in 1917 precipitated Kindelberger's departure from the prestigious Carnegie Institute in May when he joined the US Army as a private. He eventually worked his way into flight training with the rank of lieutenant because, as he later stated, "I just didn't want to end up in a trench." Over the course of the war, France built sixty-eight thousand airplanes, England produced fifty-five thousand, and German output was forty-eight thousand units. Major improvements came quickly. Some designs were obsolete within a year.

Lieutenant Kindelberger first attended ground training at Ohio State University, then Flight Familiarization at Dallas, followed by advanced flight training, which was completed in June 1918 at Park Field in Memphis, Tennessee. Any aspirations for overseas travel and assignment to aerial combat operations were dashed when he was ordered to remain at Park Field to perform flight instructor duties.

The pilot training was invaluable to Kindelberger's later success because it solidified his aviation credentials while establishing lifelong bonds with other World War I aviators like

Jimmy Doolittle, Hap Arnold, Eddie Allen, George C. Kenney, Eddie Rickenbacker, and even a German ace: Ernst Udet. Kindelberger was an accepted member of their small but elite clan whose political, military, and economic clout was destined to grow. By the time World War II broke out, many of these men were well connected and in important national leadership positions. With the exception of Udet, they became trusted friends and associates, some of whom occasionally visited with Kindelberger at the NAA facilities.

World War I hostilities ended in Paris time on the eleventh hour of the eleventh day of the eleventh month of 1918 with a volley of artillery fire. Each gun battery commander wanted the satisfaction of firing the last shot in the "war to end wars." Newly minted army air corps pilot Dutch Kindelberger found himself discharged, unemployed, and close to broke. A mere eighteen days later he was on the payroll of the Glenn L. Martin Company of Baltimore as a draftsman. Kindelberger rated himself a mediocre aviator. There is no evidence that he ever again piloted an airplane after leaving military service.

Kindelberger married his childhood sweetheart, Thelma Knarr, and the family grew with the arrival of a daughter, Joan, in 1920, and a son, Howard (nicknamed "Bud"), in 1922. Bud died tragically in an equestrian-related accident at a boarding school in 1940. The option for succession at North American by a son of Dutch Kindelberger had been eliminated.

A lifelong interest in photography grew as Kindelberger began to write articles for *Popular Mechanics* and to develop the accompanying photographs in the family bathtub. He owned as many as ten cameras at the same time. Kindelberger was also never shy about appearing in front of the camera or microphone. His face is found on countless still photographs and in industrial motion pictures. He also later spoke on nationwide radio.

Glenn L. Martin, born in 1886, played a major role in the early days of aviation. Martin sold William E. Boeing the first airplane that Boeing was to own and then taught him to fly it. Martin's company became a magnet for bright, gifted, and ambitious people with a passion for flying, and a string of aviation moguls served their apprenticeship there. It was while working at Martin that Kindelberger first met Donald Douglas. (Other alumni included Lawrence Bell of Bell Helicopter fame and James S. McDonnell.)

Douglas resigned from Martin and invited Kindelberger to accompany him to the newly founded Douglas Aircraft Company in Santa Monica, California. Kindelberger soon rose to vice president of engineering and played a significant role in the design of the iconic DC-1 and DC-2 transport planes. Kindelberger quickly found himself steering the design of progressively more sophisticated flying machines.

Business relationships of the era were incestuous. Donald Douglas was a stakeholder in the North American Aviation holding company, while General Motors, whose General Aviation (GA) division had controlling interest in NAA, held significant ownership in the Douglas Aircraft Company. When Ernest R. Breech, the GM-affiliated chairman of the board at GA, was in search of a new president and managing director in mid-1934, it was Donald Douglas who stepped forward to recommend an unlikely candidate: his own highly regarded vice president of engineering, James Howard "Dutch" Kindelberger.

Enticed in part by a generous compensation package, including GM stock options, Kindelberger departed Santa Monica in mid-1934 but remained lifelong friends with Douglas, despite frequently competing for the same contracts, talent, and other resources. For good measure, Kindelberger took two valued associates with him: Lee Atwood and the lesser-known but equally talented J. S. "Stan" Smithson, who had expertise in design and production. Nevertheless, Douglas Aircraft Company prospered as its products went on to dominate the world airliner market for nearly three decades, starting with the fourteen-seat DC-2 in 1934.

Kindelberger arrived at GA as the president and managing director. The company's former Fokker plants had been closed and operations were consolidated in Dundalk,

Donald Douglas contributed greatly to Kindelberger's success by hiring him away from the Glenn L. Martin Company and then, nine years later, nominating him to become the president of General Aviation.

RIGHT-HAND MAN

Dutch Kindelberger attracted a lifelong entourage of talented people who built a longstanding mutual loyalty among them. His closest associate was John Leland "Lee" Atwood. Atwood, the son of a Texas Baptist preacher, was a quiet mathematician who hired on as a design and structural engineer at Douglas Aircraft after drifting into the Santa Monica plant from the nearby (but failed) Moreland Aircraft Company.

The pair collaborated on the design of the DC-1 and DC-2 before accepting positions at General Aviation and heading east to Dundalk. Atwood instantly became number two in the pecking order. At age thirty-one, he was appointed vice president and remained in that position until he ascended to the presidency of NAA in 1960. Kindelberger remained as chairman of the board of directors until his death in 1962.

Either man could represent the company on important business matters. Each had attributes that offset the other and the combination of the two was the perfect mix for the sustained success of North American Aviation. Kindelberger was a boisterous, outgoing, and confident extrovert while Atwood was quiet and intellectual. Kindelberger would act on hunch, intuition, or emotion, while Atwood exercised his engineering skills by seeking out facts and numbers and organizing his managerial philosophy into six axioms:

- A good organization is as simple as the functions required of it will permit.

- A good organization is able to make decisions quickly.

- A good organization has clearly defined lines of function and responsibility.

- A good organization makes maximum use of the abilities of each individual.

- Coordinate your work with that of your associates.

- Finally, have faith in your organization.

John Leland "Lee" Atwood (1904–1999) became vice president of North American Aviation in 1934. He remained the number-two man at NAA until 1960. Kindelberger held the combined position of president and chairman of the board for most of his career. Kindelberger retired in 1960 as chief executive officer at the age of sixty-five and was succeeded by Lee Atwood. Kindelberger remained chairman of the board until his death two years later.

Maryland, a suburb of Baltimore established as a bedroom community for workers at the nearby shipyards during World War I. There were two separate factories at Dundalk: the former Curtiss-Caproni facility and the former Berliner & Joyce (sometimes abbreviated B/J) plant. The production backlog was worse than anemic.

It is ironic that Kindelberger started work at GA in mid-1934 concurrent with the departure of William E. Boeing from the industry. Both men shared a love for aviation, German heritage, business acumen, entrepreneurial drive, and the personality needed to form enduring lifelong bonds with an eclectic assortment of extraordinary people. Boeing, however, was born to a Yale lifestyle of wealth, privilege, and high society, while Kindelberger's roots were forged in the steel mill as an hourly laborer.

At the age of thirty-nine, Kindelberger's fate was sealed for the remaining twenty-eight years of his life. Times were tough. The surviving airplane builders of the 1930s—who fought tooth and nail for, then celebrated, each miniscule new order—were unable to fathom, even in their wildest dreams, the approaching decade of global conflict, when warplanes would be routinely ordered in batches of a thousand or more.

Business improved when Kindelberger, as a top priority and calling upon his first-hand experience with pilot training, aggressively took on new projects, starting with a two-seat pilot trainer. Thousands of subsequent trainer airplanes over the next twenty-plus years

NORTH AMERICAN XO-47

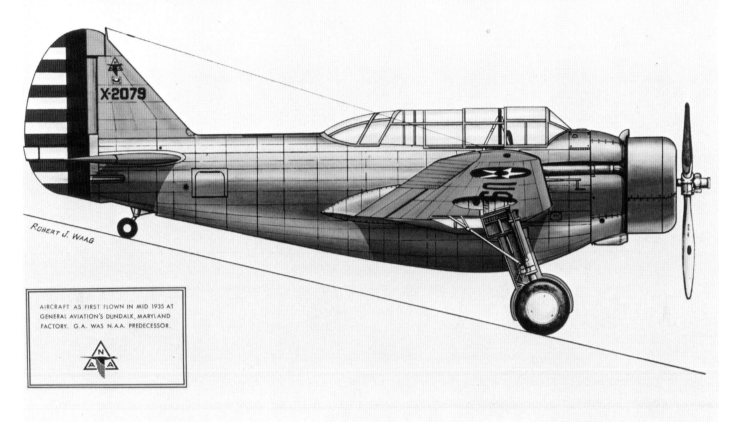

X-2079

ROBERT J. WAAG

AIRCRAFT AS FIRST FLOWN IN MID 1935 AT
GENERAL AVIATION'S DUNDALK, MARYLAND
FACTORY. G.A. WAS N.A.A. PREDECESSOR.

U.S. ARMY AIR CORPS

with designations of BT-9, BC-1, T-6, and T-28 became the foundation upon which NAA's subsequent prosperity rested.

An observation plane carrying a crew of three, the O-47, was concurrently designed for the army while operations were still at Dundalk. While the O-47 never received a name, a production run of 238 qualified it as a financial success. It earned no significant combat role in the coming hostilities.

Kindelberger next shook up the then-sleepy enterprise by discarding the General Aviation title in favor of the holding company's name of North American Aviation Inc. effective January 1, 1935. North American Aviation was now a brand name like Douglas, Boeing, Consolidated, and Martin. Frustrated by the conditions in Maryland, Kindelberger then hatched a much more significant plan. The facility was inadequate, and the weather extremes—stifling summer humidity and cold winter snow—were not conducive conditions for flight testing, working outdoors, or fitting temperature-sensitive metal parts together.

Breech and the board of directors were presented with a well-written and solidly argued justification for moving the entire enterprise across country to California. Conditional approval for the move was granted, contingent upon the win of a substantial order for new airplanes. Kindelberger went west to scout several sites for a suitable

The O-47, an army air corps observation plane, became an early success for the infant North American operation. Two hundred thirty-eight were built during the same time as the move from Dundalk to Inglewood.

ABOVE: Longer landing gear than normal provided the ground clearance necessary for the low-hanging observer's compartment of the O-47. This airplane bears the markings of the Illinois Air National Guard.

RIGHT: The crew of an O-47 numbered three: a pilot, a gunner, and an observer who could crawl below and operate a downward-looking camera. It helped establish the fledgling NAA but would have no significant wartime role.

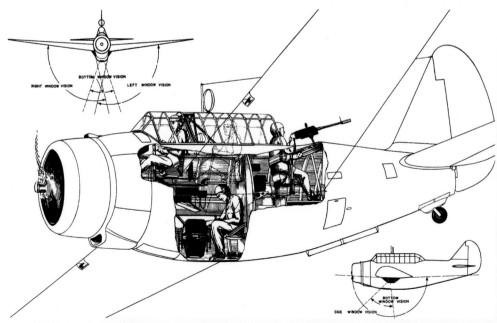

location. After evaluation, the board of directors settled on twenty acres that could be rented for $600 per year. The small parcel adjoined the Los Angeles Municipal Airport (then also known as Mines Field, now called LAX). When NAA beat out Seversky Aircraft for a contract for forty-two BT-9 trainer aircraft, the plan to relocate to the West Coast became operative.

Kindelberger convened an after-hours session in Helen's Tavern, the watering hole across the street from the Dundalk plant, one evening in the early autumn of 1935. It was with great difficulty that he persuaded the employees to move to California. "They were under the impression that there were hostile Indians west of Pittsburgh, so I fed them beer and crab cakes and lectured them on the marvels of the West," he later recounted.

The General Motors board of directors appropriated $696,000 to fund the relocation. The largest outlays were earmarked for construction of a modern plant and filling it with the latest machinery and equipment. The employee-relocation budget was only a small percentage of the allocation; those individuals deemed most worthy of retention were offered financial assistance to defray part of their expenses. Recollections of the relocation offers vary from $50 to $90. The number of families that agreed to move across the country caravan-style in their automobiles was about seventy-two. Like an earlier generation of pioneers mounting their covered wagons, the automobiles started westward in November 1935. Other Dundalk employees received nothing but the promise of a job if they got themselves to California.

Contractors working under Kindelberger's direction were hired and a huge new plant with an initial size of 550,000 square feet was constructed on the abundant, flat, and undeveloped real estate in Inglewood, southwest of downtown Los Angeles. Construction tasks included building a rail spur, extending a sewer line, and pouring concrete for aircraft parking and a taxiway to the airfield. The entire workforce of 150 moved into their new plant in January 1936. Business prospered as the backlog of unfilled orders grew to $9 million. By September 1, 1939, there were 3,400 employees.

The army air corps awarded NAA an additional order for forty more BT-9As. New features were added to further enhance aviator training: a forward facing fixed gun, a recording camera, and a flexible (swiveling) gun in the aft cockpit. Additional orders for trainer aircraft and variants flowed in from foreign countries at a surprising pace. When the Inglewood trainers were built for the British Royal Air Force (RAF), the British dubbed them "Harvards," a nod to the finest of American advanced education.

NAA had focused on small, military airplanes since the 1931 Trimotor crash. No commercial airliners were built or marketed after the move to California. (Their core competency was to be small airplanes. Kindelberger once said "Don't let them get too big too fast.") Ironically, NAA would go on to later build two very large supersonic bombers: the short-lived and ill-fated, delta-wing XB-70 Valkyrie of the 1960s and the still-serving B-1B Lancer of the 1980s.)

The unwritten strategies of the newly formed enterprise were:

- Build small planes for government customers.

- Constantly improve the product and offer new variations.

- The US military is the prime customer.

- Expand the product base by selling to foreign governments.

- A product is probably obsolete if it becomes mature and stable.

- Be forward looking and push the technology envelope.

- Work out post-delivery problems and make them right with the customer, even at the expense of profits.

The youthful Ernest Breech was the General Motors executive who recruited Kindelberger. Breech was a brilliant CPA and finance whiz who served as chairman of the board during the formative early years of North American Aviation Inc.

Dutch Kindelberger sat for numerous portraits, both painted and photographic. Photography was a hobby and he was never camera shy.

Under the cloud of the Great Depression and aware that the airplane-building business was a notorious rollercoaster of boom and bust, Kindelberger stated in an interview: "I have no ambition to head the largest plant in the industry. But I do want to head the busiest. My one thought is to sell enough of our products to keep the organization going without any layoffs. You know, there are a lot of these men to whom a layoff is a little short of a tragedy. They are raising families and need every dollar they can make. I hope to be able to keep them constantly employed and earning, for after all, that's what makes good American citizens."

Kindelberger has been described as forward thinking and possessing shrewd judgment, punctuality, a sharp wit, a generous sense of humor, and a commanding personality—with a heavy dash of salt in his language and sometimes ribald stories. Multiple sources characterized him as "a human pile driver." On rare occasions, Kindelberger exhibited the short-fused temper that lurked below the surface of his normally placid demeanor. On one instance he was observed angrily breaking golf clubs on the links because the small white ball would not accede to his expectations.

Always impeccably dressed, Kindelberger epitomized the self-made man who rose from humble beginnings. He presented an eloquent persona, and most photographs show him nattily clad in a finely-cut business suit. His automobiles, which he drove himself, were big and expensive. Consistent with the norms for businessmen of the era, photos of Kindelberger in casual attire are scarce.

His letters demonstrate the attributes of a master communicator, while face-to-face dialogue was even more persuasive. Charm offensives were normally bestowed upon friends, customers, and potential customers. The typical icy blast of bluster directed toward anybody suspected of being less than forthcoming is evident in the final paragraphs of a letter dated February 24, 1936. Kindelberger had been evaluating propulsion alternatives for a new twin-engine bomber when he sensed equivocation from Allison Engineering, the aircraft engine-builder then under the same GM corporate umbrella as NAA:

> I wish you would check into this matter and give us the information listed in the questionnaire attached hereto so that we will have something to work on. We will be going out on a limb for about $350,000.00 and if you have faith in your engine sufficient to warrant our doing this, please say so frankly at the present time as alibis are going to be hard for us to swallow if we have gone ahead depending upon you and you flop. . . .
>
> I wish you would give us immediately the complete unabridged and honest story on the engines so that we will have something to work on because the time element is such that we will not have time to kid ourselves at all and if the engine is a flop, let's understand it now and play with something else.

Kindelberger traveled to Europe in 1938 for the dual purposes of selling airplanes and assessing the state of foreign airplane production. He departed England with an order for two hundred more Harvard trainers and a better understanding of the dismal state of Britain's aviation industry. Aircraft production rates there were pathetic. The Spitfire required too many labor-intensive compound curves, and the motorcar experts only made matters worse with dies that were quickly outdated as airplane designs evolved.

In Germany, Kindelberger clicked with Ernst Udet, a kindred spirit and accomplished World War I ace who had turned barnstormer, movie stunt pilot, and playboy with a penchant for strong drink. At a 1936 airshow, the boisterous and colorful Udet performed his trademark feat of daring by plucking a scarf from the Mines Field runway with his wing tip. Only opposing national loyalties divided Udet and Kindelberger.

Udet had joined the Nazi Party in 1933 and committed his services to the Luftwaffe. Test-pilot credentials, technical expertise, and a World War I–era relationship with Hermann

Göring helped him quickly ascend to director of Luftwaffe materiel. Four thousand people toiled diligently under his command.

During his ten-day stay in Germany, Kindelberger was granted access to Heinkel, Focke-Wulf, and Messerschmitt plants, as well as a secret research lab. Little escaped his eyes. He observed that, in contrast to the British, German airplane designs were adapted for simple tooling and high-rate production.

Assembly lines were observed operating at a rapid pace. It was assumed American methods had been copied. A "chicken or egg" argument can be made. Did the Germans copy American methods or did Kindelberger bring home high-rate production ideas from Germany? Unfortunately, to date, no firsthand account of Kindelberger's 1938 European visit has been located in North American files. However, it is obvious that both sides focused on simple and repeatable manufacturing methods to achieve reliable high-rate production of military aircraft utilizing relatively unskilled labor.

Kindelberger assumed that Udet was in search of praise that could be passed along to those above him while also observing that Udet was politically savvy, and used flattering and sometimes exaggerated public relations to further his own career in the Nazi party. The German factory tours may have been an attempt to bluff the United States into staying out of the war. In any case, upon returning to America, Kindelberger (like Charles Lindbergh, who carried out a similar more highly publicized tour around the same time) reported his observations to Chief of the Air Corps Hap Arnold and his staff.

The Third Reich, however, could devour their own. Herman Göring later betrayed Udet to Adolf Hitler by blaming him for the Luftwaffe's failures during the Battle of Britain. Udet died of a fatal self-inflicted gunshot wound in 1941 at the age of forty-five. The Nazi propaganda machine falsely informed the German public that Udet had died heroically in the crash of an experimental aircraft.

Ernst Udet (in a photograph circa 1931) hosted Kindelberger's ten-day visit to Nazi Germany in 1938. Udet was a World War I ace who later became the senior Luftwaffe procurement officer. *Spaarnestad Photo*

Back in Southern California, employee communications were of vital importance to Kindelberger. Internal communication tools included a weekly newspaper at each plant site. A colorful magazine called *Skyline* covered the bigger picture. Both publications were a venue for Kindelberger to communicate directly with employees. His lengthy comments appeared in nearly every issue but the assumption is that he did not actually write everything attributed to him because there were several senior managers on the NAA payroll with the title of "special assistant to the president."

The Inglewood plant also featured the best Radio Corporation of America industrial sound system then available. There were 180 high-fidelity loudspeakers wired into the system for lunchtime entertainment, important radio broadcasts, and the transmission of

Dutch Kindelberger ensured that each plant had a huge gathering area because he wanted employees to hear directly from him and others important motivational messages. Only the best of industrial-grade public-address systems were installed.

paging messages into work areas. On December 8, 1941, workers stood down from their jobs and listened in stunned silence as Franklin D. Roosevelt declared war on Japan.

Also at Inglewood, large stadium-sized areas were available for periodic mass gatherings. Kindelberger, with a voice described as rumbling like a kettle drum, was a gifted speaker and never shy. Military leaders such as Jimmy Doolittle, as well as politicians and other luminaries of the day, all shared their stories at these gatherings in the perpetual quest to keep the workers informed and motivated.

Family events at NAA were a means to cement long-term bonds with employees. North American hosted a beachside employee picnic on August 13, 1938, with both Kindelberger and Atwood in attendance. Even during the war, an occasional weekend open house was scheduled at each of the plants. Airplanes, which constituted the latest of military marvels, were on display for close-up viewing while employees proudly boasted to youngsters, spouses, and parents of their vital roles in the unfolding drama that was leading-edge aviation.

Kindelberger was restless while at the factory and could be expected to wander out of his office into the shop areas about once an hour. Sometimes he would step outside and smoke a cigarette while pondering an issue. If he observed a production problem while pacing the floor, he retreated back to his office and would often return with a solution in a day or two. He was an inventor of numerous mechanical devices, including the "profile machine" that allowed metal parts to be fabricated in sets of ten. Occasionally, Kindelberger invited design engineers into the factory with him to watch manufacturing operations. Frequently, engineers took the hint and went back to redesign certain parts so that they could be made and assembled more efficiently.

Ever frugal, Kindelberger was also a practitioner of "management by walking around" (or MBWA, a practice still encouraged to this day). One day, he encountered an hourly worker cutting a sheet of aluminum into very small pieces. When he asked, "What are you doing?,'" the man responded that his immediate supervisor told him to cut up the piece before the "old man" found it and decided to turn it into an airplane.

Recent advances in the comfort and reliability of airplanes, performance in bad weather, and improved navigation had granted the supreme leaders of World War II a new and powerful form of mobility that could have been called "management by flying around." The horse had only recently been displaced as the traditional means of overland military travel. In fact, many senior officers were skilled equestrians who still brandished a riding crop to symbolize their authority (Hap Arnold is seen holding one as he poses for the photographer next to his four-star-adorned B-25). But if a horse could reliably travel twenty miles in a day, a twin-engined B-25 could easily go a hundred times farther and be ready to repeat the process after refueling and topping off the engine oil. Obstacles like rivers, lakes, and mountains made no difference. (However, four-engine airplanes remained the preference for transoceanic travel.)

Factory-modified versions of the B-25 were initially bestowed upon just three individuals: Hap Arnold, Dwight Eisenhower, and Dutch Kindelberger. The first B-25 off the assembly line, retained on bailment (loan) from the US Army, was assigned as a dedicated transport for NAA executives and became known as *Whiskey Express* (though the reason for the name remains a mystery).

Arnold, Eisenhower, and Kindelberger each rode their winged steed hard and with great success in their persistent quest to extend their institutional knowledge, power, influence, and effectiveness. Other important leaders, using other types of airplanes, also increasingly became frequent flyers as they hopscotched between war plants and important meetings in every corner of the country.

Constantly impatient, Kindelberger wanted things done quickly and once stated, "An airplane is like an egg. It has to be sold when it's fresh." Life in a World War II–era airplane factory was simple. The engineers, aided by draftsmen, prepared drawings of parts. The production workers made and assembled the parts. As to nitpicking engineers who could dawdle over a drawing forever, Kindelberger once stated, "It takes two men to make an airplane drawing: one to sit on his fanny and draw lines, the other to knock him on the head with a baseball bat when he's through." In an era when the technology of aviation was advancing quickly, it was Kindelberger's goal to be thinking, planning, and preparing three years ahead.

Kindelberger's blue-collar roots were always with him. "If the men in the shop are happy in their jobs, it is surprising how many more times they can hit something with a hammer than if they are sour about it," he once noted. Nothing bothered him more than an assembly mechanic uncomfortably scrunched into a fuselage while drilling overhead and having the metal shavings falling onto his face. Stan Smithson, the NAA executive responsible for manufacturing, described the evolution of "work simplification" or "design to build" at NAA:

> During the slow growth of the company, from 1934 to the period just before the war, something very important—in fact, revolutionary—happened in the aircraft industry, beginning at North American. In the old days, airplanes were tailor made, one at a time.
>
> A fuselage was built and a man crawled in through the cockpit to string wires and control cables, half the time suspended head downward while performing his job. But by the time NAA contracted with the British to build the first Mustang for the RAF, many men could work on a fuselage because it had been "designed for production" and the man who thought it up was James Kindelberger.

They called it "fuselage on the half shell" because the two halves were laid open for ease of access. The halves were joined only after all of the riveting, wiring, controls, and

continued on page 34

Stan Smithson was invited by Kindelberger to join with him and Atwood at General Aviation in mid-1934. Smithson was a manufacturing genius who enjoyed a long and productive career with North American.

THE HOME FRONT

The home was custom designed and built under Kindelberger's direction. It featured a wet bar and various gadgets from his own fertile mind. He especially relished mixing up complicated drinks for visitors.

Business obligations dictated frequent absences away from home and family for Dutch Kindelberger while he traveled an estimated eighty thousand miles per year. His wife, Thelma, kept a log, and over one three-month period Kindelberger dined at home on only four occasions because of business commitments.

Nevertheless, there was a family life. In a business letter dated October 1941, Kindelberger uncharacteristically rambled into an anecdote: "Our gardening ambition has now expanded to the point that we have bought a ranch of some three hundred acres down among the mountains of San Diego and Mrs. Kindelberger is down there practically all the time as a real dirt farmer, which I mean literally. She has bought her own tractor and roars up and down the rows of trees, plowing and cultivating like an old-time farmer."

The property eventually succumbed to Southern California developers, but not before Kindelberger gradually amassed (for his own retirement) a portfolio that came to include NAA stock, an Oklahoma oil well, stake in an automobile dealership, and patent royalties from his own inventions.

Kindelberger and Thelma divorced in 1945. The marriage had lasted twenty-six years before becoming another victim of the war. Kindelberger went on to marry Helen Louise Allen, a former model much younger than himself.

Daughter Joan was a mother with young children of her own during Kindelberger's waning years and he reveled in his newfound role as grandfather. A spacious residence was custom-built high on a palisade overlooking the Pacific Ocean, with Kindelberger taking special interest in its design and construction. It was stuffed with modern gadgets of his own creation: a slot machine was hidden in a living-room cabinet, guest beds that folded out of the walls, a pilot's microphone embedded in an impressive wet bar so he could call the kitchen for more ice, and even an automatic misting system to keep his orchids hydrated in his greenhouse.

Kindelberger and Helen enjoyed cooking and entertaining groups as large as sixty people, with two domestic servants employed to keep their large home tidy. Twenty-five years after his passing, Kindelberger's dream home was torn down after suffering structural damage in a 1987 earthquake.

The Kindelberger residence was perched on a high palisade with the Pacific Ocean in the front yard and a swimming pool behind. Kindelberger led an idyllic domestic life with his wife, daughter, and grandchildren.

RIGHT: Francis Perkins, Secretary of Labor from 1933 to 1945 and the first female cabinet member, takes interest in the work of John Hadden. She was credited with exempting women from the draft so they would be available for all forms of industrial work.

OPPOSITE: This photograph, at the Kansas City plant, was carefully staged and well executed. It also depicts the racial segregation that was considered normal at that time.

continued from page 31

tubing were in place. The resulting efficiencies could be used to either reduce cost or maximize profit. During the war years, NAA consistently delivered aircraft for less than contract prices because of manufacturing efficiencies and attention to the management of overhead costs.

When the government was confronted with too many airplane producers after the war, Kindelberger's advice was: "Let lazy companies starve to death. Keep alive only those companies which would fight for contracts with superior planes, prompt delivery, and low prices."

In spite of salty language and a gruff demeanor, Kindelberger was a polished political operative who deftly side-stepped a long string of potential pitfalls that would have confounded a less savvy executive. Examples include the strike of 1941, a US Senate investigation into production problems at Dallas in 1943, and the crash of an experimental B-25 (the NA-98X) in 1944. However, Kindelberger made at least one public relations stumble by not living up to public expectations for workplace opportunity, even by the norms of 1941.

His staffing plan for a newly conceived Kansas City plant was limited to white males between the ages of eighteen and thirty-five. That thinking raised public ire and brought protests from local politicians. Wartime labor shortages quickly forced the expansion of that demographic to include older people, women, and minorities. The first women arrived at work on January 19, 1942. However, the sad reality was that the modicum of

black employees at the Kansas City plant never exceeded ten percent of the workforce and a disproportionate number of them were assigned to janitorial or service jobs, unfairly banned from upwardly mobile positions.

Kindelberger normally refrained from sounding off to the press but his temper was piqued early in the war when Edsel Ford and Charlie Sorenson, another Ford executive, made assertions regarding the ability of auto companies to mass-produce large airplanes. The Consolidated B-24 Liberator heavy bomber was to be the test case. NAA was gearing up for production at their new Dallas plant while the Ford-produced versions were to come from Willow Run, Michigan. Ford struggled at first, but ultimately succeeded with a peak production rate of 650 per month. Just over eighteen thousand Liberators were constructed, making it the most-produced American airplane of the war.

Walter Reuther, leader of the United Auto Workers (UAW), further roiled the waters with his well-publicized "Reuther Plan," which asserted UAW members at the automobile plants, in collaboration with management, could quickly retool and turn out five hundred fighter planes per day. The plan, released on December 23, 1940, was ludicrous and ultimately rejected by the wiser men of the National Defense Advisory Council. Autoworkers worked with steel, not aluminum; less than 10 percent of the required tooling was common, and automobile assembly bays were far too narrow to allow the passage of airplanes. Furthermore, the army was in dire need of long-range heavy bombers, not fighters.

With uncharacteristic bombast, Kindelberger was publicly critical of the auto industry's plane-making assertions. In the end, the cross-country verbal altercation consumed newspaper ink by the barrel, but appeared to do no lasting damage as both the Ford people and Kindelberger withdrew to their respective corners to concentrate on the business at hand: gearing up for war.

Iris Mahone (left) and a co-worker are seen in shirt sleeve comfort at the Kansas City B-25 factory, which was air-conditioned, a feature then more frequently found in motion picture theaters.

CHAPTER 3

WAR AT HAND

There has been in general a great disappointment among the people of this country regarding airplane production. When the President said fifty thousand airplanes per year, this meant four thousand airplanes per month, and when orders were placed it was hard for the average person with no knowledge whatever of the requirements for production to realize why we did not instantly start producing four thousand airplanes per month.

—Dutch Kindelberger, November 30, 1941

Workers scramble to get this B-25 ready for delivery as Dutch Kindelberger shakes hands with freshly minted Lt. Gen. William Knudsen in February 1942. It was during this early-war timeframe when the Doolittle Raiders were being prepared in secrecy for their airborne assault upon Tokyo.

A Santa Fe Railway steam locomotive pauses at the Inglewood plant as workers depart the plant. The puffing smoke-belchers were deemed "good enough" to keep the trains moving. In fact, scores of new steam-powered locomotives were fabricated during the war years.

The prewar North American Aviation business base began to grow with the sale of ever larger numbers of military aircraft to the army and navy. The export of trainer aircraft and fighter derivatives to various foreign countries augmented the profitability at a time when many other companies were just starting to shake off the lingering effects of the Great Depression. NAA products found homes in countries around the world, and the company was consistently profitable during the prewar years at Inglewood.

By 1940, the US government was beginning to stake out an amazing amount of discretionary powers that would allow it to redirect all forms of heavy industry for the duration of the war years. Scarce resources and other military essentials were managed with an iron fist. For instance, because the 1,350-horsepower General Motors Model 567 diesel engine was perfect for submarine propulsion, steam locomotive builders, who still retained ample capacity to augment and replace worn-out Depression-era locomotives, were called upon to step up production of their smoke-belching iron contraptions. The Model 567 was reserved for use in submarines and other marine applications, and railroad dieselization was deferred for a decade.

During World War II the United States, Mexico, and Canada were spared the infrastructure damage inflicted upon Germany, Japan, Russia, and many other countries. Essentials like food and fuel remained plentiful compared to other parts of the world. Gasoline was rationed only because rubber for tires was in short supply. The vast railroad system remained intact to transport the surge of passengers and everything else necessary for domestic consumption during sustained military operations on two war fronts.

Rail transportation was of vital importance to airplane production. Industrial plants and major military bases of the era were always located on rail lines. For instance, at NAA's Kansas City B-25 factory, five hundred carloads of freight arrived per month, while three

THE CALM BEFORE THE CHAOS

In prewar Southern California, abundant cheap real estate, a great climate, aircraft manufacturing, and moviemaking all had combined to fuel economic growth. It would take decades before all of the farmland and orange groves were lost to development. But the year 1939 was a watershed throughout the world, as well:

- The entertainment industry prospered. Three movies of particular note were in production or released: *Gone With the Wind*, *The Wizard of Oz*, and *The Grapes of Wrath*.

- New York hosted a World's Fair where breakthroughs like television, super highways, and dishwashers were demonstrated for the first time.

- The pace of airplane orders exploded as war and rumors of war in Europe and Asia drove the demand for strengthening the anemic US military and sating the needs of allies. New products evolved, plants expanded, and a surge of new employees came onto the payroll.

- Los Angeles Union Station opened for business as the last of the nation's grand railway stations. Rail traffic expanded as the railroads were called upon to move the freight necessary for military production and to deliver thousands of uniformed troops to their ports of embarkation.

- Intercity trucks and buses were busy but inadequate to shoulder the nation's military efforts because tires were in short supply and roads were primitive by today's standards.

- Electro-Motive Division (EMD) of General Motors demonstrated to railroad management the operating advantages of modern diesel-electric locomotives over steam-powered locomotion when pulling lengthy freight trains.

hundred carloads of spare parts, scrap metal, and reusable shipping containers departed. Smaller aircraft, including the AT-6 and British Mustangs, were packed into wooden crates for shipment aboard railroad flatcars to seaports for loading aboard ships. American Mustangs, trainers, and medium bombers were usually flown by Ferry Command to their next destination. In the interest of security, production employees were instructed not to speculate about destinations after aircraft were accepted by the government.

After years of work, two massive concrete dams were constructed. In 1936, the Hoover Dam, on the Colorado River near Las Vegas, was completed. The Grand Coulee Dam, on the Columbia River in Washington state, followed in 1942. The government agencies and private contractors involved honed their skills at overseeing and accomplishing massive public-works projects. Sprawling housing developments sprouted near each of them for workers and their families. These experiences gained facilitated the building of shipyards and new airplane factories, along with much needed residential units for workers.

Both dams supplied the West with water for irrigation, but more significant was the abundant, reliable, and low-cost hydroelectric power that each provided. These massive amounts of electricity would energize not only shipyards and aircraft plants, but also help process mountains of bauxite ore into aircraft-grade alloyed sheet aluminum, plate aluminum, and ingots for castings essential for aircraft construction.

After Great Britain declared war on Germany in September 1939, President Franklin D. Roosevelt recognized that the world was sliding toward an ever broader conflict and that the United States would be swept into the fray. He initiated military assistance to Britain while laying the groundwork for national mobilization. Roosevelt's mastermind for the ramp-up of industrial production to unprecedented wartime levels was Danish immigrant and master of automobile production William Knudsen (sometimes called the "Great Dane").

In 1940, Roosevelt called Knudsen, a senior General Motors executive, to Washington, DC, and engaged him on war preparations before appointing him as chairman of the Wartime Office of Production Management. GM President Alfred P. Sloan, a longtime foe of Roosevelt, took umbrage and immediately terminated Knudsen from the GM payroll. Knudsen felt a deep obligation to the United States because of the success he had achieved. He became the first of the "dollar-a-year" men—individuals of means and accomplishment who contributed their time and talents to the US government in exchange for a dollar.

Knudsen was the only person in US military history to go directly from civilian to the rank of lieutenant general, adroitly trading in his fedora and business suits for an army uniform adorned with three stars. Upon commissioning in January 1942, he oversaw army production strategies, set priorities, resolved wartime industrial problems, and was a frequent visitor at the three NAA factories and many other defense plants. The self-imposed travel, long hours, and unremitting stress of resolving the plethora of production problems took a visible toll on his health. He passed away in 1948, a month after his sixty-ninth birthday.

Industrialists, as a whole, disapproved of Roosevelt's policies, his cabinet members, and almost every aspect of the New Deal. The popular Democrat's pro-union stance and the rapid progress of organized labor under his watch were especially galling to the automobile builders. After the downfall of William Boeing following the Senate Air Mail hearing of 1934, there is no evidence that Dutch Kindelberger did or said anything to antagonize the New Dealers, while luminaries like Sloan, Henry Ford, and Charles Lindbergh were more outspoken in their disdain. They remained leery of the Roosevelt administration and did not fully embrace the war effort until after the attack on Pearl Harbor. Historians have long agreed that the American miracle of World War II was the incredible increase of war materiel, and like a puppeteer pulling strings, Knudsen was in the middle of most of it.

Every aircraft builder confronted the financial challenge of unprecedented expansion to meet the exploding demand for planes. NAA utilized internally generated funds (i.e., profits) not only for product development but also for plant construction up until November 1940, when another agency, the Defense Plant Corporation, first made government money available. Airplane producers could not anticipate the duration of the war, nor could they afford to bear the cost of huge but empty plants when hostilities ended. Government financing paid for 74 percent of the space utilized by NAA at peak. In addition, separate financing in the form of government-guaranteed bank loans was available to fund inventory.

NAA was building toward its apex during the war years from 1938 to 1945 when more than forty thousand warplanes were assembled—more than any other United States company. Their headquarters, general offices, labs, manufacturing spaces, and airfield accesses were located in Inglewood, where engineering, flight testing, and other developmental work was also accomplished.

It was important that the Inglewood plant was situated adjacent to ample tracts of vacant real estate because the facility would be expanded a total of thirty-three times between 1935 and 1944 as additional factory, office, laboratory, and warehouse spaces were added to meet demands. The quest for more space resulted in the lease of additional nearby facilities suitable for industrial purposes. The idled Hollywood Park horse-racing track was obtained in April 1943. The clubhouse areas and grandstand became additional office space and a huge warehouse, respectively, for government-furnished equipment.

The eight Southern California airplane builders—Consolidated, Douglas, Lockheed, North American, Northrop, Ryan, Vega, and Vultee—banded together, establishing the Aircraft War Production Council, and collaborated on matters of mutual interest, including the construction of a shared wind tunnel.

The US aircraft companies also struck a pact that allowed the sharing of proprietary designs so that needed models could be built where production capacity existed or could be quickly created. For example, both Douglas and Vega built Boeing B-17s in Southern California. However, only NAA built NAA-designed aircraft in the United States. (As a footnote, NAA trainers were licensed for assembly in Australia, and the ultimate version of the T-6 trainer, dubbed the Harvard 4, was built by Canadian Car and Foundry, successor to Noorduyn, in the 1950s.)

Aircraft builders also freely exchanged design concepts. For example, NAA borrowed the dive brakes (upper and lower wing surface panels that could open to slow a speeding airplane while engaged in a ground attack) from Vultee for the A-36 (a version of the P-51), but also provided their B-25 landing gear design for use in Northrop's P-61 night fighter. High-shear rivets, a 1943 invention, replaced most structural fasteners in all airplane designs.

The National Airplane Division of the National Defense Advisory Commission (NDAC) made recommendations for preparations for war. Created by President Roosevelt in 1940, the NDAC was an ad hoc prewar group of visionaries, including Bill Knudsen and Gen. Henry "Hap" Arnold who foresaw and communicated the immediate need to begin the construction of massive new factories that would be required to achieve the desired national production rate of fifty thousand airplanes per year.

The NDAC further recommended that new plants be located far from the coasts, behind the mountains in multiple Midwestern cities to ensure the urban infrastructure of

The Hollywood Park horse-racing track was idled by the war and leased by North American for office space and the warehousing of Government Furnished Equipment (GFE).

ABOVE: This example of wartime housing was constructed in Kansas City to house North American workers. Some of the quickly-assembled temporary structures, which were found nationwide, lasted for decades.

RIGHT: The visitor entrances at Kansas City and Dallas (shown here) were of impressive modernistic design.

any single location would not be overwhelmed. NAA operated two of these new plants, at Dallas and Kansas City.

Roosevelt's appeal for increased aircraft and other wartime production was taken seriously by everybody—even his detractors. Unlike today, when presidential goals are often considered rhetoric, frequently ignored, and then forgotten, military and industrial leaders accepted the challenge and set about to meet it because they knew Roosevelt frequently looked at the production figures and would act decisively if expectations were missed.

Work started on the Dallas plant (actually located near Grand Prairie) in 1940 and the first factory building was ready for occupancy in a mere 120 days. The name of this business entity was North American Aviation, Inc. of Texas, and it operated as a subsidiary from September 30, 1940, to December 31, 1941, when it became part of the parent. Dallas would ultimately be the home for AT-6 Texan trainer assembly, a second P-51 production line, and the fabrication of almost 900 B-24 Liberator heavy bombers under license from Consolidated of San Diego.

The Kansas City industrial area called Fairfax was home to another government-owned and funded plant. It was constructed by McDonald, Tarleton, and Patti of Kansas City and St. Louis, and management oversight was shared with the army corps of engineers. Construction began in early 1941 with the driving of telephone pole–sized pilings into the bottom land adjacent to the Missouri River. Reinforced concrete was poured over the top of the pilings. Windowless steel walls surrounded the entire plant, requiring air conditioning, an emerging technology more frequently found in movie theaters than factories. But it would ensure minimal part-fit problems caused by expansion and contraction of metal as it was heated or cooled.

The business would be operated as North American Aviation Inc. of Kansas and focus on high-volume B-25 Mitchell production. A startling number (6,608) of the medium bombers were produced during the plant's brief four-year run. A large but separate modification center located on another part of the Fairfax airport was constructed of wood in 1942 because of a shortage of steel. B-25s from Inglewood were flown to the modification center for mission- or customer-specific changes and engineering updates received too late for incorporation on the assembly line.

In March 1941, Kindelberger arranged the wartime executive talent at North American headquarters to his satisfaction, with him and Lee Atwood at the top of the organizational chart. The other vice presidents were: R. H. Rice (engineering), J. S. Smithson (manufacturing), R. A. Lambeth (finance), L. R. Taylor (industrial relations), R. L. Burla (public relations), and R. E. Dawe (quality control). Kindelberger also included three additional executive positions: C. J. Gallant (technical assignments), Noble Shopshire (contracts), and Harold Raynor (special assignments).

Further, Kindelberger called upon his deep bench to provide a small nucleus of skilled managers necessary to organize and lead the two new plants. H. V. Schwallenberg was a marine architect with an impressive academic resume that included a stint at Massachusetts Institute of Technology. "Schwally" was one of the original gang from Dundalk and was first employed by Bethlehem Shipbuilding in 1914 before joining Berliner & Joyce midcareer. He was dispatched to the Kansas City plant in 1941 to become the facility's senior manager, and was accompanied by experienced test pilot Paul Balfour. Other managers and specialists would join them, some on permanent assignment, others on a short-term basis.

Harold F. Schwedes was assigned to Dallas as the leader of North American Aviation Inc. of Texas. The assistant factory manager was Englishman Kenneth Bowen. Another former Berliner & Joyce employee, Bowen had recently achieved recognition for his role as project engineer on the P-51 developmental team, credited with the aircraft's design-to-build features, ease of maintenance, and serviceability attributes.

Parts shortages were common. Airplanes were lined up outside pending arrival of needed component. This is sometimes called "traveling the work" and the out-of-sequence installations are a labor-wasting symptom of an unhealthy factory.

The Carnegie Institute of Technology would have been Kindelberger's alma mater had he stayed to graduate. On November 30, 1941, he returned to speak there. Noting that, prior to ramping up production capacity, the nation would have topped out at six to seven hundred airplanes a month, he also stated:

There has been in general a great disappointment among the people of this country regarding airplane production. When the President said fifty thousand airplanes per year, this meant four thousand airplanes per month, and when orders were placed it was hard for the average person with no knowledge whatever of the requirements for production to realize why we did not instantly start producing four thousand airplanes per month. . . .

The fact that it takes from nine months to a year to build an airplane plant or an engine plant and even begin to get the equipment in it, the fact that it takes as much as six months to a year to obtain the necessary materials to begin construction after an order is placed, the fact that the tooling is intricate and time-consuming, are always overlooked.

It is hard now to realize that the aircraft industry has had the green light for little more than a year. . . . [T]he American aircraft industry has been able to do so much in that period as Germany did in five years—and it is only the beginning.

The December 7, 1941, attack on Pearl Harbor galvanized American resolve as nothing else could. The United Kingdom and British Commonwealth nations (including Canada) expanded their involvement in the fray, declaring war on Japan. On December 11,

Germany declared war on the United States and a hurriedly prepared statement appeared in all three NAA plant newspapers that day:

> To the North American family: America has united solidly to meet an issue forced upon us by unprovoked aggression. We at North American are in the thick of the toughest fight we have ever faced. Neither I nor anyone else need tell you the seriousness of the situation. You all recognize it and I am keenly aware that each of you is determined to do his job better and faster than ever before. These bombers, fighters, and trainers which have been moving down our assembly lines are real and tangible things which can contribute to our war effort. Let's keep them rolling out the door.
>
> — J. H. Kindelberger, President

In the hectic months that followed, Kindelberger quickly found himself not only managing North American, he also became a leader of the entire aviation manufacturing industry: "Dutch was embroiled in the mobilization turmoil," reads an NAA corporate history commissioned by the company's Columbus Division in 1959 or 1960. "He was airborne much of the time, hopping between his three plants coordinating everything from hand tools to housing, with side trips to Washington quiz bees.

"Because of his dominant personality and acumen, Dutch unofficially represented airpower from the producer's standpoint. Officially he was the first president of the Aircraft War Production Control Council and spoke for the entire aviation industry."

The problems endemic to NAA and all other aircraft plants included serious material shortages, shallow planning, and a chronic dearth of labor. Human resources challenges at the newly established and recently expanded plants included: severe shortages of

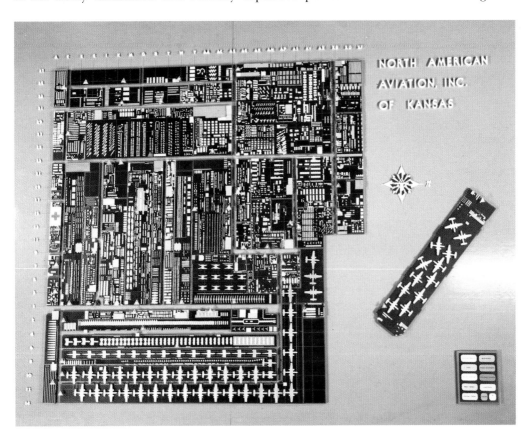

Industrial engineers maintained large graphic displays of the factory arrangement. It was subject to frequent updating as the product mix changed, the plant was expanded, or more moving assembly lines were implemented.

suitable housing; a lack of local transportation for workers; inadequate parking for private automobiles; a need for personal services like laundry, check cashing, and tool purchases; employee assistance for medical and emotional support; and insufficient on-site meal services. Eventually, various food vendors won and lost the Inglewood contract, including Studio Commissary Services, Sprott & Company, and Canteen Food Service of Chicago. Any one of these factors could contribute to employee dissatisfaction, which in turn might manifest itself in absenteeism or high turnover. The investments in training and experience were lost when a valued employee quit over avoidable workplace frustrations.

An especially irritating issue for management was the drafting of skilled workers from airplane plants into the military for mundane duties. Absenteeism also occurred when skilled men attended to personal affairs in response to a pending military induction notice. Kindelberger testified at hearings in early August 1943, "The government must decide whether it wants airplanes or soldiers from aircraft plants." A few days later, the California draft director announced a blanket deferment for aircraft workers.

It has been estimated that it took two wartime workers to equal the productivity of an experienced prewar employee. However, the pounds of airplane produced per labor hour doubled between 1938 and 1943 thanks to a combination of work simplification and automobile-style assembly methods, more than making up for the skills dilution caused by the recent arrival of large numbers of new people into the industry. Labor-saving devices that made their way into aircraft plants during the late 1930s and beyond included high-speed presses for forming sheet aluminum, metal-shearing devices called "brakes," and band saws for sheet cutting. There were also new precision finishing machines for honing, lapping, and polishing. Pneumatic riveting devices and electric spot-welding equipment further decreased labor hours while increasing accuracy and consistency of joined parts.

The English wheel was another novel device that allowed the operator to feed sheet-metal stock between two power-operated crowned wheels and form curved sections of sheet with skillful manipulation. Huge new presses, some rated at 5,500 tons, were introduced and could turn out sheet-metal parts of far greater size and complexity than ever before. And because airplanes are made of much softer materials than automobiles, tools could be fabricated more cheaply and be more quickly updated as designs changed.

A different problem arose at Dallas when whistleblowers complained to Congress of overstaffing and featherbedding (i.e., people on the payroll who were not productive). Other allegations included cronyism, unfair promotions, and inept management—none of which were surprising, given the fact that tens of thousands of employees of every ilk were newly hired. The Truman Commission, headed by Senator Harry S. Truman, investigated the allegations.

As usual, when a problem arose in Dallas or Kansas City, Kindelberger climbed aboard the corporate airplane. On arrival, he did a masterful job of explaining, addressing, and resolving site-specific issues. Employees were invited to submit suggestions; in fact, each received a blank suggestion form in their weekly plant newspaper. Serious consideration was given to the responses, and action was taken when warranted. There is no evidence that anybody was fired over the Dallas allegations and the investigation soon faded from memory.

Meanwhile, the federal government, in dire need of more military hardware, made sincere and sustained efforts to address all issues. Substitutions of materials were made when necessary until output increased. In rare instances, thin carbon steel or plywood was substituted for aluminum (e.g., B-25 aircrew seats and AT-6 aft fuselages were fabricated of wood). The huge modification center at Kansas City was constructed using laminated wood beams. Fast-running semitrailer trucks were pressed into service hauling parts to where they were most desperately needed.

Despite federal help, airplane factories also found themselves trapped in a bureaucratic nightmare caused by traditional governmental practices. Wartime procurement

started with fixed-price contracts that stipulated all of the labor and parts that went into an airplane had to be thoroughly tracked. As production rates accelerated, there were not enough inventory clerks and accountants in the workforce. When first implemented on the B-24 program at Dallas, fixed-price contracting resulted in the immediate redeployment of 1,800 people who were previously engaged solely in property accounting and inventory management. In another instance, the typed-up bill of material for a portion of one contract created a stack of paper fourteen feet tall. As usual, NAA was on the leading edge of implementing a better method, this in the form of a mechanism for subsequent price adjustments if needed.

As far as all that money was concerned, Treasury Secretary and famed financier Henry Morgenthau was called upon to raise funds to fight World War II through tools like War Bonds and "buy a bomber" programs in which communities and other groups raised the funds to purchase an aircraft. (The Museum of the Air Force in Dayton estimates that a B-25 cost $109,670 in 1943.) At the start of the program, an airplane's nose was adorned with the name of the contributing group. But the exigencies of war caused deception to creep into the program. At Kansas City, a ruse was carried out in the photo department with a master photo of a B-25 and a skilled calligrapher using a bit of white ink. The resulting 8x10 photograph seemed to depict an actual B-25 with each group's name decorating the nose. In fact, every group received a photograph of one of just a few airplanes. Many people have attempted to research the combat fate of "their" bomber, only to be told that no such airplane ever existed.

The assignment of mid-level managers and specialists ebbed and flowed among the three plants depending on shifting priorities and needs. A party was held in Inglewood in June 1942 to mark the departure of sixteen engineers to new jobs in Kansas City and

Jack Fox, a Field Service representative who earned fame for his wartime service in Australia in 1942, was assigned as the traveling crew chief aboard *Whiskey Express* (see opposite page) in late 1943. At 5 feet 4 inches and 140 pounds, he was the right size for traveling in an airplane that many found claustrophobic.

Dallas. Challenging assignments, sometimes with too much responsibility, were handed to individuals with the hope and expectation they would rise to the occasion. Those who floundered were soon shunted aside. Weekly plant newspapers of the era make frequent reference to the arrival and departure of mid-level managers and specialists.

Harold Raynor, a native of Greenport, Long Island, was a marine engineer and a veteran of the Glenn Curtiss Company who boasted that he was hired into Atlantic Aviation by none other than Anthony Fokker. He earned his status as a long-time trusted member of the NAA inner circle by being part of the small team that took on the NA-16 trainer project of 1934. His tall, thin frame and protruding ears make him easy to recognize in many photographs from the late 1930s when he was responsible for international marketing.

A company that grows from small to huge in a short period of time needs documented procedures to ensure policies are communicated and consistently applied. Raynor's leadership role in the creation of the NAA "Procedures Manual" dated July 1, 1943, is evident because his name appears on the cover.

Production quotas were not being met at Kansas City and the plant was in trouble. With manager Schwallenberg having been on sick leave for six weeks, Kindelberger and Atwood

WHISKEY EXPRESS

NAA's B-25-platform VIP transport was in constant use as it frequently whisked company executives between California, Texas, Kansas, Dayton, and Washington, DC, among other business destinations. Rare during the early war years, transport versions of the B-25 became common thereafter. With an optional bomb-bay fuel tank, they had a range of 2,400 nonstop miles.

Jack Fox, the field-service representative who earned fame for his wartime service in Australia during 1942, did a midwar stint in late 1943 as the traveling crew chief aboard *Whiskey Express*. A fast-attack bomber dedicated to VIP transport was an important symbol of power and prestige. Fox noted that the airplane was an attention grabber when they arrived at airports. Fox who had received limited private pilot flight instruction during the 1930s, was an acknowledged expert on all aspects of B-25 operation. He reported that the airplane had been flown hard and that his predecessor had scrimped on engine and airframe maintenance. Fox expressed appreciation for the generous assistance rendered at the various NAA plants as much-needed parts and repairs were sought out during brief layovers.

Workplace politics aboard *Whiskey Express* contrasted with Fox's straight-arrow ethics and simple upbringing. Fox reported that during one late-evening flight back to Los Angeles the pilot had departed the cockpit to scramble head first through the tight passageway (where the wing spars spanned the fuselage on the top of the bomb bay) to "schmooze" with the passengers riding in the aft fuselage. When the pilot failed to return, it was Fox who landed the B-25 in darkness at the busy Los Angeles Municipal Airport. His irritation level spiked when coworkers scowled after seeing him at the controls.

The assignment to *Whiskey Express* was a source of constant frustration to Fox and his job satisfaction improved when he voluntarily returned to overseas war-zone field-service work.

The B-25 known as *Whiskey Express* was on bailment from army air forces to North American as an executive transport. In constant use, it allowed Dutch Kindelberger to simultaneously manage major plants located in three distant states while making frequent side trips to Washington, DC, and Wright Field.

jumped aboard *Whiskey Express* and flew to Kansas City where they settled in to assess the situation. The stress level was palpable. Schwallenberg was relieved of his assignment and shunted off to Inglewood as a corporate-level quality-assurance director. (Kindelberger ensured there was a safety net for members of the inner circle who had given their best effort.) Memories faded over time and Schwallenberg went on to retire from NAA in 1957 as a celebrated executive.

The Kansas City plant newspaper, the *North Ameri-Kansan* reported on December 3, 1943, that acting plant manager Harold Raynor had been appointed new permanent plant manager. Raynor now had responsibility for more than twenty thousand employees. Using a carrot rather than a stick, Raynor's management style, combined with the manufacturing improvements he sponsored, were credited for exceeding production targets with a sustained production rate of about three hundred B-25s per month. Raynor would return to Inglewood postwar as corporate director of material. He left the company in mid-1951 but later reappeared at NAA's Downey, California, plant as an executive on the *Apollo* manned-spacecraft project in the 1960s.

Product development at NAA was aggressive during the war years and annual financial results were favorable until 1947, when postwar net earnings first encountered turbulence. Cost accountants were assigned to compute detailed profit or loss statements on each airplane project. General Motors remained the largest stakeholder in NAA, but the aircraft business was different from their other holdings.

In his autobiography, Alfred Sloan wrote: "Dutch Kindelberger was an extremely capable engineer and demonstrated great technical competence in aircraft design and manufacturing. He developed into a fine administrator, came to be recognized as a man who could produce outstanding military airplanes at low cost. But he had very little general administrative experience before coming to North American, and recognizing his own limitations, he relied on Ernest Breech and Henry Hogan of General Motors as an informal executive committee and they regularly consulted each other on important problems which arose between meetings of the Board of Directors."

With the passage of time and an increase in self-confidence, Kindelberger came to manage NAA with the style and swagger of a sole proprietor. He was empowered to make quick and unilateral decisions when necessary to seize an opportunity. An army air forces report of 1945 commended his decisiveness: "When President Roosevelt called for an output of fifty thousand planes, Mr. Kindelberger bought very heavily of everything needed to take care of their share of the fifty thousand. It was fortunate for our later needs that he had the foresight and nerve to go immediately into the market with $600,000 of North American funds. . . ."

In 1943, the NAA board of directors comprised only seven men. Henry M. Hogan was the chairman, and also a board member, vice president, and general counsel at General Motors. Henry B. du Pont of the E. I. du Pont de Nemours Company of Wilmington, Delaware, was also a board member at both companies. Kindelberger held the majority vote: him, Atwood, Chief Financial Officer R. A. Lambeth, and the person who recruited him—GM stakeholder Ernest R. Breech.

The chemistry between Breech and Kindelberger was excellent. Breech, two years younger than his subordinate, brought formidable accounting and financial skills to the table while judiciously exercising another vital attribute: the ability to reach into the deep pockets of GM and pull out cash when most needed. North American would have stalled in the early, formative years without the financial backing of GM—one of the wealthiest private enterprises on the planet.

Kindelberger delivered technical expertise and marketing genius specific to aviation. If the enterprise were an automobile, Kindelberger would have been the gas pedal, always pushing forward and striving to get there faster. Lee Atwood was analogous to the brake,

slowing things down long enough to ask questions while double-checking facts and data. Ernest Breech, meanwhile, was the steering wheel who oversaw the ledgers and ensured the sustained profitability necessary to keep an enterprise viable over the long haul.

Breech eventually departed to assume executive control of another GM affiliate: the Bendix Corporation, whose components were found in virtually every American-built airplane and automobile of that era. In the postwar era, Breech would make the reverse course of William Knudsen by departing GM to assume the presidency of Ford Motor Company, where he mentored young Henry Ford II. Breech and Kindelberger remained lifelong friends.

Meetings of the board and annual shareholder events always went smoothly on Kindelberger's watch. The ownership of NAA was spread over thirty thousand investors. GM's stake slowly fell with the passage of time from 40 to less than 30 percent before it was completely divested by 1958. By mutual consent, the two companies were on separate paths as North American became progressively less dependent upon General Motors for either financial assistance or management direction in the pre–World War II era. In fact, by 1947 North American was no longer controlled by General Motors.

There was never evidence or allegation that GM meddled in NAA affairs. However, important business interdependencies did arise from time to time. GM's Allison Division provided early P-51 engines while the Fisher Body Division plant in Memphis was a major provider of B-25 airframe parts and assemblies. GM rendered considerable assistance during North American's rapid expansion at the start of the war by loaning key manufacturing methods personnel to facilitate the rapid ramp-up of production.

As is the practice to this day, many aircraft parts were not built by the prime contractor. The government wisely provided externally sourced components like engines, radios, tires, guns, turrets, and bomb sights as "government-furnished equipment" (GFE). This avoided bidding wars and allowed the government to engage multiple vendors, manage standard designs, and allocate any shortages depending on shifting priorities.

An early war photo of a British B-24 Liberator, B-25 Mitchell, and B-17 Flying Fortress together. The B-24, designed by Consolidated Aircraft of San Diego, was the most produced airplane of the war. North American built about nine hundred of them at Dallas. Nearly ten thousand Mitchells were constructed by North American while several companies built about a combined total of 12,731 of the Boeing-designed B-17 Flying Fortress.

This early war-era internal chart was crafted to depict the shortfall of parts needed for the rapid expansion of airplane production. Subcontracting was the buying of parts. Feeder plants were established in leased space to alleviate congestion at the main plants.

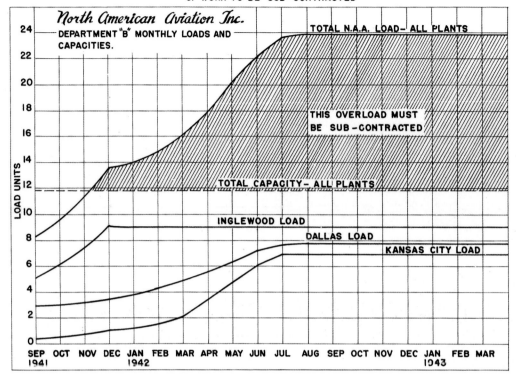

THIS IS AN EXAMPLE OF THE DEPARTMENTAL LOAD STUDIES WHICH DETERMINE THE AMOUNT OF WORK TO BE SUB-CONTRACTED

North American Aviation Inc. DEPARTMENT "B" MONTHLY LOADS AND CAPACITIES.

TOTAL N.A.A. LOAD- ALL PLANTS

THIS OVERLOAD MUST BE SUB-CONTRACTED

TOTAL CAPACITY- ALL PLANTS

INGLEWOOD LOAD

DALLAS LOAD

KANSAS CITY LOAD

Cross-procurement could also hinder high-rate production and create inter-service friction. Production of AT-6 trainer aircraft, for example, was owned by the army but the navy also used the airplane, calling it the "SNJ." If the navy wanted a tailhook installed on a SNJ, the army might balk since it would slow production for all users and the navy would therefore need to retrofit the SNJ. Meanwhile, because the navy owned the procurement for Norden bombsights, army air forces could be slighted in their requests for changes.

Main plants were suffering every form of shortage, from work space to parking for both airplanes and autos. The war couldn't wait for more new nearby housing and further plant expansion. An innovative solution, called "feeder plants," was devised to reduce workforce and space shortages at the main plants. Under the system, work was brought closer to the workers by renting buildings that were converted into small factories. Feeder plants were soon humming nationwide. North American-operated examples were found in downtown Dallas, Waco, Pasadena, on Figueroa Street in Los Angeles, at a vacant Chevrolet factory near Kansas City, and elsewhere. Outsized trucks, custom-built to deal with the bulky (but lightweight) airplane parts moved the parts from feeder factories to main plants.

In the quest for optimization, the production process was constantly adjusted. New variants of existing products were introduced as engineering improvements were incorporated into production lines. The B-25D at Kansas City was phased out in favor of the B-25J, for example. And on Memorial Day 1944, it was announced that B-25 production at Inglewood would end. P-51 production, for the first time, was able to hit full stride as space and labor constraints were finally alleviated.

It was a struggle to implement automobile-style mass production in warbird factories, however. What evolved was described by NAA as the "component breakdown" method of

production. The key was a steady, uninterrupted forward march of a moving assembly line. It required orderly thinking and advanced planning. It demanded that each job be done in its proper place and time with a minimum of confusion. The concept was used at all North American plants.

A unique feature of the Fairfax plant in Kansas City was an elevated continuous chain conveyor that carried B-25 tail assemblies near the ceiling and high above the assembly line. The conveyor brought the assemblies down to the aft fuselages where they were permanently attached. Each piece or component, in turn, was added as the aircraft continued its forward progress toward the factory exit. Any missing pieces would catch up to be properly installed Fairfax sustained a production rate in the range of three hundred per month during the last two years of operation.

The Kansas City B-25 factory sprouted on a former seventy-five acre alfalfa field in the Fairfax industrial district.

CHAPTER 4

TRAINERS AND TRAINING

Probably no airplane ever designed was more perfect for its purpose. It cost little to build and fly, it was simple and trustworthy, it was safe and it simulated the combat aircraft of its period. . . . Here, undoubtedly, is one of the truly greats. Brought out in volume batches, never pampered, driven to dilapidation, and still always flying with charity for mothers' sons, the AT-6 will be forever celebrated.

—AT-6 description written by
North American Aviation plant
historian, circa 1960

The lengthy ammunition belts make it evident that the student pilots will be engaged in a live-fire exercise. The guns installed in trainers were not for combat but to expedite pilot training in the more lethal fighter aircraft of the day.

Well-trained pilots with aptitude, self-confidence, and an aggressive attitude have always been the foundation upon which decisive military airpower rests. Trainer airplanes are vital tools for honing competent combat pilots. They were also the first market niche North American sought to fill.

In 1934, while operations were still called General Aviation and located at Dundalk, Maryland, the three new hires—Dutch Kindelberger, Lee Atwood, and Stan Smithson—arrived fresh from the Douglas Aircraft Corporation at Santa Monica, eager to do well at their newfound opportunity. General Aviation stress engineer Dick Schleicher was himself feeling stressed-out at the sad state of the business:

Work in the stress department had fallen off to less than a dribble. There were five of us left under Elmer Bruhn and we needed work or else. So, Bill Miller, our chief engineer from the Berliner and Joyce days, got into his torpedo-body sports car and drove to Washington, DC, to see Commander McCart. He came home with a contract for a full stress analysis report on the OJ-2 [Navy airplane] we had just built, with Zap flaps. The last thing we needed was

LEFT: Richard "Dick" Schleicher was the principal stress engineer at North American during most of his tenure from 1934 to 1971. His eyewitness accounts of several memorable events are preserved in the North American files.

OPPOSITE: Dutch Kindelberger arrived at Dundalk, Maryland, in July of 1934 in an Oldsmobile. Kindelberger cursed the heat and the entire operation would be relocated to Inglewood, California, within two years.

NA-16, the prototype for over twenty thousand military trainer airplanes that followed it, is photographed in the mud at Dundalk, Maryland, on April 5, 1935. Twin canopies were later fitted over the open cockpits.

more proof the OJ-2 was structurally sound. Nevertheless, this small contract kept the four of us employed until we became North American Aviation.

Just before Dutch arrived in Dundalk to take up his new position, rumors were a dime a dozen about what might happen to us. My desk was at a window overlooking the executive parking space. It was July and hot! A new Oldsmobile pulled up and out sprang a big man cussing the heat. He had parked his car in space No. 1 (no one ever dared park there). I turned to the stress group and yelled, "Here he is," and we all made sure we looked busy.

The void left by a lack of work occasionally was filled by horseplay. W. B. "Bill" Smith recalled some of the antics of the crew:

Shop workers were generally left alone and trusted by supervision to do their thing. Rules came into being as things got out of hand or went too far. Horseplay was not uncommon. A cranky, heavyset, Navy inspector, Mr. Hull, with very little sense of humor, was often the target of shop horseplay. He could all too often be seen grabbing at the back of his neck after being hit by a rivet; blown through a piece of tubing. [Matters turned ugly when floats for Navy planes failed leak testing because of small holes.] Government inspectors were powerful people in those days and it took all the apologies our factory manager could come up with to keep from getting shut down.

Kindelberger took stock of the situation upon arrival at the old Curtiss-Caproni hangar that housed the entire General Aviation operation. "It couldn't have been much worse," he later recalled. It was like a dusty museum with the vestiges of former Berliner & Joyce and Fokker greatness lingering in the decay. Schleicher continued:

> After Dutch, Lee, and Stan arrived from the Douglas Company in Santa Monica, one day the word went out that we were to witness a demonstration of that wonderful new manufacturing technique called the drop hammer (it was actually invented in the Stone Age). Dutch had acquired the equipment from somewhere and we didn't have an operator. A phone call from Dutch to Donald Douglas, and a sheet metal worker was on his way east. For several days after his arrival no one could find him, but he finally did show up. We all stood by as he raised the head after placing the die on the bed with a piece of aluminum on it. Bang! The first piece of cowling was made. That worker was kept sober after that.

At the time, no new military airplane types were in gestation, the commercial models had been unsuccessful, and there was only a little sustaining work to be done on some navy planes. Kindelberger pondered their next move. Douglas, Martin, Boeing, and Consolidated had a lock on the big airplanes. Employees looked askance as Kindelberger sold the prototype of an airliner then under development to a junk dealer for $1,500.

The new arrivals still needed something else and they needed it quickly. It was while in the backseat of a New York taxi cab that Kindelberger asked his new boss, Ernest Breech, who was chairman of the board at General Aviation and the General Motors envoy, for $36,000 to design a low-wing, two-seat basic monoplane trainer and enter it into the army air corps competition to be held in three months (all previous American military trainers were bi-wing). A trainer airplane was a match for Kindelberger's World War I–era flying experience and knowledge base. The shortness of time and the small sum requested seemed rather optimistic to Breech, but he had hired Kindelberger because the man was sincere, motivated, and capable. Funding and the project were approved.

GM under Alfred Sloan in the 1930s demanded excellence of its managers in order for their careers to advance. The newcomers, augmented by a small cadre of the Fokker brain trust, went to work on the high-stakes new product. They knew their futures hinged on a successful design.

Kindelberger donned his marketing hat and traveled the short distance south to Washington, DC, to meet with his lifelong colleague, (then) Col. Henry "Hap" Arnold, a rapidly rising star in the army air corps with his finger on the pulse of procurement and a host of other modernization issues. As the pair dined at the Mayflower Hotel, Arnold cautioned his friend that the deadline for the fly-off was looming and that other competitors—Curtiss-Wright Airplane Division (with the model 19R) and Seversky Aircraft Corporation—were well along with their designs.

Kindelberger was hell-bent for success and his enthusiasm was contagious. An engineer, Gordon Throne, recalled, "He was really a top organizer that could inspire people to do a job. You didn't mind working your butt off for Dutch."

Dundalk shop personnel would sometimes come to the plant on Saturdays in an effort to make schedule on the trainer project. One Saturday Kindelberger happened to stop by his office, and noted that the shop was humming with activity. When the New Dealers were swept into office in 1932 with no end to the Great Depression in sight, Congress had quickly passed an alphabet soup of labor-oriented legislation, including the Fair Labor Standards Act that required employers to pay hourly wage earners overtime pay for weekly hours in excess of forty. With Kindelberger's notorious anger starting to flare, plant manager Bob McCulloch was confronted with, "Do you guys want to get me in trouble with the government? We could be fined and lose our contract!" McCulloch calmly took Kindelberger

Edmond T. "Eddie" Allen earned fame by taking many aircraft designs (for various builders) aloft for the first time, including NA-16. Eddie Allen died while piloting an experimental B-29 in 1943. The flaming aircraft crashed into a meat packing plant in an industrial area of Seattle.

to the timecard rack. None of the cards were punched in. One of the workers gathered around spoke up: "We didn't punch in, we're here just having fun. Is that against the law?" The NA-16 trainer prototype was designed and built in a breathtaking sixty-two days.

The Dundalk operation was run on a shoestring. Kindelberger's wife, Thelma, for example, handled translations from Spanish for South American customers. Coworkers, in their oral histories, later stated there was no dedicated test pilot. Edmond T. "Eddie" Allen, an experienced freelance pilot and consulting aeronautical engineer with a résumé that included taking the first Douglas DC-2 airliner aloft, first flew the NA-16 on April 1, 1935, before ferrying it to Dayton for evaluation by army air corps engineers, procurement specialists, and test pilots.

Allen was another resource whom Kindelberger had spirited away from his recent mentor, Donald Douglas. In a small company, on a hot project with relaxed work rules, it is likely that Allen's contribution to the NA-16 included a combination of design, maintenance, and flying tasks.

Alexander de Seversky was a Russian expatriate and another World War I pilot who designed, built, and flew airplanes. His company's entrant into the trainer competition proved to be NAA's only other serious contender, but the army evaluation eventually found the NA-16 to be superior. Lacking the steady financial hand of an Ernest Breech, the Seversky Aircraft Company lost $550,000 in 1939 and Alexander de Seversky was forced out of his company, though it would reappear as Republic Aviation Corporation with a long string of successful airplanes, including the P-47 Thunderbolt, the F-105 Thunderchief, and the A-10 Thunderbolt II of Gulf War fame.

The NA-16's modern attributes were noted, including an all-metal cantilevered wing attached low on the fuselage, with no external bracing—features that would find their way into subsequent North American models. The fuselage was covered in fabric that could be removed for ease of maintenance or repair, and the aircraft was skillfully designed to mimic the handling characteristics of a fighter plane from the era. NA-16 was returned to Dundalk upon flight-test completion, where it was refurbished and received a new Pratt & Whitney engine. (An interesting footnote: the airplane was ultimately sold to the Republic of Argentina and flown there.)

If the goal of a prototype airplane is to demonstrate the attributes of the design and collect needed engineering enhancements, the NA-16 was a smashing success. A significant production order was awarded, but the list of needed changes was formidable. Allen wrote the following in a letter dated May 15, 1935:

To: Mr. J. H. Kindelberger
From: E. T. Allen
Subject: Report of basic trainer flights at Dayton

This was the first time I had flown the airplane with full load, and the first time I had been really violent with the controls. The characteristics change considerably with both of these factors. Incidental observations are as follows:
   1: Buffeting: When the stick is jerked back at 80 to 100 m.p.h. the buffeting and stalling of the wing became very evident. It occurs to me that a larger fillet might have some affect upon delaying the appearance of buffeting.
   2: Shimmy: Tail wheel shimmy developed several times during fast taxiing.
   3: Ground looping: The tendency to ground loop was much more evident with a full load. Several times it was very difficult to stop a ground loop. . . .

The letter went on to point out issues with ailerons, spinning, landing-gear struts, excessive takeoff roll when heavily loaded, and poor ventilation when the open-air twin cockpits

were covered by a canopy. The army stipulations filled six typed pages and included the need for a more powerful engine and fairings on the leading edge of the fixed main landing gear. A desperately needed production contract for forty-two airplanes worth about $1 million was awarded to North American.

Kindelberger exchanged friendly letters with Allen, who was in Buenos Aires during 1936 and receiving consulting payments from NAA. He invited Allen to Inglewood to perform flight testing on an XB-21 experimental bomber. However, it was not uncommon for people with aviation-manufacturing experience in any facet (managerial, engineering, piloting, or assembly) to move among military service and various airframe builders, and Allen took a post as a Boeing engineering test pilot in Seattle where he was engaged in the flight testing of a number of new and significant models, including versions of the

Pilots train in BT-9s over the Lone Star State. Prewar pilot training was conducted at just three airfields, all of them in Texas. The number of airfields was greatly expanded when the war arrived. The requirement for year-around good flying weather dictated that all of them be located in the warmer parts of America.

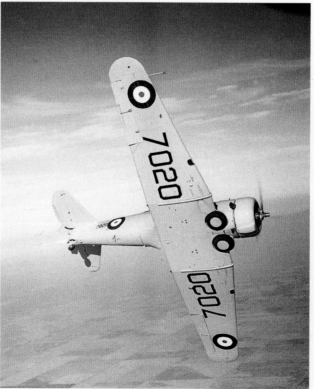

ABOVE: With its fuselage skin removed, the light and delicate internal structure of this North American trainer barely obstructs the view of surrounding scenery. Exposing the underlying structure was intended to ease maintenance and facilitate repairs.

LEFT: The graceful lines of the North American trainer family are visible in this in-flight photo.

B-17, the Model 307 airliner, the Model 314 (best known as the boat-hulled Pan American Clipper), and later the XB-29.

While there was no shortage of capable people to design, build, and test aircraft in the 1930s, the supply of military pilots was another issue. The number of US Army–trained pilots had fallen to just 184 by 1937 and all pilot training was limited to three locations, all in the state of Texas: Randolph, Brooks, and Kelly fields. Much of the public attitude toward war preparedness could be described as indifferent. From 1937 to 1940, with an order backlog in the $9 million range, NAA sold more military aircraft to foreign governments than to the US Army and Navy combined.

The BT-9, as the production NA-16 became designated, established the fundamental design of NAA trainers for many years. A plethora of variants followed, marketed as basic trainers, advanced trainers, and basic combat trainers. Some adaptations were even built for export as combatants. Many NAA trainers were overhauled and widely used by the US military as late as 1953. All were powered by a Pratt & Whitney air-cooled R-1340 radial engine. Propellers were provided by Hamilton Standard. Cruising speed was a leisurely 130 miles per hour.

Engineering innovations and design enhancements added to the original NA-16 yielded many variants. Improvements found in the subsequent AT-6 Texan, for example, included all-metal construction and a retractable landing gear. Hydraulic power for flaps and landing gear was provided by a pilot-operated manual pump. Important controls such as throttle mixture, prop, elevator, aileron, rudder trim, and landing gear and flap actuators were found on the left side of the cockpit. The AT-6's complex systems were a challenge for the student pilot to master, thus easing their transition into single-seat combat aircraft in which there would be no instructor to intervene when a potentially lethal mistake was imminent.

The demands of war dictated that the traditional curriculum for pilots be shortened. Brigadier General George Stratemeyer was responsible for aircrew training. In a 1942 article in the company's *Skyline* magazine he boasted, "At the end of ten weeks [a cadet pilot] should be proficient in all fundamental maneuvers in a primary trainer. A recent class of 146 members flew an aggregate of 3.8 million miles without a fatality. . . . No other country in the world can spare aviation gasoline for anywhere near that much cadet flying; but we feel that it is essential for good pilotage and we have the gasoline."

Pilots and other aircrew members are best trained with a rigid, rigorous, and consistently applied curriculum. Prewar flight training followed three phases, each of a three-month duration: primary training (sixty-five flight hours); basic flying training (seventy-five flight hours); advanced training (seventy-five flight hours).

Flight time in smaller and simpler airplanes was followed by bigger, faster, and more challenging aircraft. As the war approached, new training fields were established across the warmer parts of the country until thirty-one airfields were dedicated to training. By 1943, up to sixty-three civilian flying schools were also under contract to train pilots.

Robert "Bob" Hutton (1921–2015), an Air Force retiree and pilot, was interviewed for this book at his residence in Madison, Wisconsin. Even at age ninety-two, his pilot's log-book remained a treasured document kept close at hand. He quickly retrieved it from a nearby drawer and made frequent reference to ensure the dates and events were accurately recounted.

Hutton grew up in Iowa and attended college for eighteen months before taking and passing the rigorous pilot aptitude tests. To shield him from the draft, army recruiters enlisted him as a private but directed that he stay safely at home with his parents for two months until his pilot-training class could be fully assembled, scheduled, and commenced. Primary training at Visalia, California, was followed by advanced training at Merced, California, where Hutton was awarded his wings and commissioned as a second lieutenant on March 10, 1943.

The 1934 vintage design of the North American trainer was durable, and after considerable updating, was still viable a decade later. In fact, the AT-6 and other North American models remain the darlings of the air show circuit. Some were repainted and adapted to portray Japanese Zeros in the movie *Tora! Tora! Tora!* and other war films.

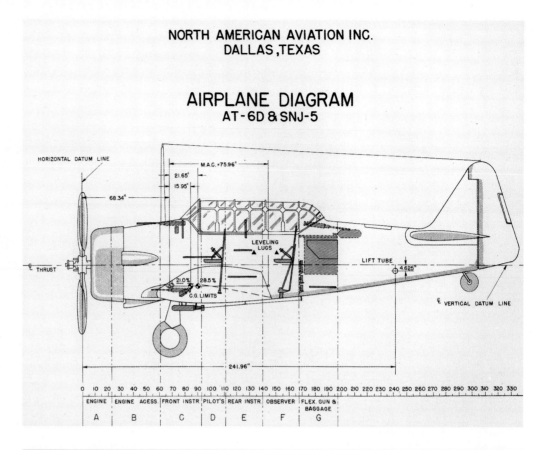

The compass on this trainer is being calibrated on a portion of the Inglewood tarmac called "compass rose." The magnetic compass was a critical navigational component in the decades before GPS and inertial navigation. It was one of many preflight tasks performed on each new aircraft in accordance with strict procedures.

.025 ALCLAD RIBS AFTER FAILURE
176% H A A LOAD
3-5-41   77-90-3

During the era prior to the invention of the computer, primary structural parts were stress tested to destruction. Lead weights were piled upon a part, in this case a horizontal stabilizer for an AT-6 trainer, until it failed. A part that broke at less than 100 percent of design strength would go back to the drawing board for re-work. A pilot who flies an airplane beyond its design limits is inviting disaster.

Even at the peak of the war, no corners were cut and there were no shortcuts for Lieutenant Hutton. Despite his strong desire for assignment to a fighter squadron, Hutton was destined to serve as an instructor pilot, first attending sixty days of advanced instructor training at Randolph Field, then another sixty days of instrument instructor training at Roswell, New Mexico. Military duty at Lemoore Army Airfield began in August 1943, with marriage and the starting of a family soon to follow.

The first half of a normal duty day was spent with student pilots in the classroom as they performed flight planning. The afternoon hours were aloft in the cockpit with a trainee. Hutton's unfulfilled wish for assignment to fighters was further dashed when he was relocated to Pecos, Texas, as an instructor on twin-engine planes. Students assigned to receive multi-engine training were on a trajectory to become either bomber or transport pilots.

Cadet pilots could be eliminated from training at any step along the way if they lacked aptitude, developed chronic motion sickness, or were unable to multitask. Frank Priebe, a civilian flight instructor from Rhinelander, Wisconsin, earned the nickname "Maytag" because he washed out so many cadets. The attrition rate varied depending on the demand for pilots in war zones. Hutton recalled that at Lemoore and Pecos he and the other instructors were urged to minimize the washout rate because of the high demand for bomber co-pilots.

A washed-out pilot could expect to remain in the military, possibly in another aircrew position such as navigator or bombardier. Others, with more education, could be assigned to non-flying officer positions such as finance, supply, or logistics. Those with less education would remain enlisted men, but a military job as a uniformed mechanic, munitions handler, fuel specialist, or other ground crew member was considered by many to be preferable to the infantry.

Hutton later found himself as a ferry pilot moving surplus aircraft about the country for Air Training Command as the war wound down and training bases were closed. His first military service commitment ended on October 22, 1945, when he mustered out of the army air force as a captain at Dayton, Ohio. He returned to the family-run home construction and carpentry business in Iowa, but the desire to again occupy the pilot's seat tugged at him. With the passage of time, the urge to return to the freedom of the sky and the comradeship of military service grew more compelling than sawing boards and pounding nails.

Regardless of the curriculum, student pilots destined to fly fighter aircraft could expect to encounter a North American trainer, at some point. And these airplanes went by many names: the SNJ in the US Navy, the AT-6 in the Army Air Corps, the Wirraway in Australia, and the Harvard in Great Britain and Canada. As one British RAF flying instructor stated: "What I think is so good is their marvelous cockpit layout. It's like a car. In some airplanes the controls seem to be put anywhere there is space. The result is knobs, buttons, and levers everywhere; under the seat, behind your back, over your head, under your arms.

ABOVE: A mechanic prepares to hand-spin the propeller to start the engine of the North American trainer. An abundance of well-trained pilots, plenty of fuel, and thousands of combat aircraft help seal the Allied victory.

OPPOSITE: Enlisted mechanics remove the engine cowl from a trainer plane. The North American trainers were flown hard during the war years. A plant was established in Fresno, California, for the purpose of refurbishing them in the early 1950s.

OPPOSITE: Lieutenant Colonel Charles E. Branshaw, in civilian attire, explains the attributes of an AT-6 trainer plane to Senator Harry S. Truman at Inglewood during August 1941. Truman led the senate commission to investigate problems with wartime production until stepping down to run for vice president.

The Harvard trainer gives the impression that the designer sat down and made a plan of his controls before he began to build the machine. It was decided that one place was just right for every instrument and gadget where it went. We call it the 'Yankee Layout.'"

One hundred eleven trainers (NAA designation NA-64) were destined for France when it fell to Germany. The British purchased these and delivered them to Canada, where they were called the "Yale." The next version (NAA designation NA-66) were called "Harvard" when delivered anywhere in the commonwealth, including Canada.

The goodwill the North American executives established with their offshore customers is evident in a letter from one Mr. Meadowbrook, British Air Minister of Contracts, to Kindelberger dated August 22, 1938: "I should like to reciprocate, very sincerely, your remarks as to cooperation on the contract discussions. In breaking new ground we were both working under difficulties which, however, thanks to your attitude, turned out to be much less formidable they would other otherwise have been. We all felt that it was a pleasure to work with you and were only sorry that the necessity for speed was so insistent."

continued on page 76

INGLEWOOD MECHANIC TRAINING SCHOOL

In addition to pilots, mechanics also needed to be trained. Established in the summer of 1941, the North American Field Services department operated a contract factory school at Inglewood with the military designation of 3716 Army Air Forces Base Unit. Two course offerings were open to enlisted men determined, by army-administered testing, to have mechanical aptitude. They were focused on either the B-25 Mitchell or the P-51 Mustang. The curriculum was structured to provide twenty-eight days of training over five weeks. The 525 young soldiers were instructed six days per week and split into three shifts. Each of the five phases of training lasted one week: airplane (general); hydraulics; electrical; power plant; engine change out and run-up.

The students slept in open-bay barracks at the school site, and the instructors were a mix of thirty-nine NAA civilian employees augmented by sergeants from army air forces. Classrooms were utilized for the academic training while "hands on" assignments were performed on dedicated non-flying airplanes permanently parked on campus.

The daily routine was reveille at 6:50 a.m., physical training at 3:45 p.m., and singing while marching to and from physical training. Retreat was at 5:15 p.m. Sundays were unscheduled and left open for worship, rest, or recreation.

There would be no backsliding while at the 3716th Technical School. Sustained military indoctrination was a vital component of the daily routine that included care of clothing and equipment, display of equipment, military courtesy, first aid, articles of war, sexual morality, personal hygiene and sanitation, small-arms familiarization, air-raid drill, fire drill, and orientation on military discipline and leadership.

By the end of 1944, an estimated 13,500 young men had been converted at the Inglewood factory school from awkward and naive American teenagers into qualified crew chiefs who were fit, prepared, eager, and ready to be deployed anywhere in the world.

Many would return to civilian life and use their newfound skills earning a good livelihood in aircraft manufacturing, general aviation, or as airline mechanics.

ABOVE: The mechanic's school was partially camouflaged. The survival of the aircrew members depends upon the ground crew's ability to keep their airplane combat ready and in good repair.

RIGHT: A non-airworthy B-25 was used to train Army Air Forces mechanics as the young troops, under the watchful eye of a white-lab-coated instructor, accomplish another hands-on training assignment.

ABOVE RIGHT: Students at the mechanics' school stand formation. Most of these men will soon find themselves at a distant (sometimes exotic) overseas airbase.

ABOVE: Harvard trainers are crated for shipment by rail to a port (often Newark, New Jersey) and ocean shipment to Britain.

RIGHT: A Harvard trainer is tucked into a crate destined to be loaded on a railcar.

OPPOSITE: Harvard number one thousand takes shape as British officials look on.

continued from page 71

ABOVE: To abide by the Neutrality Act, Harvard trainers were flown to an airfield near the Canadian border and taxied to the border crossing. A rope was thrown across the border and attached to the Harvard. A tow truck pulled it into province of Manitoba where it was taxied by a Canadian pilot for departure from a nearby local airfield.

OPPOSITE: The legacy product of North American was a long line of top-notch trainers. All production of the AT-6 was moved to Dallas in 1941 where the name "Texan" was attached. This ad touts the aircraft's appeal to air forces around the world.

Relations with the army air corps during this same period were testier. Concerns regarding the BC-1 variants built under production order NA-36 addressed faults like the tendency of the landing gear to jam and the awkward location of the pilot's lever to lower it.

Exported trainer aircraft were normally disassembled and loaded into crates for shipment overseas, traveling to seaport aboard railroad flatcars. Logistics got more complicated when the Germans began to sink ships in the Atlantic Ocean. The anxiety of the British is almost palpable in a directive dated August 28, 1939, from Air Ministry Group Captain Pirie: "Clear all Harvards awaiting shipment, by any ships available other than German, Italian, Japanese, and United States. Any equipment or planes which could not be shipped [are] to be railed to Vancouver. If the international situation eases, a return to the normal shipping program should be made."

Two prewar combat airplane projects based on the trainer design were undertaken for foreign customers: the NA-50 for Peru and the NA-68 for Siam (now Thailand). The number of pilot seats was reduced to one, the fuselage shortened, and a more powerful engine installed. The aircraft themselves represented somewhat of a departure from other aircraft that North American had designed and manufactured, and were perhaps the most heavily armored aircraft yet produced by NAA (with the exception of the twin-engine bombers). Both combat types carried machine guns, 20mm cannons, and several alternate provisions for bomb racks on the wings and under the fuselage.

Both airplanes were sturdy to excess, strengthened to withstand load factors of +12g and −6g (trainers were stressed for +8.5g). Both load forces are at the limits of human

A SQUADRON OF NORTH AMERICAN AT-6 TEXAN TRAINERS "PEELING OFF" FROM ECHELON FORMATION

PILOTS OF 24 NATIONS TRAIN IN "TEXANS"

The most widely used trainer in the world today is the North American Texan, formerly known as the Harvard. More than 10,000 airplanes—believed to be a world's record—have been built in North American Aviation's trainer series. Twenty-four nations have chosen the Texan as their own combat trainer. Their wing insignia adorn this page.

In gunnery and bombing practice; in formation and instrument flying; in coast patrol and semi-combat duty the Texan has proved its versatility.

A pilot trained in a Texan is equal to any job in modern air war. He feels as much at home in a P-51 Mustang fighter or B-25 Mitchell Bomber as in a North American trainer. For the instrument panels and controls in all three North American planes have been specially designed to make the transition "painless" from trainer to fighter or bomber— helping give young pilots full confidence on their first flight in a heavier plane.

In the United States Army Air Forces almost every pilot of a fighter or bomber —whether single-engine or twin-engine —won his wings in a North American trainer. That's a mighty important fact that we, the men and women of North American, are proud of.

Free! Reprint of this page. Send post-card to North American Aviation, Inc., Dept. G, Inglewood, California.

NORTH AMERICAN AVIATION, INC.
Inglewood, California
Dallas   Kansas City
Member, Aircraft War Production Council, Inc.

AT-6A TEXAN TRAINER

CREW: Two

ENGINE: Pratt & Whitney R-1340-49 600-hp radial

WINGSPAN: 42 ft. 0 in.

LENGTH: 29 ft. 0 in.

HEIGHT: 11 ft. 9 in.

WEIGHT: 3,900 lb. empty; 5,700 lb. loaded

SPEED: 210 mph at 5,000 ft.

RANGE: 750 miles

CEILING: 24,200 ft.

ARMAMENT: Two 0.3-in. (7.72mm) machine guns, one fixed, one trainable

COST: $25,672

NUMBER BUILT: 21,342 (all models)

BELOW: The painting depicts the bond between an aviator and the airplane he is assigned to fly. For most military pilots, a trainer is a rung on the ladder to something more challenging.

OPPOSITE: Even in the days before digital photographic manipulation, people working in the darkroom could create fanciful spoof images.

endurance, which is often rated at 9g, and then only if wearing special variably inflated pneumatic chaps called g-suits that force blood from the legs to the upper body and brain. (G-suits were not available until the jet age.)

Under threat of Japanese invasion, the government of Siam reluctantly consented to an uncomfortable collaboration. The shipment of six P-64s (the army air corps designation for the NA-68) was in transit at Hawaii during the Pearl Harbor attack and was promptly seized by the US government for use as trainers. Some later became the prized and much sought-after personal perks of flight-qualified senior officers.

CHAPTER 5

B-25 MITCHELL MEDIUM BOMBER

One of the latest additions to our air forces, the husky 12-ton baby we know as the North American B-25C. This hard hitting member of our striking power is one of the speediest bombers in the world, with speed approaching that of the standard fighter-planes in use abroad. It carries a very healthy load of bombs and operates at high altitude. The tricycle landing gear makes for excellent take-off and landing qualities and, for a large ship, it handles beautifully in the air.

—General Henry "Hap" Arnold, January 1942

Brass bullets of .50-caliber size are fed into the Bendix-built top turret of the B-25. The red-ringed insignia is evidence this image dates to the late summer of 1943.

The XB-21 Dragon was a predecessor to the B-25 Mitchell. North American lost the competition to Douglas but gained valuable insights into the design of medium bombers.

The Glenn L. Martin Company of Baltimore built the B-10 bomber from 1933 to 1940. It was an all metal twin-engine monoplane that made obsolete all bombers that preceded it. However, by 1936 the army air corps was in search of something still newer, bigger, and better. The procurement officers issued a fresh written specification and two companies responded.

North American, with an appetite to move into bigger airplanes, leaped at the project. The result became known as the XB-21 Dragon, which first flew on December 22, 1936, and competed with a DC-2 variant from Douglas Aircraft Company designated the B-18 Bolo. The XB-21, a tail-dragger like the DC-2, was considered the superior aircraft, but it lost the competition because of basic economics. Douglas quoted a unit price for the B-18 of $64,000, while each NAA XB-21 Dragon was estimated to cost $122,000.

It was an important lesson, which NAA took to heart.

Depression-era military budgets motivated procurement officers to emphasize affordability. Subsequent NAA models, including the B-25 and P-51, would be conceived with an eye toward ease of manufacture, facilitating automobile-style assembly-line production at rates previously inconceivable.

The B-18 Bolo proved underpowered and inadequately armed. Many were destroyed on the ground in the Pearl Harbor attack, and the B-18s assigned to McChord Field near Tacoma, Washington, were relegated to anti-submarine duties, coastal patrol, and occasional transport missions.

In 1939, another medium-bomber competition was held among North American, Douglas, and Martin. The designers at NAA by then had valuable medium-bomber design experience, combined with enhanced understanding of the military's need for range, bomb load, reliability, and defensive armament. The best features of the B-21 were carried forward into a new prototype design called the NA-40.

An innovative underslung engine cowl contributed to low drag, and a modern tricycle landing-gear configuration was accomplished by moving the center of balance forward

ABOVE: A wind-tunnel technician attaches a torpedo to a B-25 scale model. The bottom turret was eliminated by mid-war and skip bombing became a common weapon against shipping because torpedoes were expensive and in short supply.

LEFT: A team of B-25 engineers compare an aircrew member seat and what appears to be a piece of wing leading edge to drawings.

Three dour-faced mechanics tend the fire bottle (i.e., an industrial-sized fire extinguisher) in this rare photograph of a preliminary B-25. The upward slope of the entire wings (i.e., "constant dihedral") is clearly visible. The gull-winged appearance of all subsequent B-25s emerged after flight testing determined the wings outboard of the engine nacelles needed to be at zero degrees (or parallel with the ground) to provide a stable aerial-bombing platform.

and replacing the tail-wheel with a nose-wheel. Pilot-forward visibility while taxiing was much improved. The nose wheel was free to pivot; however, directional control during taxi was accomplished by a combination of variable engine thrust and selective main-gear braking. (Powered nose-wheel steering was still a decade away.)

The NA-40 departed Mines Field in Los Angeles toward Wright Field near Dayton, Ohio, for testing and evaluation by the army air corps. The testing went well and was mostly completed when the NA-40 crashed at 7:30 p.m. on April 11, 1939. Standard military protocol dictated an unbiased investigation of all serious accidents.

Kindelberger arrived at Wright Field a week later to conduct his own investigation. Base officials, under instructions from Materiel Command's Brigadier General George Brett, were cooperative, and Kindelberger reported back to the North American board of directors on April 20, 1939, that the root cause of the accident was "100 percent pilot failure."

The pilot, an experienced lieutenant, was flying at low altitude (700 feet) below a cloud bank when he deliberately ran one engine dry and feathered the propeller in an apparent unscripted test of engine-out performance. Contrary to the written flight manual procedure, he attempted a windmill engine restart by unfeathering the prop. The added drag, as the propeller blades moved obliquely to airflow, reduced airspeed, stalling the airplane at an altitude too low for recovery. Fortunately, all three crewmembers survived, but the airframe was destroyed.

Meanwhile, the Glenn L. Martin Company was diligently at work developing the competing B-26. The Marauder, as it was known, was endowed with more powerful R-2800 engines that allowed it to fly faster and higher. The wing, however, was less forgiving of weight gain, and the landing and takeoff speeds were considered excessive. There were crashes and groundings before all of the technical issues were resolved. In contrast, the B-25, with its R-2600 engines, was a bit underpowered but stable and easy to fly and maintain.

In spite of the NA-40 crash, NAA remained committed to win the contract as Lee Atwood, Ray Rice, and the other engineers continued to refine and polish their vision of the ultimate medium bomber. On August 16, 1939, the air corps made a momentous public announcement that would fundamentally define the mix of the American airpower for the approaching war. Only the companies were announced; the models (in parentheses) were revealed later:

TWO-ENGINE BOMBER:

- Glenn L. Martin Company (B-26)
- North American Aviation (B-25)
- Douglas Aircraft Company (B-23)

FOUR-ENGINE BOMBER:

- Consolidated Aircraft (B-24)
- Boeing Aircraft Company (B-17)

TRAINER AIRCRAFT:

- North American Aircraft (AT-6)
- Vultee Aircraft Division (BT-13 and BT-19)
- Curtiss-Wright Corporation (AT-9)

TWO-ENGINE INTERCEPTOR PURSUIT AIRCRAFT:

- Lockheed Aircraft (P-38)
- Grumman Aircraft (the aborted XP-50)

Army aircrews from the 17th Bomb Group of McChord AFB, Washington, arrive in the summer of 1941 to ferry home a new B-25, serial number 40-2170, the sixth B-25 off the assembly line. Their bags are piled upon the roof of a Pontiac station wagon. Many aircrew members serving in the Northwest (but not this airplane) would participate in the Doolittle Raid.

The rule book had been thrown away because of the tenuous international situation. Contrary to normal times, when a single model from a specific supplier was selected, multiple models of all types of military airplanes from several companies were simultaneously ordered into production by the army. The navy was concurrently, but separately, gearing up for air war with massive orders for new aircraft.

A sparely worded one-page document dated September 5, 1939, found in the North American files, bears the signature of James F. Kindelberger: "General Order NA-62: Proceed with fabrication of 184 model B-25 bombers plus one static test (skeleton) airplane plus spare parts for US Air Corps."

The B-25 design was approved by the army on September 10, 1939, and the maiden flight was on February 25, 1941. It is unlikely that anybody anticipated that production would continue until nearly ten thousand units had been assembled. Lee Atwood and Ray Rice were credited as co-designers of the B-25, but it was Atwood who first suggested the name: "Very early in the project several us were having a bull session in Kindelberger's office and the subject of a name for the new bomber was brought up," he later recalled. "I suggested that it be named after General 'Billy' Mitchell but nothing was decided at that time. In later conversation, we settled on Mitchell."

The B-25 is the only airplane named for a person. Brigadier General "Billy" Mitchell was another World War I aviator who rose to prominence between the wars as a staunch advocate of airpower in his role as assistant chief of the army air service from 1919 to 1925. Mitchell tenaciously pushed for the further development of parachutes and other aviation advancements by constantly demanding ever more from the staff at McCook Field near

STARS AND BARS

In 1942 the aviation portion of the US Army was renamed from US Army Air Corps (USAAC) to US Army Air Forces (USAAF), and in July 1943 adopted a new insignia that replaced the previous star-in-a-circle design with a star in a circle that also featured horizontal bars on each side. The new version was said to be visible at greater distances and less likely to be confused with the circular insignias of Japan and other countries. Insignias evolved as follows:

- **PREWAR TO MAY 1942:** White five-point star on blue circle; red circle in center of the star

- **MAY 1942–JULY 1943:** White five-point star on blue circle; red circle eliminated

- **JULY–SEPTEMBER 1943:** White five-point on blue circle; horizontal blue and white rectangles on both sides with entire insignia outlined in red

- **SEPTEMBER 1943 ON:** White five-point on blue circle; horizontal blue and white rectangles on both sides; red outline eliminated

Existing airplanes were updated and paint shops applied the new marking to newly produced airplanes. In addition, camouflage paint was abandoned starting in early 1944, and subsequent airplanes were delivered in unpainted aluminum. Nonmetal surfaces except glass were routinely painted silver. That decision was premature, however, ground-support warplanes in the European Theater of Operations (ETO) were ordered locally camouflaged in June 1944 in addition to "invasion stripes" of alternating white and black starting on May 17 (intended to minimize friendly-fire incidents on the crowded beaches of Normandy on and after D-Day). The resulting camouflage was a hodgepodge of colors and patterns.

James Pendleton paints an older-style insignia on an airplane in 1942.

TECHNICAL NOTES
B-25B MITCHELL MEDIUM BOMBER

CREW: Six

ENGINES: Two Wright R-2600s 1,700 hp each

WINGSPAN: 67 ft. 6 in.

LENGTH: 53 ft. 0 in.

HEIGHT: 16 ft. 9 in.

WEIGHT: 29,300 lb. maximum

CRUISING SPEED: 233 mph

MAXIMUM SPEED: 328 mph

RANGE: 2,500 miles (with auxiliary tanks)

CEILING: 21,200 ft.

ARMAMENT: Six .50-cal. machine guns; 3,000 lb. of bombs

COST: $109,670 (1943)

NUMBER BUILT: Almost 10,000 (all models)

Dayton (dismantled in 1927). In an effort called Project B, he sponsored the sinking of seized World War I German warships by aerial bombardment in February 1921. Senior navy admirals took umbrage at Mitchell's scathing criticism of their spending of limited defense funds on battleships, which Mitchell considered obsolete and ineffective in any future faceoff with evolving air power. The general was demoted to colonel and then court-martialed for insubordination. He was later vindicated but died at age fifty-six in 1936.

The B-25 would become the signature Inglewood product and an object of adoration for Inglewood employees when Jimmy Doolittle's Raiders chose it to deliver the first meaningful offensive blow to the Japanese homeland in the April 1942 bombing raid on Tokyo.

The B-25 design evolved as the war progressed and constant engineering changes were applied. Some originated with army air force engineering offices or operating crews, while others were conceived by North American. Engineering revisions were often frozen with only the most critical of them scheduled for later at postproduction modification centers. Then, as today, out-of-sequence work was the enemy of efficient airplane-building.

The B-25 was a workaday, everyman type of airplane that was relatively inexpensive to build, plentiful, reliable, easy to maintain, and adaptable. There were reconnaissance versions, bombers, strafers, trainers, transports, and more. As it evolved, the Mitchell went from a lighter aircraft to a slower, heavier warplane bristling with ever-more firepower and armor plating that added drag and weight. The interior of the airplane was so noisy, with thin insulation and engines near the flight crew stations, that many crewmen suffered hearing loss. NAA experimented with various exhaust manifolds to no avail. It was said that a B-25 was the best way to turn aviation gasoline into noise.

Early versions of the B-25 were equipped with a lower turret but this proved a chronic source of problems. It was retractable and designed to be lowered when needed, but the mechanism's micro-switches malfunctioned when the turret was lowered too quickly and the turret would jam in the down position, resulting in excess drag. Jimmy Doolittle ordered them removed from the Raiders' airplanes as he traded decreased firepower for increased fuel. Factory installation of lower turrets ceased effective with the first G variant.

An optional removable bomb bay fuel tank was also available. In the days before midair refueling, it gave the B-25 the range necessary to fly the long and lonely 10.5-hour nonstop 2,400-mile slog from Southern California to Hickam Field on Oahu in the Hawaiian Islands.

By midwar, the term "medium bomber" was a bit of a misnomer for the B-25. "Ground-attack gunship" may have been a more accurate description of many Mitchell missions. While every B-25 was built with a bomb bay, many were outfitted at the factory with an array of firepower—sometimes as many as eighteen Browning .50-caliber machine guns that could deliver a withering nine thousand rounds per minute. Some iterations of the B-25 were documented to be the most heavily armed aircraft of World War II. Their weapons mix was frequently altered and updated as production continued. Weapons that could be swiveled and aimed by a crewmember were referred to as flexible guns, and guns that were built into the airplane and bore-sighted to fire straight ahead were called fixed guns—the pilot aimed the airplane's nose while tracer rounds helped him home in on the target.

ABOVE: General Hap Arnold proudly poses with his B-25 transport bearing an emblem with four stars. The riding crop, a symbol of military authority, is a vestige from the days of horseback cavalry.

OPPOSITE: Nicely-dressed workers (both in need of adequate ear protection) test fire a .30-caliber flexible gun. First installed in the nose of the early B-25s, it was later deemed inadequate and replaced by a larger .50-caliber model. With constant riveting, gun fire, engine testing, and drop hammers, airplane factory workers, no doubt, suffered significant avoidable hearing loss.

Twelve forward-facing guns could deliver a withering nine thousand half-inch slugs per minute, which would be formidable in any war.

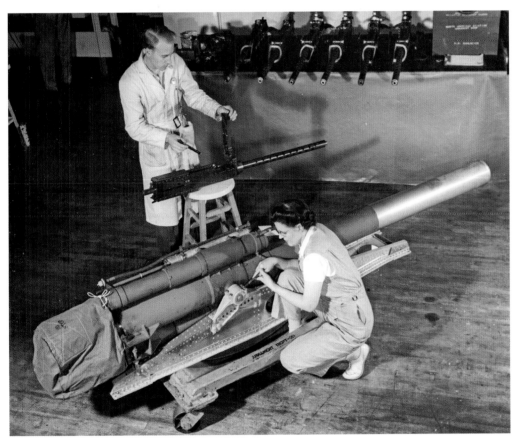

LEFT: The optional 75mm cannon was built by Oldsmobile Division of General Motors and it proved to be lethal against ships or other substantial surface targets. The pilot needed the skill to aim the centerline of the airplane at the target. The gun was firmly affixed into the airplane.

OPPOSITE: A mechanic has the unenviable job of working behind the 12-foot 7-inch spinning propeller. The variable pitch is no doubt set to neutral to minimize the wind blast that would otherwise hurl him onto the tarmac.

In the B-25's case, this could be ground troops, an airfield, a ship, or an aircraft. Some Inglewood-built Mitchells carried a 9-foot-long 75mm cannon built by Oldsmobile. These were used with great success in the Pacific, as Mitchells were credited for eleven of the twenty-two Japanese ships sunk at the Battle of the Bismarck Sea in 1943.

On Memorial Day weekend in 1944 it was announced that B-25 production would be phased out at Inglewood, allowing all production resources to be fully devoted to P-51 Mustang production. The Kansas City plant would become the world's sole source of B-25s. By war's end, two-thirds (6,608) of the nearly ten thousand B-25s built had come from the Kansas City Fairfax plant.

XB-28 DRAGON

In 1940, North American was awarded a contract for the design of next generation of medium bombers. The initial goal was to update the B-25, then itself barely on the cusp of entering military service, with a variant boasting more powerful engines and a pressurized crew compartment. As frequently happens, the design evolved into a totally new aircraft that first took flight on April 26, 1942. The XB-28 was of similar size and configuration as the Mitchell but had a single, rather than dual tail. A pair of 2,000-horsepower Pratt & Whitney R-2800 engines made it faster, while pressurization enhanced aircrew safety and comfort at higher altitudes. Like the earlier XB-21, the XB-28 was also named "Dragon."

The expected benefit of bombing from higher altitudes was a measure of safety from ground-based artillery, and from fighters incapable of similar altitudes. However, high-altitude bombing was problematic before the invention of modern guided (or "smart") bombs. The ability to destroy small targets like bridges, dams, radio transmitters, and electrical sub stations while avoiding collateral damage was especially vexing. It was said the famed Norden bombsight could "drop a bomb in a barrel from 18,000 feet," an assertion that may have had a placebo effect on any crewmen harboring qualms of innocent civilian deaths caused by bombing errors. However, the phrase "high-altitude precision aerial bombardment" is oxymoronic. While the Norden bombsight was an invaluable aiming tool, the combination of altitude, clouds, human error, and winds all too frequently combined to yield unfavorable margins for error that could translate to civilian deaths.

The XB-28 project was eventually terminated as military strategy evolved and there was no longer sufficient need for a pressurized high-altitude medium bomber. External decisions impacting NAA were always filed under "lessons learned" and tempered by the realities of ongoing national and global events. In any case, line workers at Inglewood were fully immersed in warbird construction and, most likely, completely uninterested in debating theories of ethical warfare or the technical complications of aerial bombardment.

However, Gen. Hap Arnold would cite the XB-28 as an important precursor to the eagerly awaited pressurized Boeing B-29 long-range heavy bomber then in development. More money was spent on the B-29 program than any other wartime project—including the Manhattan project that yielded the first atomic bombs. Arnold described the XB-28 as a miniature B-29, noting, "Some experimental planes are never mass produced, although we learn valuable things from them." The XB-28 had, in fact, furthered the science of aerial bombardment even though it never dropped a single bomb in combat.

The XB-28 was just one example of the numerous designs conceived, tested, and abandoned during the war. The government wisely limited the proliferation of new designs to allow manufacturers to focus on high-rate production of a limited array of airplanes.

The XB-28 featured a pressurized cabin, R-2800 engines, and four-bladed propellers. It was a well-engineered aircraft, but never ordered into production because the need for it faded as the war progressed. The first prototype is pictured in the cold and snow at Wright Field. The army was impressed with the design and a second prototype for reconnaissance missions was constructed.

TECHNICAL NOTES
XB-28 DRAGON

CREW: Five

ENGINES: Two Pratt & Whitney R-2800-27 radials 2,000 hp each (takeoff power)

WINGSPAN: 72 ft. 7 in.

LENGTH: 56 ft. 5 in.

HEIGHT: 14 ft. 0 in.

WEIGHT: 35,740 lb. (gross)

CRUISING SPEED: 255 mph

MAXIMUM SPEED: 372 mph

RANGE: 2,040 miles

CEILING: 33,500 ft.

ARMAMENT: Six .50-cal. machine guns; 4,000 lb. of bombs

SERIAL NUMBERS: 40-3056 (XB-28) and 40-3058 (XB-28A)

15-gun salute from American flyers

There's "no future" for Japs and Nazis who tangle with the crushing firepower of the 15 guns packed by the new B-25 Mitchell bomber. Today's Mitchell—6000 design improvements more deadly than the model in which General Doolittle bombed Tokyo—bristles with heavy armament. From the 75-mm. cannon in its nose to the "stingers" in its tail, the Mitchell's guns blast the enemy on land and sea, protect its five-man crew against air attack. As they shoot to win on eleven fronts of this global war, the victorious B-25s are helping mightily to soften up the enemy, to make the job of American fighting men all over the world easier, safer.

North American B-25 Mitchell

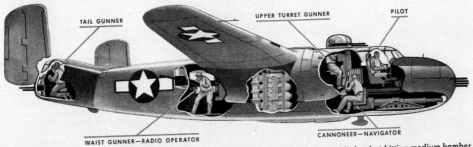

TAIL GUNNER

UPPER TURRET GUNNER

PILOT

WAIST GUNNER—RADIO OPERATOR

CANNONEER—NAVIGATOR

FIREPOWER *PLUS* **MANPOWER!** The B-25 Mitchell and its 5-man crew fight together as the world's hardest-hitting medium bomber team!

North American Aviation *Sets the Pace*

WE MAKE PLANES THAT MAKE HEADLINES . . . *the B-25 Mitchell bomber, AT-6 Texan combat trainer, P-51 Mustang fighter (A-36 fighter-bomber), and the B-24 Liberator bomber, North American Aviation, Inc. Member, Aircraft War Production Council, Inc.*

One of several wartime magazine advertisements from North American touted the B-25 and its firepower.

CHAPTER 6

STRIKE

In conclusion, to sum up all observation, there is apparently great lack of proper attitude, that is, personal movement is too slow and lacks energy, an attitude that what does not get done today will be done tomorrow, and with the younger men there is little or no conception of seriousness or thought or importance to their work. There seems to be a tendency of riding a crest of a boom and buck passing is the password of the day.

—Inglewood plant internal management report, mid-1941

Well-disciplined troops rush onto plant premises in a wedge formation on the morning of June 9, 1941.

Kindelberger (seated) attended a labor union meeting for reasons not fully understood. Two separate unions vied to organize the Inglewood workforce.

A malaise was simmering among the many mostly young male workers employed at Inglewood during early 1941. Plant leadership noted the lackadaisical attitude of the workers and their morale was in a slump. North American entry level hourly wage rates were kept low in spite of hefty profits. Other industries were unionizing. New laws and actions by the Roosevelt Administration were favorable towards unions and, with a large, young, and restless workforce, the Inglewood plant was ripe for organizers. Two separate and competing unions went after the prize.

A bitter struggle had started in December 1940 between the United Auto Workers of American (UAW), affiliated with the Congress of Industrial Organizations (CIO), and the International Association of Machinists, affiliated with the American Federation of Labor (AFL). The National Labor Relations Board sponsored a runoff election and the CIO won by a tiny fraction of the vote. The AFL challenged many of the ballots. The situation was further complicated by allegations that communist sympathizers were striving to hobble American war production at the behest of the Russians then aligned with the Nazis in Germany.

Labor unions grew during the 1930s with the support of President Franklin Roosevelt's "New Dealers," who nurtured a supportive attitude towards organized labor, but the administration reversed course as a spate of strikes across all of America became a serious impediment to the ramp-up of war-related production. Labor stoppages in early 1941 impacted the shipbuilding, steel, and coal industries.

Bargaining for the first contract at North American began in May. The rank and file workers at Inglewood were unfamiliar with the time lags, drama, and frustrations inherent in the collective bargaining process. They voted to strike on May 23, 1941, but stayed on the job for thirteen days past their strike deadline. The issue went to the National Defense Mediation Board when it quickly became evident that an indefinite stall was just beginning. The members ignored pleas from national union leaders to keep working, and walked off the job on Thursday, June 5, 1941.

The North American Inglewood plant then accounted for 20 percent of all military aircraft in June 1941—including vitally needed trainers and medium bombers. The company held $196 million in contracts. A work stoppage would do incalculable damage to the British war effort and interfere seriously with United States defense preparations.

Discussion at President Roosevelt's cabinet meeting of Friday, June 6, centered on the California walkout and it was decided that the government would seize the plant on Monday, June 9, if the strike continued. The president made that announcement on Saturday, June 7, and the War Department stated it was ready to act. However, nobody in government or army service had any ideas about how to take over, let alone operate, a major airplane factory. They were without precedent.

The weekend was spent making hasty plans. Lieutenant Colonel Charles E. Branshaw, the chief air corps procurement officer on the West Coast, was called upon to be the government's agent to operate the plant with assistance from army legal, fiscal, and contractual experts. The mayor of Los Angeles offered up the "entire" police department to resolve the strike but military planning continued because the track record of local police at strike resolution was unfavorable.

The nation's top union leaders were in a serious dilemma. In the aftermath of the president's freshly declared "unlimited national defense emergency" dated May 27, 1941, they had firmly committed to their political friends in Washington, DC, that there would be no strike. However, the newly organized North American West Coast union local, lacking the

Richard Frankensteen, a labor
union senior official from Detroit, is
disrespected, mocked, and jeered
at the meeting with strikers on
Sunday, June 8, 1941.

experience and maturity level of the Michigan-based auto workers, had mutinied against their leadership.

Richard "Dick" Frankensteen, a union president who earned his clout at Chrysler's Dodge plant, was flown from union headquarters in Detroit. He arrived in Los Angeles for a face-to-face gathering with union members in a desperate quest to promptly defuse the situation, but was, instead, mocked and jeered at the mass meeting on Sunday, June 8. Spiced-up with dramatic photographs and gripping newsreel images, the labor confrontation at Inglewood received coast-to-coast coverage on newspaper and radio. Army forces, already standing by, were mobilized when officials received the news that the impasse remained unresolved.

continued on page 101

LEFT: Lieutenant Colonel Charles E. Branshaw is seated at what appears to be the executive desk of Dutch Kindelberger after directing 2,600 army troops to seize the North American Aviation Inc. Inglewood plant in response to an unsanctioned wild-cat strike on June 9, 1941. Just two years later, in mid-1943, Branshaw would be wearing the two stars of a major general on his uniform.

ABOVE: About twenty of the most militant agitators were taken into the custody. The name of this flag-waver has been lost to history. None of them were charged or taken to court. The matter ended peacefully.

LEFT: The army troops brought their tents and settled in as an occupying force until all further threat of labor disruption had passed.

OPPOSITE: The situation is tense as strikers help an older woman scramble across a gully ahead of advancing army troops.

continued from page 97

Under cover of darkness, 2,600 troops—mostly from the nearby 3rd Coastal Artillery, augmented by two battalions from the 15th Infantry— were organized into three motorized columns, and then dispatched with orders to halt temporarily within thirty minutes of the plant to await further instructions.

President Roosevelt signed Executive Order 8773 at 10:30 a.m. Eastern time (7:30 a.m. Pacific time) on Monday, June 9, 1941. A small army spotter airplane circled quietly overhead in the crystal-clear Inglewood morning sky, sending radio reports on the troop convoys and the rapidly developing mob scene at the plant every fifteen minutes to commanders on the ground.

Workers started arriving for their shift at 6:30 a.m. It was presumed that most were intending to work because they arrived holding lunch buckets; however, picketers, agitators, and other hotheads used intimidation to block the plant entrances. Fights soon broke out. Police intervened at 7:43 a.m. tossing tear gas into the crowd. The canisters were seized by strikers and thrown back over the chain-link fences which completely surrounded the plant. The Los Angeles Police Department (LAPD), retreated, cowering under a hailstorm of rocks and bottles.

At 8:10 a.m. Lieutenant Colonel Branshaw concluded that the efforts of local authorities had failed. With the situation deemed to be out of control, he ordered army forces into action. The troops rolled in fully equipped for battle, dismounting their vehicles with bayonets affixed to rifles. Live ammunition, and machine guns had been issued. There was to be no delay, no negotiations, and no nonsense. Soldiers, in their World War I–style helmets, marched smartly onto the plant premises in disciplined formations and advanced directly towards the strikers.

LEFT: On the morning of June 9, 1941, a small army spotter airplane circled above the North American Inglewood plant. The pilot radioed observations to commanders on the ground at fifteen-minute intervals as the largest labor clash of World War II unfolded below.

OPPOSITE: The strike at North American's Inglewood plant merited major nationwide press coverage as the biggest event involving organized labor of the World War II era.

The wildcat strikers could only briefly savor their victory over the LAPD. The force of 2,600 well-disciplined army troops was overwhelming. At the east entrance, a picket line, manned on the leading edge by the most militant of the strike agitators, was soon pushed back across Aviation Boulevard, clearing an unobstructed pathway to the factory gates. About twenty of those who did not abide by orders were instantly taken into custody and taken aboard army trucks to nearby Fort MacArthur for holding.

Before noon, North American security guards were able to open access gates. Most employees streamed back to work when it became evident they were protected from further violence and intimidation at the hands of the strike proponents. Photographs show police then assisting with security by screening employees as they approached the plant gates.

At a press conference in Washington, DC, on Monday afternoon, June 9, Secretary of War Stimston stated: "Mr. Kindelberger, president of this company, has a very good reputation with the government for making airplanes and is a square shooter. There are not enough like him. We do not want to do any injury to such a man. You may draw your own inferences from this." The confusion within the War Department was evident when Branshaw, their on-site commander, was simultaneously stating: "North American has no voice in the operation. We are calling upon the company executives for information because they are familiar with the plant but we are calling up machinery for more extensive operation by government men."

The seizure of the North American plant by the US Army had turned out to be quick and easy. A graceful exit would prove more challenging. The government found itself in an awkward position without precedent. Howard Petersen, a War Department special assistant quickly penned some wise objectives for such actions:

The strikers must not gain an advantage. Otherwise, every American war plant will have a strike to force a takeover.

The company has in this case had a completely clear record and must not be penalized by the takeover.

If the government becomes the direct employer of labor an infinite number of technical difficulties arise . . .

In order to produce planes, complete management cooperation must be obtained . . .

The general question of methods of operation was addressed at a White House meeting on June 10, 1941. Secretary of War Stimson later asserted: "The President's views coincided with the others . . . [I]n this case it was desirable to assume as little of the relationship of direct management to the operations of the company and its labor relations as possible, and that the company should be treated as the agent of the government for that purpose."

There were no deaths, and only one serious injury was recorded when a striker was accidently bayoneted. The army established its temporary presence at Inglewood with an occupation force of 1,500 soldiers bivouacking on the grounds adjacent to the plant as production resumed inside. The soldiers utilized the washroom facilities within the plant, making themselves at home as they settled in. Until emotions had time to subside, the temporary military presence would ensure that employees were safe from intimidation, sabotage was discouraged, and sit-down strikes would not occur.

The overwhelming demonstration of military might against unruly civilian citizens was deemed a success. The image of soldiers aiming machine guns towards striking fellow Americans was a sobering sight. The situation was tense but the consequence of decisive action was workers who, with the exception of local union local leaders, accepted their lot and returned to work without excessive lingering anger.

Collaboration between union leader Richard Frankensteen and company executives would, on the surface, seem unlikely; however, dialogue with the army regarding

insubordinate union members was another matter. After consultation between Lieutenant Colonel Branshaw and Frankensteen, nine of the most militant strike organizers were forever banished from not only the plant but also the union. Their cases were reviewed by prosecutors but nobody was brought to trial for their actions.

Utilizing the hardball playbook of labor relations, the company obtained pictures from their own photographers, newspapers, and freelancers who extensively photographed the events of June 9, 1941, to ferret out systematically, identify, fire, and blacklist the strike instigators. The 8-by-10 prints remain in company files and the penciled names of suspected strike organizers can still be seen annotated on the backs of the prints. One fellow photographed on the picket line with his young daughter was determined to be an employee of Vultee Aircraft, another Southern California airframe builder also in the process of unionization.

After three weeks, the situation returned to normal, allowing the remaining army troops to break camp and return to their barracks on July 3, 1941. An agreement between the union and North American was signed on July 18. The concern about communist influence on the union had faded when Germany turned on their previous ally and attacked the USSR starting on June 21, 1941. An army air forces report dated August, 1945 stated: "The original realignment of wage rates at North American Inglewood was a direct result of the dramatic and significant labor disturbance of June 1941. This strike has been termed the most significant in the nation. The strike did not seriously affect production but it created a tremendous wave of national indignation directed solely at the strikers and other strike instigators."

The Japanese attack on Pearl Harbor was the lightning bolt that galvanized pro-war public opinion. Sporadic labor work stoppages continued during the war years but the wave of patriotism that swept the country mitigated them. The war effort was never again seriously threatened by an organized labor disruption.

CHAPTER 7

WORKING ON THE SUNSHINE ASSEMBLY LINE

The Axis' far-flung spy system, employing infinite patience has operatives who concentrate on sifting hundreds of apparently unrelated, fragmentary items of information and weaving them into a pattern which may enable them to sabotage a plant, sink a convoy of ships, or repel a "surprise" invasion on some foreign shore. If you hear it, don't repeat it. If you see it, don't talk about it.

—Plant weekly newspaper *Skyline*,
December 24, 1942

Riveting is a two-person activity. A rivet is installed in a predrilled hole. One person operates an air-driven hammer and the other holds the bucking bar on the backside. Alice (Huckleberry) Howlett (left) and Ernestine (Bounce) Hargis are riveting a center beam at the Kansas City plant. Both remained local area residents for the balance of their lives.

ABOVE: Working on the sunshine assembly line was intermixed with playing on the Southern California beaches.

RIGHT: Newly hired unskilled workers were assigned to a rented storefront facility away from the main plant. They were paid entry-level hourly wage rate—giving rise to the expression "earn while you learn."

Manufacturers faced an acute labor shortage when boatloads of workers marched off to war at the same time demand for warplanes skyrocketed. The solution was to woo women and people from other groups previously seldom found in aviation manufacturing. The strategy was successful. Others came from many assorted lines of work like agriculture, retailing, and the service industries, drawn to the higher wages and better benefits. However, the work could be difficult and dangerous.

Many Americans were forced by the hard times of the Great Depression to depart their homes and families in search of work. Urban legend has it that the drifters were admonished to "write, if you find work." Some of those who ended up in the aircraft factories of Southern California responded with letters making reference to "working on the sunshine assembly line"—a combined reference to the balmy Mediterranean climate and the fact that much of the wartime work at Inglewood was performed out-of-doors and in the shade of camouflage netting.

In spite of chronic serious labor shortages, the Inglewood payroll was totally devoid of representation from a large, capable, and well-educated group of American citizens—those of Japanese heritage. President Roosevelt signed Executive Order 9066 on February 19, 1942, which had the effect of evicting approximately 120,000 people of Japanese ancestry from the West Coast. (The order was actually much broader than that; people of German and Italian ancestry were also interned, though not

A worker on a stepladder tends to a B-25 at North American's Inglewood facility. Southern California's dry, sunny Mediterranean climate was certainly an advantage for aviation industries that located there.

nearly on the same scale.) One photograph in the North American collection shows an Asian woman at work but it is labeled to make it clear that Mom Hee Lin was Korean.

Americans, generally males between the ages of eighteen and twenty-three, who were called upon to serve their country in the military usually received an induction notice from their local draft board. They could expect a structured process consisting of a haircut, issue and fitting of uniforms, and a rigorous physical training routine to augment classes and their life in the barracks. Workers in the various war plants too, could expect to encounter a structured process as they moved from unskilled "new-hire" to assume positions of greater challenge, responsibility, and reward (both monetary and psychological).

There was no maximum age limit for obtaining a job at NAA. A company medical doctor performed a physical examination. If declared fit, the applicant was interviewed to verify the conditions and terms of employment, nature of the work, and pay. Fingerprints and photographs were taken, and three documents were in-hand as they departed the hiring hall: written instructions on when, where, and to whom they would initially report for work, training, or orientation; a copy of the NAA employee handbook; and the employee version of the collective bargaining agreement between the company and the UAW.

ABOVE: Women comprised a significant portion of the North American security department. They were called "Plant Police" and were frequently armed, sometimes deputized, and always treated with respect.

RIGHT: Clarket industrial tugs, then called jeeps, are posed for a group photo. They pulled wheeled dollies (called cars) which, when filled with parts and assemblies, were moved along established routes as needed anywhere in or around the plant.

With the deafening noise of constant riveting in many areas, an airplane factory can be a daunting, dangerous, and bewildering place for a new employee. Engines were test run and tuned before each aircraft was flight tested. Flashing red lights warned of gunfire, which frequently crackled as heavy-caliber aircraft machine guns were bore-sighted and then test fired into earthen pits.

Like the military, the training process at NAA varied depending on the work experience and educational background of the applicant. Training was administered by the Human Relations department and provided to unskilled shop laborers in a vocational school environment away from the main factory, sometimes in abandoned retail stores. Preparatory training included shop mathematics, blueprint reading, sheet-metal work, riveting, pattern making, machine operation, and jig building. New employees earned hourly pay and seniority during training while remaining eligible for health care and other benefits. Students developed aviation manufacturing skills while being exposed to the rigors of factory work.

The second phase, called inductance training or orientation, was typically conducted at the plant, and would include shop rules and regulations, good work habits, accident prevention, first aid and industrial safety, and job simplification. Some of the photographs created for new-hire orientation at Inglewood can be seen on these pages.

The poster reminds employees that their work may expose them to government classified information and that the penalties for unauthorized disclosure of it are steep. "Loose lips sink ships" was a common wartime motto.

The third phase consisted of off-hour courses on trade extension or supplementary training to improve the skills of those workers already employed, and to expand the knowledge of their specialty (e.g., advanced welding for welders, tool fabrication, electrical theory for electricians).

Leadership training was offered to those with the potential to take on more responsibility. It featured the latest theories of motivational management and industrial psychology. Maslow's hierarchy of needs was first published in 1943 and it was soon being explained to North American's most eager management trainees.

The need for expanded medical departments combined with enhanced employee assistance programs evolved because long hours at work, combined with the stress of family members absent and gone to war, could push a person to tears. Other company-provided services developed during wartime. Welfare nurses made house calls. The employer would assist with the handling of traffic violations. Child care, package check, income tax assistance, check cashing, cafeteria, and notary public services were available.

The strategy to bring women into the workplace was ready for implementation by the first week of January 1942 when the first ten women arrived for work in the Inglewood wire shop. They wore specially designed uniforms with slacks as they prepared to perform

continued on page 112

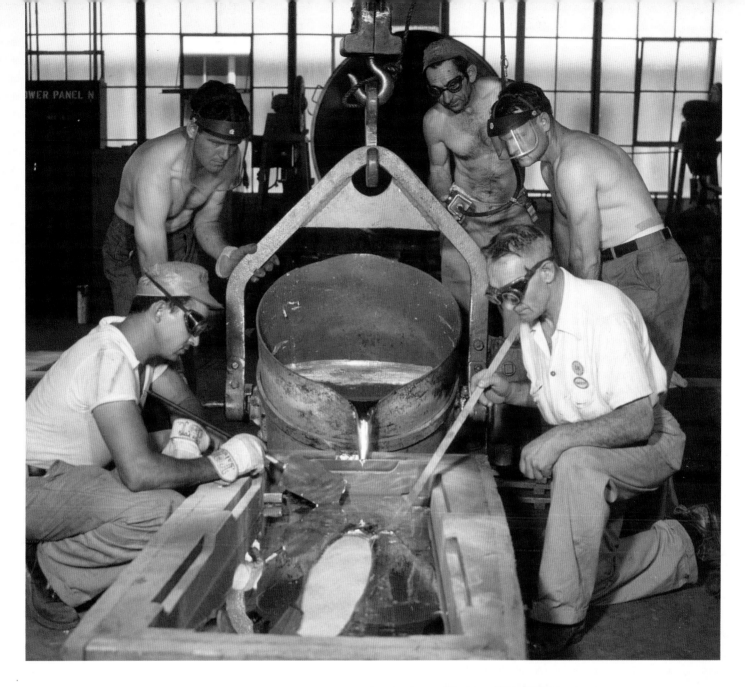

ABOVE: Molten aluminum pours from the cauldron as foundry employees cast aircraft parts at the North American Inglewood plant. The work was hot, dangerous, and dirty.

RIGHT: Mounting tires is one of the most miserable, physically demanding, and dirty jobs in an aircraft factory. Aircraft tires have more plies than automobile tires because they operate at higher speeds and endure heavier loads.

OPPOSITE: This woman operates her forklift truck proudly under blue skies. Her attire and angle of the sun suggests it is winter in Southern California.

RIGHT: Tall vertical bins were built as factory parts storage space became scarce. The plank is narrow and there are no hand rails: a condition that would make a modern-day safety inspector cringe.

OPPOSITE: The large tires on the B-25 made it possible to operate from unpaved surfaces but placed a weight penalty on the design. The entire sub-assembly includes brakes and the sturdy landing gear.

continued from page 109

electrical sub-assembly. Other women were already employed sewing or in the offices and at the telephone switchboards.

A small number of uniformed military personnel were found at defense plants. Lieutenant Colonel Donald F. Stace was the government flight representative at Inglewood in 1941, responsible for an office with about two dozen staff members. There were three other uniformed officers, while the others were civilian employees of the army. Their responsibilities included contract administration, quality control and inspection, fiscal and technical publication oversight, factory and engineering liaison, field support, and the requisitioning of spare parts.

‡

Up through the summer of 1941, flying units at the various airfields dispatched their own pilots to Inglewood to accept new warbirds from the factory. With the outbreak of hostilities, delivery of airplanes to the RAF in England, and the expansion of American flying units into the various theaters of the war, Hap Arnold created Air Corps Ferrying

A simulated disaster drill exercise was conducted in the plant emergency command center. The plant was vulnerable to enemy attack, plane crash, major fire, accidental explosion, or earthquake.

Command on May 29, 1941, to move the airplanes to where they were next needed, with initial emphasis on flights over the North Atlantic. By the fall of 1941, Ferry Command had expanded into domestic deliveries. Military pilots were frequently augmented by civilian contractors, especially earlier in the war.

As both production rates and design changes accelerated, an increasing number of airplanes were sent to modification centers for rework and/or customizations. Effective on May 28, 1942, the 6th Ferrying Group was established at the Long Beach Municipal Airport to process new military airplanes being assembled in Southern California. Dallas and Kansas City plant output was handled by the 5th Ferrying Group at Hensley Field, also located in Dallas.

Furthermore, under Arnold's guidance, a quasi-military organization which evolved into the WASPs (Women Airforce Service Pilots) was established, and at peak, 1,704 women pilots who had obtained their flying skills outside of the military were engaged to ferry airplanes within the North American continent. Arnold's goal was to free up a like number of male pilots for combat duty overseas. In the United States, work rules, initially intended to protect women from overly strenuous work, were mitigated with the passage of time; however, certain especially arduous jobs were reserved for men, including foundry work and the mounting of tires. Tire irons were used to finesse the rubber tires onto trims, which was dirty and exhausting work. (Wartime airplanes were equipped with tires that now appear to be oversized. The balloon tires allowed the relatively light B-25 to operate from unpaved runways or, when needed, depart pavement for taxi or parking on sodden surfaces.)

Human resource practices were updated to address the labor shortages faced by all wartime employers:

- **Absenteeism**: It was soon discovered that excessive overtime was counterproductive. Errors increased while output decreased as employees become fatigued. It was difficult for them to accomplish necessary personal chores. The solution was to limit work schedules to five days a week, and shift duration to nine or ten hours. Also, scheduling one or more days of rest on weekdays provided convenient time for addressing personal issues.

- **Military service**: Many employees required job-related training before they could be productive. Many young men were lost to the draft after being trained. NAA

continued on page 118

This photograph was annotated to make it clear that Mom Hee Lin was Korean. Some 120,000 persons of Japanese ancestry were confined to internment camps.

OPPOSITE: Artists were employed to crank out depictions of North American products at war. The renderings depicted the enemy in an unflattering light and bore racial stereotypes.

RIGHT: The recruiting billboard was to attract workers but was not intended to entice them into leaving other defense contractors.

BELOW: This shop scene depicts average people performing the important but mundane tasks necessary to get an airplane assembled.

continued from page 115

maintained on-site office space for Selective Service representatives to administer deferments. Plant newspaper articles advised employees in receipt of a draft notice to report it to their supervisor. An employee with a deferment was prohibited from enlisting for military service. Threats to cancel deferments were made to those young men with poor attendance.

- **Poaching:** Employers soon learned that enticing the employees of others was a bad practice. The government controlled entry-level wage rates to encourage employees to stay put. Meanwhile, non-wage incentives, including health care, paid holidays, and vacation time, were offered to enhance employee loyalty.

- **Child care:** Mothers could work confidently when their children were safely cared for in day care during times when other family members were on military duty.

- **Part-time shifts:** Stay-at-home mothers and high school students were offered four-hour daily work shifts.

Mechanics were expected to provide their own hand tools and this vendor sold them to the newly hired men and women.

Some parts of the plant were restricted. This B-25 is on jack stands and access to the area has been limited in the interest of safety.

‡

It took smart, capable, and seasoned engineers to bring a new airplane design to fruition. An overall designer was needed to rough out the general plan and parameters. A wooden model plus an artist rendering were useful tools to communicate the idea to others. (The archives are rife with examples that never made it beyond that stage.) Only a few were handed to an aerodynamicist. Specialized scale models were then assembled and taken to the wind tunnel for testing; sometimes a scaled-down wing would be tested separately from the balance of the design.

If the project was still proceeding, work on the airplane would be divided among a host of specialists. Design engineers would work out the details iteratively with draftsmen. The result was hundreds of hand-drawn blueprints and specifications to guide the shop workers as they fabricated and assembled the components.

The primary structure such as wings, fuselage, and control surfaces including the empennage (tail surfaces) are critical for providing the strength needed to keep an airframe safely aloft and reliably under control. Examples of secondary structure include the fairings that provide aerodynamic smoothing where the wing and fuselage join. Selection of the material for an aircraft component is a balancing act between availability, cost, strength, durability, longevity, and the current state of technology for its fabrication.

Stress engineers are responsible for ensuring the parts are strong enough to withstand the anticipated loads. Richard L. "Dick" Schleicher, a 1929 graduate of Villanova University, was the principal stress engineer at NAA for most of his career, which started in 1934 and ended in 1971, and an eyewitness to many of the historic events described in this book.

Schleicher was popular with co-workers, who sometimes called him the "head sandbagger." The primary means to validate materials during his career was by destructive testing.

continued on page 123

WHEN TO DUCK FOR COVER?

Military officials considered plants located near the coasts, such as like Inglewood, vulnerable to enemy attack. Defensive measures included soldiers, anti-aircraft artillery, searchlights, barrage balloons, and camouflage.

The North American Inglewood warbird factory was located adjacent to the Pacific Ocean and within easy reach of heavy naval guns or the same enemy aircraft carriers that had recently pummeled Pearl Harbor. Enemy attack was of serious concern to officials. The military establishment was chronically uncomfortable with airplane factories near the coast and they remained so into the 1950s.

In January 1942, foremen were requested to familiarize themselves with blackout procedures. Bomb shelters were prepared and employees were instructed to switch machinery off during bombing attacks. There was even concern of a chemical attack. Barrage balloons were constantly in the skies overhead as anti-aircraft crews from the 3rd Coastal Artillery manned guns on the nearby Playa del Ray Beach sand dunes.

Camouflage netting was installed over concrete aircraft parking aprons as rooftop

modifications were added to conceal the plant. Vigilant soldiers bearing rifles were photographed as they patrolled the rooftops. Bob Chilton, engineering test pilot, complained of wartime jitters: "Every time the Army alerted the front office [of a potential attack], we had to get a bunch of pilots together and fly all the airplanes down to Phoenix. Then, in a day or two, we would fly them all back to the [Inglewood] plant."

In the era before radar, powerful searchlights aimed aloft were used to sweep the nighttime skies over Los Angeles. The impressive pillars of light then became a signature of Hollywood movie premiers in the following decades. The army went into a panic on one cartoonish evening in an event that inspired director Stephen Spielberg to produce the 1979 comedy motion picture entitled *1941*. The event, remembered by some as "the Japanese attack on Los Angeles," was recounted in letters to the *South Bay Daily Breeze* newspaper commemorating the fiftieth anniversary of the war:

Had the invasion started? Was the airport under attack? Was Douglas, where I worked, being bombed?

Those were some of the thoughts as we ran outside to see what the shooting was all about in the early morning hours of February 25, 1942.

I lived only about a mile from the edge of the airport, Douglas Aircraft Plant, which was turning out S.B.D. Dauntless dive bombers, was on one side of the airport, North American Aviation, which was building B-25 bombers, was just across the road.

Once we got outside of the house that night we could see many searchlights all converging on a single object. Was it a plane, a squadron of planes, or what?

It was right over the airport, I don't know how many anti-aircraft guns were within two or three miles of our house but all of them must have been firing as fast as they could. They made on heck of a racket that went on for forty-five minutes to an hour as near as I can remember. The "Thing" moved southeast from the airport towards Signal Hill with all of its oil fields and on over to the shipyards with every gun along the way opening up.

Everybody had theories. One guy actually saw "a squadron of enemy planes" flying low over his house. I have my own theory. I definitely saw a speck in the center of all of the searchlights, possibly a weather balloon that some searchlight operator picked up and couldn't account for its presence. The "Thing" took forty-five minutes or more to move the distance of about twenty miles, much too slow for any airplane. Also it was very high. All of the shells exploded below it.

That morning I started to work a little early but I didn't get very far until I ran into a colossal road jam. I wheeled my car around, drove home, hopped on my bike, and managed to arrive at work on time. The crew straggled in during the next couple of hours, each with his own theory and his own story.

E. Wayne Mathews
Inglewood

Another *South Bay* reader wrote:

. . . I was awakened by thunder and lightning. As I lay there listening, it sounded very strange—a steady roar and flashes of light against the curtains. It went on and on. I became really frightened. I thought it was the end of the world.

I got out of bed and took my little girl (about age three) from her crib. I sat on the bed praying and waiting for the end. Finally, it stopped and I put her back to bed.

The next morning I ran to meet my husband as he returned from the night shift at North American.

I said, "Did you hear that funny thunderstorm last night?"

He replied: "Funny, hell. I got hit in the head with it."

In my excitement, I had not noticed his bandaged head.

My husband received a head wound (from falling shrapnel). We were most gratified that it was not serious.

Norma Vinsonhaler
Torrance

Dick Schleicher recalled that the only damage North American had was sweeping up the shrapnel from the anti-aircraft guns and repairing a few dented wings of the airplanes on the tarmac that evening.

Barrage balloons constantly flew over the airfield. They were intended to defend the airfield and factory by complicating a low level aerial approach. Some had explosive charges that would detonate on contact.

ABOVE: In an enduring tradition, workers pour out of the plant and into their cars during the daily ritual known as shift change.

RIGHT: The plant medical department employed doctors and nurses. They could perform a flight physical, tend to ailing workers, and render first aid.

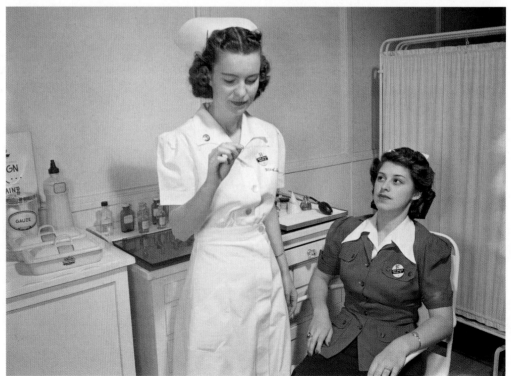

continued from page 119

Everything from individual parts like a rudder pedal to entire wing assemblies were tested to destruction by piling lead bars or bags of sand upon them until they broke. Each test was carefully planned, executed, and documented with photographs.

Landing gear was tested by hoisting the entire airplane into the air and dropping it from progressively increasing heights. Weight was piled upon other parts until they broke. Instruments, sometimes as primitive as a common scale, were used to measure loads or forces. Each part was designed to endure a maximum load, defined as 100 percent. A part that broke at less than the maximum load was deemed a failure and subject to redesign or other corrective measures. Exceeding 100 percent was generally deemed a success; however, greatly exceeding the maximum might indicate a part that was too heavy, expensive, or otherwise over-built.

The sight of a new hire wielding a drill motor would bring shudders to a grizzled shop foreman. Expensive parts can be turned into scrap metal because of an errantly drilled hole. Jigs were used to simplify drilling. The message is to wear your safety equipment.

continued on page 127

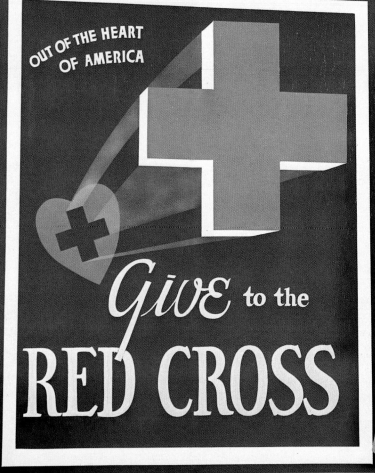

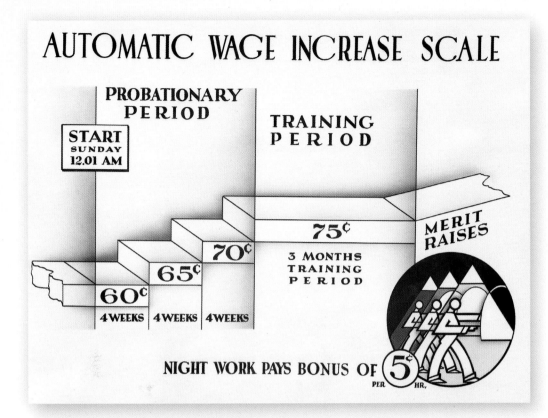

AUTOMATIC WAGE INCREASE SCALE

PROBATIONARY PERIOD

TRAINING PERIOD

START SUNDAY 12.01 AM

60¢ — 4 WEEKS
65¢ — 4 WEEKS
70¢ — 4 WEEKS
75¢ — 3 MONTHS TRAINING PERIOD

MERIT RAISES

NIGHT WORK PAYS BONUS OF 5¢ PER HR.

The chart explained wage rates to employees. The rates were managed by the Office of Price Administration (OPA) and were universally applied—to avoid bidding competition between employers in the never-ending quest for enough workers.

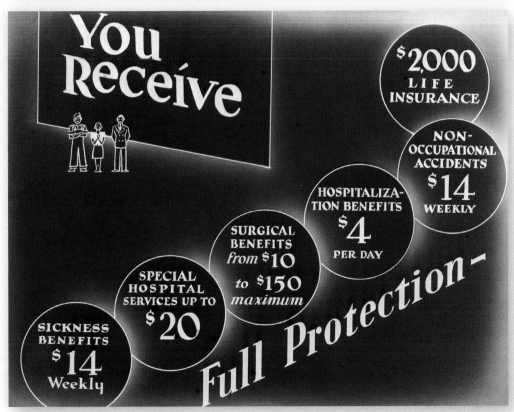

You Receive

$2,000 LIFE INSURANCE

NON-OCCUPATIONAL ACCIDENTS $14 WEEKLY

HOSPITALIZATION BENEFITS $4 PER DAY

SURGICAL BENEFITS from $10 to $150 maximum

SPECIAL HOSPITAL SERVICES UP TO $20

SICKNESS BENEFITS $14 Weekly

Full Protection–

LEFT: Healthcare benefits were explained. Employer-provided health care was a loophole that allowed some employers to differentiate themselves from others. The tradition of employer-provided healthcare was started during the war.

OPPOSITE: Mary Hogan was a Red Cross volunteer at the North American Inglewood plant.

Carpooling was encouraged because aircraft plants were often not well served by public transit systems and fuel and tires were rationed.

THE WARTIME MOTORIST

Based upon the number of articles in the plant weekly newspaper, tires were the biggest challenge drivers faced in 1942. The scarcity of rubber forced the rationing of gasoline, but airplane plants were at airports on the edge of the urban areas and not well served by public transportation. One photograph depicted a tire neatly stenciled in white paint "Defense Worker—Stolen Tires Impede Defense." A number of automobiles caught fire in the parking lot prompting a reminder to *not* leave smoldering cigarettes in the upholstery. Car-pooling came with recommendations for riders:

- Change out of your greasy clothing before getting into the car.
- Be on time.
- Pay the driver for expenses timely.

- Don't kid about his car or driving.
- Go to bat to help the driver obtain tires.
- Use patience and care in conversation.
- Don't monkey with the radio.

There was similar advice for the drivers:

- Be on time.
- Maintain the car and keep it clean inside and out.
- Follow a regular route.

- Don't presume lady guests have any interest in you.
- Fuel the car on your own time.

continued from page 123

The workplace injury and mortality rate in American industry was higher than normal during the war. Aggressive production quotas, long hours, and workplace shortcuts combined with an influx of new and unskilled workers all contributed to make industrial accidents common. Women were to wear company-prescribed uniforms, drill press operators were to wear caps, bandanas, or suitable head gear to keep long hair out of the machinery, hand or neck jewelry was banned, and footwear appropriate for the factory was required.

Compared to other companies, the wartime safety record at the NAA plants was considered good, despite a number of on-the-job fatalities. Two industrial deaths were recorded

Keeping work areas tidy and transportation aisles clear is the timeless message of this posed image.

ABOVE: Manufacturing laborers were expected to provide their own small hand tools. Specialized and larger tools were borrowed from the tool crib in exchange for a chit. The tool room attendants then had accountability for the tools for which they were responsible.

RIGHT: The normal boundaries of industrial photography were exceeded in a series of images by a gifted (but unknown) portrait maker. The identities of the subjects also remain a mystery.

OPPOSITE: Photographs of WASPs (Women Airforce Service Pilots) in factory collections are rare. WASP Florene Miller of the 6th Ferrying Group, Long Beach (California) Airport, is seen lifting her seat-style parachute into the cockpit of a P-51 Mustang. The date is early 1944 and her stylish uniform bears an Army Air Forces patch. The WASPs were called upon to ferry new aircraft about the United States to free up male pilots for overseas combat service.

at the NAA Kansas City plant: a flight line mechanic walked into a spinning propeller, and a woman was killed in an explosion when an extension cord light bulb was thrust into a tank rife with vapors from sealant.

Flying accidents claimed other employees. Five died when the thirteenth B-25 airplane off the assembly line crashed on April 25, 1942. Later, the three-person crew of airplane number 87 was forced to jump for their lives when in-flight control was lost, resulting in one leg injury from the parachute landing. Manufacturing defects caused by inexperienced assembly workers was the suspected cause of both accidents. Henceforth, and to focus attention on the mechanical readiness of the airplane, the crew chief (i.e., head flight-line mechanic) was required to be a participant in all B-25 Fairfax test hops.

All of the airplanes of the era were fueled by volatile aviation gasoline, and cigarette smoking was ubiquitous. Each of the thousands of Browning machine guns installed on the combat airplanes was test fired prior to delivery. With the massive influx of unskilled and youthful labor, it is amazing that research into North American files has yet to uncover an instance of workplace conflagration or accidental gunfire.

CHAPTER 8

THE P-51 MUSTANG

The Focke-Wolf FW 190D re-engined with the Junkers Jumo 213A was the best German fighter to be used in large numbers during the war, but it did not have better performance than later models of the Spitfire or the USAAF's North American P-51D: the latter, fast, maneuverable, pleasant to fly and with more than twice the range of the Bf 109 or Spitfire even without drop tanks, probably has the best claim to be the outstanding piston-engined fighter aircraft of the Second World War.

—Noted aviation historian A. D. Harvey,
Air Power History magazine, 2014

The Mustang was an exceptional escort fighter, but could also provide close air support, when called upon. Munitions specialists prepare to load a general-purpose bomb under the wing of a P-51B.

Brilliant aircraft designer, Austrian-born Edgar Schmued (right), looks like a proud father as he shows off his new baby, known as NA-35, to Lt. Col. S. P. Chang, Commander of the Chinese Central Aviation School, in January 1940 as test pilot Vance Breese looks on. No sale was made as Schmued moved onto his next assignment: NA-73X, which evolved into the P-51 Mustang.

England and France were in dire straits in early 1940. Dutch Kindelberger had forged a strong business relationship with the British and French military with the successful sale of earlier trainer airplanes. Purchasing agents representing the two countries approached him and asked: Could North American build P-40 Warhawk fighter planes on license from Curtiss?

Contrary to the wishes of Army Air Corps Materiel Command, Kindelberger instead counter-offered to design and build a brand new airplane that would leapfrog the P-40—a rapidly aging prewar design. Engineers at NAA had been privately mulling the prospect of a new fighter for a number of months. By building its own airplane, the company could try out the "design-for-production" methodology that would ultimately yield higher production rates at lower unit cost. A deal was struck; but, France disappeared into the Third Reich before the new model could be delivered.

NAA had dabbled with fighter aircraft for export previously. Some trainer aircraft, like the NA-50 and NA-68, were fitted with guns and hard points for bombs and marketed for export as combatants. The airplane envisioned by Kindelberger and his chief designer, Edgar O. Schmued, was destined to become a legend. It would fly faster and farther and be more nimble in an aerial joust than any other fighter aircraft that preceded it.

Born in 1899, Schmued was an Austrian who served on the German side in World War I. He designed an airplane after that war but it could not be built because of the restrictions imposed on Germany by the Treaty of Versailles. He joined Fokker operations in Brazil where his genius was recognized. Immigration to the United States at that time was severely restricted, but he accomplished it with the sponsorship of General Motors.

Schmued reported to work at Fokker in 1931. When his wife, Louisa, balked at the move to California, he resigned for a brief period and accepted a post at Bellanca, a Delaware-based builder of smaller-sized airplanes. Unhappy there, Schmued soon accepted Kindelberger's open-ended offer of employment and departed for California by automobile in early 1936. Tragically, a grinding head-on collision on California's Highway 60 killed Louisa and left Schmued seriously injured.

After recovering sufficiently, Schmued worked at Inglewood as the chief of preliminary design for most of his twenty-two years with NAA. His genius for airplane design touched many aircraft models over his four-decade career: the Peruvian fighter (NA-50), XB-21, B-25, F-86 Sabre, F-100 Super-Sabre and, years later after leaving North American, the Northrop T-38 Talon. He achieved enduring aviation fame as the leader of the legendary Mustang project at NAA.

Company records reveal that the design of the new NAA fighter was heavily influenced by a little-known tiny two-seat trainer airplane that was designed and built under general order NA-35. It first flew only five months before initial design work commenced on NA-73, the internal designation for the first iteration of the design that finally emerged as the legendary P-51 Mustang.

Schmued was at the heart of the NA-35 design. The entire airplane was simple but innovative. It was the first NAA airplane to be powered by a liquid-cooled engine, an advance that yielded a greatly diminished frontal area for the fuselage. Schmued also incorporated the recently released National Advisory Committee for Aeronautics (NACA) laminar flow wing specification: a single sheet of smooth aluminum comprised the entire upper wing surface, thus ensuring minimal drag and a clean airflow.

Freelance pilot Vance Breese, one of a number of Southern Californian test pilots who were richly rewarded for taking new models aloft for the first time, deftly handled the NA-35's maiden flight on December 9, 1939, while fabrication work commenced on a

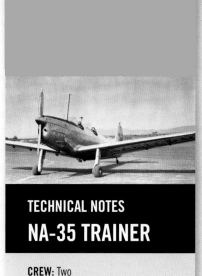

TECHNICAL NOTES
NA-35 TRAINER

CREW: Two

ENGINE: Menasco C4S-2, 150 hp

WINGSPAN: 29 ft. 10 in.

LENGTH: 25 ft. 6 in.

HEIGHT: 6 ft. 11 in.

EMPTY WEIGHT: 1,218 lb.

GROSS WEIGHT: 1,760 lb.

MAXIMUM SPEED: 140 mph

CRUISE SPEED: 124 mph

RANGE: 305 miles

CEILING: 18,500 ft.

This drawing was intended to illustrate the aerodynamic advantages of the Mustang's wing profile.

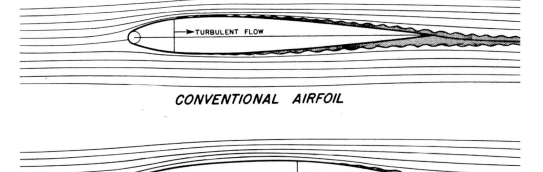

CONVENTIONAL AIRFOIL

LOW-DRAG AIRFOIL

The unusual lines of the Mustang's low-drag laminar flow wing, lower drawing, are revealed in contrast with the conventional type. The maximum thickness of the low-drag airfoil is nearer the center of the chord, which "thins out" the bulbous leading edge of the customary wing type almost to a point.

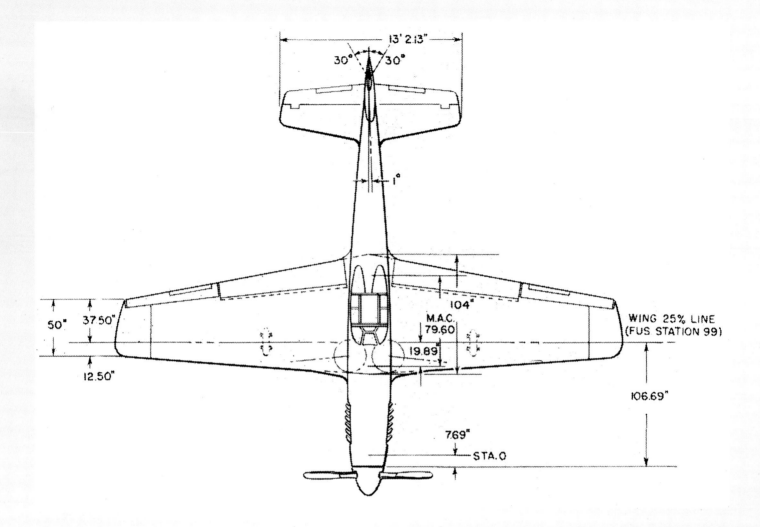

13' 2.13"

30° 30°

1°

104"

M.A.C.
79.60

19.89"

50" 37.50"

WING 25% LINE
(FUS STATION 99)

12.50"

106.69"

7.69"

STA.0

Another Mustang drawing illustrates the aircraft's thin fuselage and touts it as a chief reason for its remarkable speed.

second airplane. A standard NAA marketing campaign was mounted during January 1940. Potential customers included the US military, foreign governments (i.e., the Chinese), and potential civilian buyers. The demand was tepid. The design, while not intended to meet an air corps requirement, was declined outright by the US military establishment.

Unfortunately, work on the basic trainer diminished as 1940 progressed because of plant expansion and other rapidly evolving projects out-prioritizing NA-35. Acting with the audacity of a sole proprietor, Kindelberger informed the board of directors at their meeting of July 12, 1940, that he had abandoned NA-35 and sold the design to Vega for $100,000 cash. As expected, the board expressed no qualms. The design then became known as the Vega 35. A handful of additional 35s were produced before Vega's resources were also commandeered to produce military airplanes.

Kindelberger gave Schmued instructions to design the new British fighter airplane starting with the pilot and moving outward. The hypothetical pilot was to be 5 feet 10 inches tall and weigh 140 pounds. Schmued found such a man already on the payroll, sat him in a chair, and then began calculating the requisite man/machine interfaces. His name was Art Chester.

The new airplane would benefit from four important design features that were to be validated by wind tunnel testing: The new NACA laminar flow wing design, which remained efficient even when abused in rigorous wartime service; elegantly crafted fuselage contours to further minimize drag; low frontal area of the fuselage, made possible by the selection of a liquid-cooled engine; and an innovative engine cooling system which placed the radiators behind the pilot, thus yielding the distinctive air scoop aft of the cockpit and under the fuselage.

American combat aircraft of the World War II era were most frequently powered by radial engines. The pistons were arranged in a circle about the propeller shaft and each cylinder was exposed to the oncoming airflow so heat could be dissipated by metal fins—similar to many modern day motorcycles, chainsaws, or rotary lawn mower engines. The pistons on a liquid-cooled engine were neatly lined up in a row behind the propeller. The choice of a liquid-cooled engine eliminated the need for a wider drag-inducing engine and the associated broad circumference fuselage. Initial versions of the new airplane, powered by an Allison engine turning a Curtiss three-bladed propeller, were best suited for flying at lower altitudes.

Heat dissipation is a vital aircraft design consideration. Only about 25 to 30 percent of the energy derived from aviation gasoline becomes shaft horsepower. The balance of the energy is either expelled as hot exhaust gas or must be dissipated by the cooling system. Also, the generation of heat varies depending on the engine throttle setting. Fuel consumption soars during takeoff and climb-out while continuously declining during cruise at altitude as the fuel load decreases as it is burned.

Both the oil and coolant radiators were to be located at the bottom of the airplane, aft of the pilot, to provide a better center of balance. As cold air was heated by the radiators, it would expand and be forced out of a variable constricted vent at the rear of the airplane yielding just enough thrust to offset about half of the drag created by the Mustang's

continued on page 138

An early Mustang is posed with white-clad mechanics and soldiers. The visual clues include the three-bladed propeller and birdcage canopy. Later Mustangs evolved four-bladed propellers and bubble canopies.

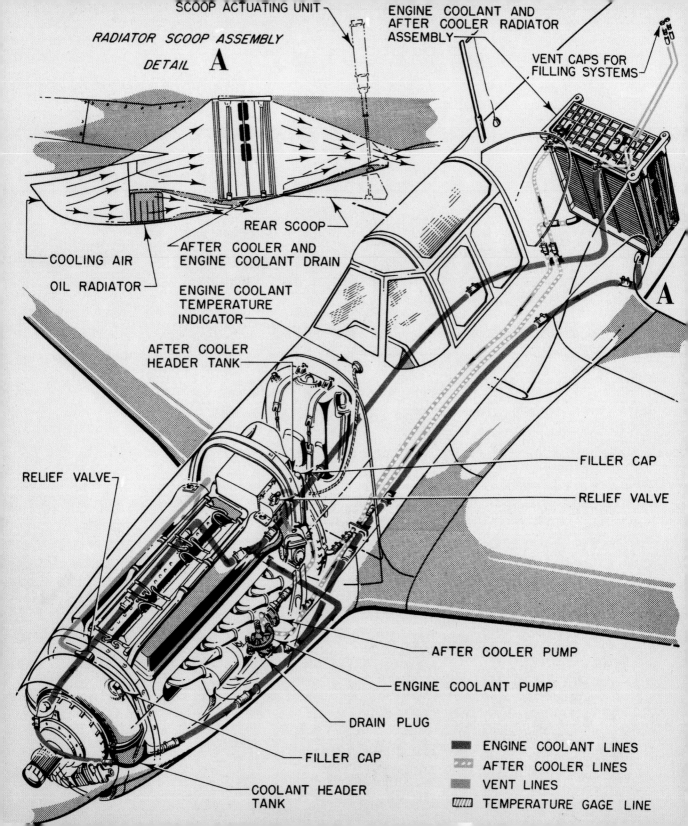

SCOOP ACTUATING UNIT

ENGINE COOLANT AND
AFTER COOLER RADIATOR
ASSEMBLY

RADIATOR SCOOP ASSEMBLY

DETAIL **A**

VENT CAPS FOR
FILLING SYSTEMS

REAR SCOOP

AFTER COOLER AND
ENGINE COOLANT DRAIN

COOLING AIR

OIL RADIATOR

ENGINE COOLANT
TEMPERATURE
INDICATOR

AFTER COOLER
HEADER TANK

A

FILLER CAP

RELIEF VALUE

RELIEF VALVE

AFTER COOLER PUMP

ENGINE COOLANT PUMP

DRAIN PLUG

FILLER CAP

COOLANT HEADER
TANK

ENGINE COOLANT LINES
AFTER COOLER LINES
VENT LINES
TEMPERATURE GAGE LINE

LEFT: An unidentified air corps officer consults with Edgar Schmued. The topic, no doubt, is the P-51 because there are Mustang related items behind them.

BELOW: Robert "Bob" Chilton was a primary Mustang test pilot. Here, he sits in an older model equipped with the "birdcage" canopy.

OPPOSITE: The cooling system was vital to the Mustang. This schematic depicts the multiple radiators to include the oil cooler.

continued from page 135

ABOVE: This Mustang is approaching the wing-to-body-join step on the moving assembly line.

OPPOSITE: The central spinner is attached to the four-bladed Hamilton Standard propeller as this airplane rolls to the end of the moving assembly line.

signature protruding air scoop. The phenomenon was called the Meredith effect, and it was discovered by North American engineers in the NACA-published scientific papers.

While the air scoop was the secret ingredient yielding a notable performance advantage, it was also a serious detriment in case of ditching—crash landing on water. Most other airplanes of the era were smooth on the bottom when the landing gear was retracted, and, with optimum landing pitch attitude, the aircraft's velocity was safely dissipated by bouncing atop the waves. However, the low-hanging scoop of the Mustang dug into the water on impact, abruptly pitching the aircraft nose down resulting in a very sudden stop. Set against that, a wheels-up landing on a runway was most often survivable because the scoop acted as a handy landing skid to be ground away by abrasion with the pavement.

The team started laying out the new airplane on May 5, 1940. Kindelberger granted Schmued the authority to handpick each staff member for NAA's highest priority project. Ed Horkey, a gifted aerodynamicist, was hired to perform the wind tunnel work. The team devoted themselves solely to the task and nothing else. Only on Sunday did they wrap up their work early (at 6:00 p.m.) to acknowledge the weekend.

FLIGHT TESTING

Flight testing can be a pressure cooker of inflated expectations and abbreviated schedules but many engineers find it a rewarding place to work. Louis Waite was hired away from Boeing to establish a flight-test organization for North American, so that the company would no longer need to rely on external consulting pilots, like Vance Breese.

Waite's initial focus was instrumentation, so he hired Ed Virgin, an army-trained pilot and engineer, on February 6, 1941. It fell upon Virgin's shoulders to become chief of test pilots as he went about the recruitment of others and organized them into a professional, self-sufficient group.

The primary goal of flight testing is to demonstrate that new models and variations to existing designs may reliably be certified as suitable for their intended military or civil use. As operations grew, North American company pilots came to be organized into three groups:

- **EXPERIMENTAL TEST PILOTS.** They are at the top of the flight-test pecking order. They are educated as engineers and are usually very pragmatic, logical, and easy to work with; however, there are sometimes individuals with prickly egos. Test pilots are expected to fly aircraft of all types and sizes while line-pilots often spend their entire careers in a single model. Robert "Bob" Chilton was the test pilot most often associated with P-51 flight testing.

- **PRODUCTION TEST PILOTS.** They take new airplanes up on their maiden flights to ensure everything is working properly. After any in-flight "squawks" are resolved, the customer is invited to participate in an acceptance flight. Production pilots can ferry airplanes between locations and may also deliver airplanes to their next destination.

- **PILOT INSTRUCTORS.** They team with other field services professionals to ensure customer cockpit crews, maintainers, and other flight crew members are properly trained in the operation of new models and often follow airplanes of a new type into service.

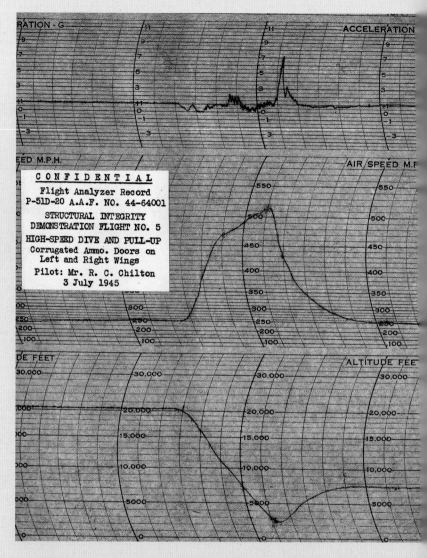

The working attire of military aircrew members evolved with the passage of time. Neck ties were ubiquitous to accompany the commonly worn suit or sport jacket during the early days. As the parachute became an important

The classic directive for streamlining airplanes, "Get all the humps and bumps inside," is credited to Schmued. Excessive overtime was endured and the end result was nothing less than a miracle. The design and shop fabrication of the completed prototype was completed on September 9, 1940, a mere 117 days after project initiation. There were problems: the Allison engine arrived late, and, contrary to the drawings, the wiring harness was positioned such that the motor mounts required rework before the engine could be installed.

life-saving device, it was noted that the wind blast at altitude could separate pants and shirts from the wearer and send them floating earthward in mutually exclusive directions. No surviving aircrew member wanted to greet his rescuers in a state of nakedness while shivering; therefore, it was noted that, by late in the war, aviator attire had evolved into one-piece cotton coveralls. Depending on season and temperature, street clothing could then be safely worn under the coveralls. It would not be until 1970 that military aviators switched from cotton flight suits to those fabricated from flame-resistant Nomex. Meanwhile, airliner pilots remained clad in business suits and neckties as reassurance to any white-knuckle potential passengers.

More substantial crash helmets began to appear as leather skull caps were replaced by hard-shell versions. These served multiple purposes: head protection in a crash, a more substantial foundation to keep an oxygen mask securely tethered to the wearer's face, and headset not only for radio communication but also for noise attenuation. Progressive hearing loss is too common among those who earn their livelihood in or around airplanes.

Flight-test engineers meticulously script the validation testing, participate in the execution, before performing and documenting the subsequent analysis. An aeronautical engineer who is actively involved in the certification of modern advanced military aircraft was invited to interpret a sixty-nine-year-old analog three-axis analog graph that documented a P-51 test flight of 1945. It is stated using contemporary technical terms and concepts:

The maneuver description appears to be accurate: HIGH SPEED DIVE AND PULL UP.

It appears the pilot sets-up at 20,000 feet / 250 mph, accelerates in a dive to 500 mph, then completes a wings level pull of some sort to load the aircraft with 7g, ultimately recovering the aircraft to 8,000 feet / 250 mph.

As expected, the maximum g load is lined up right after he hits his top airspeed and airspeed bleeds significantly as he puts on g. Fast and low is the easiest place to load the aircraft with g due to the higher dynamic pressure at lower altitudes (i.e., dense air). Modern fighter programs do "wind-up turns" and "loaded rolls," among other maneuvers, to test the structural integrity of the airframe and efficacy of the digital flight Control Laws (CLAW). In a modern aircraft, the CLAW keeps the pilot within the structural limits of the airframe based on aircraft configuration, gross weight, and other factors.

Of interest is that the pilot pushes the aircraft to 0g to initiate his dive, which means he's likely doing a wings level push. Modern test pilots prefer to bank or roll inverted and pull into the dive to keeping positive g on the aircraft. Engines also don't like operating at 0g for more than a few seconds at a time, so the engineers for modern programs prefer the test pilot to avoid that region unless doing specific 0g / negative g testing.

It is also interesting to see the buffet/g-transients/turbulence induced on the aircraft as it exceeds 450 mph in the dive. It appears the aircraft doesn't like being in this state and it is doubtful if the pilot can read his instruments accurately.

Flight testing was to remain a potentially lethal business for the next generation of test pilots. The war years were followed by the headlong rush to break the sound barrier and perfect jet-powered fighter aircraft in the military's quest for more speed, maneuverability, and altitude.

Chuck Yeager, the first human to break the sound barrier, spoke to the graduating class of the USAF Test Pilot School in June 2012. Even at an advanced age, he crisply recounted his own escape from France after being shot down in a P-51, his later exploits as an ace, and of "forty streets" at Edwards AFB named after test pilots who died pursuing the headlong quest for ever greater speed, range, capacity, altitude, and maneuverability with evolving (but sometimes unstable) aircraft designs and engines that were too often either unreliable and/or underpowered. However, evolving technology has mitigated the dangers of the World War II era to the point where some consider driving to the airfield is more dangerous than executing the test conditions.

After the arrival and installation of the first Allison engine, the NA-73 prototype quickly moved into flight test. Bearing the civil registration of NX19998, it first flew on October 26, 1940, with freelance pilot Breese at the controls.

Kindelberger later stated that the delay caused by waiting for the engine actually gave the NA-73 team breathing room to work out some of the kinks still remaining after the rushed development. The prototype (internally designated NA-73X) ingloriously came to earth on its fifth flight at 7:15 a.m. on November 20, 1940. It was the day prior to Thanksgiving when test pilot Paul Balfour was forced down by fuel-related engine failure.

Paul Balfour was born in 1908 and was employed by North American as a test pilot starting on March 1, 1936. During the era when the company was still small, he also performed drafting duties when not piloting. Balfour departed Inglewood for a sales demonstration in Mexicali, Mexico, in a BT-9 on May 12, 1936. and was joined there by Dutch Kindelberger. The shared travel experience with Kindelberger most likely spared Balfour's reputation and career. One year later Balfour would accompany Schwalenberg, as the pair assumed the important positions of chief pilot and plant manager at the newly established Kansas City B-25 factory.

"Dick" Schleicher, North American's principal stress engineer, was an eyewitness:

> Paul Balfour had just taken off from Mines Field and crossed Sepulveda Boulevard when he disappeared from sight. CRASH!!! We all jumped in our cars and headed along the Imperial Highway. There it was—our beautiful NA-73X lying upside down in a plowed field, and Paul standing nearby wondering what happened. It seemed that a fuel valve had stuck, or was never operated. Everybody was wringing their hands.
>
> I looked at the broken propeller shaft, scratched windshield, crushed vertical fin, and bent wing; turned to Lee Atwood and suggested that we wash off the mud, replace all the damaged parts, and try again. We did and the P-51 was born!

Since NA-73X flew under civilian registration, the accident report was filed with the Civil Aeronautics Authority in Washington, DC. The probable cause was stated to be "not determined"; however, there were eighteen gallons of fuel found in the auxiliary tank, 32 gallons in the right wing, but only 5 pints in the left wing tank. It is likely Balfour caused the accident by mismanaging the fuel tank selector, which starved the engine. Balfour received treatment for minor injuries and a mobile crane was summoned to retrieve the damaged airplane before sundown.

Given the magnitude of the damage visible in the photographs, NA-73X was repaired surprisingly quickly. The engine was ready for a test run on December 31, 1940, and the aircraft next flew on January 11, 1941. Test flights of 7.5 hour duration were undertaken in California before the Mustang was consigned to European bomber-escort combat operations. Advancing the throttle during mid-mission simulated dog-fights demonstrated that the Mustang's cooling system, containing a mixture of water and glycol (NAA documents sometimes refer to the brand name of Prestone), was adequate for rugged service.

North American was convinced at an early date that the Mustang design was monumental. Schmued and Horkey were jointly, but unsuccessfully, nominated on March 25, 1941, to receive the prestigious Daniel Guggenheim Medal for aeronautical accomplishment, an annual award established in 1928.

The recognitions, if awarded, were to read:

> Mr. Schmued [is recognized for] the rapid and precise design work in connection with the NA-73 fighter airplane with special regard for military efficiency and aerodynamic refinement as well as clever design for the application of quality production. This airplane is without a doubt the simplest fighter to build that has ever been conceived.
>
> Mr. Horkey [is recognized for] the critical calculations and aerodynamic testing relating to the successful and practical development of the laminar flow wing for the NA-73 fighter, materially reducing the drag, increasing the speed, and improving the stall characteristics of the newly designed combat airplane.

The final conveyor system a Mustang would encounter was located outdoors. It is where radio and engine testing was accomplished. The airplane was tethered to the moving line and the engine run at full power as the airplanes slowly moved sideways.

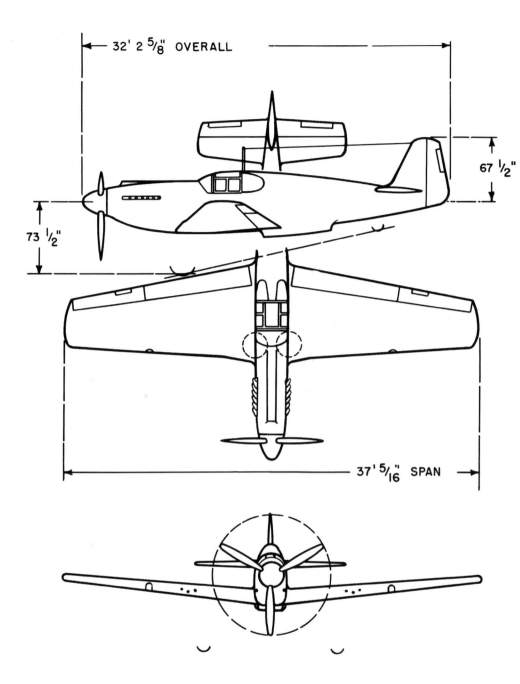

32' 2 5/8" OVERALL

67 1/2"

73 1/2"

37' 5/16" SPAN

The outline and dimensions of the British NA-73 Mustang. The P-51 would follow as the design evolved and important improvements were applied.

Production of 320 Mustangs for the RAF began as NAA engineers desperately sought solutions to improve the high altitude speed and performance of the Allison engine. As stipulated in the military aircraft export requirements, two examples (the fourth and tenth units off the assembly line) were redesignated XP-51 and handed over to the air corps for evaluation in August and December, 1941.

No further orders for the Mustang were immediately forthcoming. Kindelberger later lamented, "We thought we had the best airplane in the world and wanted to keep building it but we didn't get orders." The early disdain of the army air corps bureaucrats at Materiel Command toward the Mustang is clear and obvious. They had no intention to evaluate the two test items they had been provided. The reasons behind the rejection are

more difficult to decipher. The North American people at Inglewood rationalized the problem thus:

- NA-73 was undertaken by North American for export. There was no sponsorship within Army Air Forces Materiel Command at Dayton or their Santa Monica office. It was an unwanted military orphan that fell into the category of "not invented here."

- North American did not have the legacy of a pursuit airplane builder enjoyed by Bell, Curtiss, and Lockheed. It had been decided in the massive production awards of August 16, 1939, that the primary role of North American was fabrication of trainers and medium bombers.

- Pursuit airplanes with air-cooled radial engines were faster, lighter, simpler, and more nimble than liquid-cooled models, which were burdened with extra weight of the mixture of water and anti-freeze, radiators, air scoops, and all of the associated plumbing.

- The Allison engine limited Mustang operations to the lower altitudes. Installation of a supercharger was needed to perform at the higher altitudes where the heavy bombers were found. Unfortunately, the supercharger did not exist or, if invented, it would ruin the aerodynamics.

- The feared German invasion of England was becoming less likely, thus mitigating the need for a low-altitude fighter.

Another theory is that Maj. Gen. Oliver Echols, who had power over procurement, was angered by Kindelberger's insubordinate decision to design the Mustang, rather than build the P-40 on license. The theory continues that Echols, still holding a grudge, was on a vindictive quest to punish NAA for their audacity, by turning off the engine supply

FIELD SERVICE BULLETIN
73-95

MODIFICATION OF P-51 SERIES AIRPLANES FOR LONG RANGE OPERATION

stream. NAA was then producing two P-51s and two B-25s per day. Echols wanted more fast attack bombers and no further pursuit airplanes from the company.

Lee Atwood believed the Mustang had at least one friend working behind the scenes within the army air corps procurement system. He wrote the following in 1981 about Benjamin Kelsey, an MIT educated engineer who became an accomplished and famed military pilot, then rose to the brevet (temporary) rank of brigadier general before retiring from the USAF in 1955: "Ben Kelsey, in my opinion, was among the most effective Air Corps officers of World War II. His active liaison between combat and aircraft engineering was extremely productive and resulted in aircraft and weapons improvements in a timely manner and when most critically needed. I first met Ben when he was the project officer on the [Lockheed] P-38 and he became interested in the P-51 at an early stage. Undoubtedly, he did all he could to bring it along. He had a low key, but very convincing approach."

Other authors contend that Kelsey did nothing favorable for the P-51 because he was solely committed to the P-38. His true role remains open to speculation since very little he put in writing on the subject has been preserved.

ABOVE: The wheel chocks tell us this P-51B (circa late summer 1943) is enduring a full-throttle engine test on a remote part of Mines Field (now LAX) and is not about to become airborne.

OPPOSITE: Field Service Bulletin 73-95 conveyed to field mechanics 109 pages of rework instructions necessary to increase the Mustang's range by the installation of an optional 85-gallon fuel tank in the aft-fuselage.

Work on this Mustang is performed outdoors and under camouflage netting. The presence of the men with neckties makes it likely that experimental engineering work may be underway.

When the air corps expressed need for a dive bomber, Kindelberger told them he had one. Upper- and lower-wing dive-brakes were borrowed from Vultee Aircraft and cannons were added to the Mustang design as it was adapted for the air-to-ground attack role. Five hundred of the newly designated A-36 Apaches were ordered on April 28, 1942, further inflaming Echols. The Mustangs destined for the RAF were crated up and dispatched by sea. With assistance some would later attribute to Ben Kelsey, an additional 150 Mustangs, funded by American taxpayers under Lend-Lease, were ordered on British behalf under contract NA-91.

General Hap Arnold decisively sliced through the fallacies that fueled the army air force's qualms about the Mustang. He first intervened by directing the acquisition of reconnaissance versions. Arnold's adamant insistence on proceeding with production of the Mustang is evident in a very blunt letter dated August 31, 1942, signed by Maj. Gen. Muir S. Fairchild. The last sentence stated ". . . by command of Lieutenant General Arnold." The initial order for 310 combat Mustangs for army air forces was dated October 20, 1942, but they would not become ubiquitous in European skies until late 1943 and into 1944.

It could be argued that many heavy bombers and aircrew lives were lost over Europe for lack of Mustang escort; however, when asked about that at the end of the war, North American representatives again responded that they had needed the time to perfect the design. A telegram dated July 5, 1943, from Materiel Command Headquarters at Wright Field to NAA at Inglewood conveys the intensity of the newly found interest in the Mustang: "An urgent directive has been received from the chief of Army Air Forces to provide the maximum combat range at the earliest possible date. It is requested that an immediate study be made to determine the method by which the maximum possible internal protected fuel can be carried in (model P-51B and subsequent) airplanes and that the contractor submit a plan for the incorporation of such provisions."

On August 17, 1943, a two-pronged attack employing nearly four hundred heavy bombers was launched from England. Colonel Curtis LeMay led the contingent attacking the Messerschmitt aircraft factory at Regensburg while the other force was directed against a ball bearing plant at Schweinfurt. Both targets were beyond the range of the escort fighters then available.

General Arnold winced when he read the after-action report stating that sixty Flying Fortresses had been shot down and nearly six hundred airmen were killed or captured. Arnold knew the Eighth Air Force bomber fleet could not sustain that level of combat loss. Fighter protection was needed and only the P-51 Mustang was best suited to provide it—but a new 85-gallon fuel tank would need to be installed in the aft fuselage.

A North American internal memorandum dated August 25, 1943 stated: "The Army is requesting fuselage self-sealing fuel tanks in as many P-51 airplanes as possible. The urgency of the request is based principally upon the recent loss the [Allies] have experienced on long range bombing ventures without fighter protection. . . . It is proposed that a change point be established as soon as possible in the P-51 airplanes. . . ." The installation of an 85-gallon fuel tank in the aft fuselage increased the endurance by about two hours. The modification, documented by Field Service Bulletin 73-95, was also available as an optional retrofit. The 109-page set of instructions detailed how to make room for the additional fuel tank by relocating the oxygen tank, radio, battery, wiring, and other electrical components.

The requested changes were not to be fully implemented until the P-51D models rolled out of Inglewood and Dallas plants; however, improvements appeared incrementally as all aspects of the design were evaluated, then re-evaluated.

There were three iterations of canopy. The original "birdcage" canopy comprised sections of glass secured to a metal frame. Later, the Malcolm Hood was also applied to the P-51B and P-51C models. Invented by the British for the Supermarine Spitfire and manufactured by R. Malcolm and Company, it offered improved pilot's visibility. However, starting with the P-51D, an aerodynamically conformal canopy became an externally visible trademark of the newer Mustangs. This was manufactured by heating acrylic and then vacuum forming it over a mold.

Armor was installed in the firewall to protect engine cooling components and additional armor plate was located behind the pilot's seat. The heavier copper radiator was replaced by a lighter aluminum version. Sealed balanced ailerons were installed on the wing tips. Important fuel system changes were also made and a rubber-like self-sealing material was installed in the fuel tanks to stem the loss of fuel to bullet holes.

A different engine was the most significant improvement to the Mustang. When later asked about this, NAA replied that when the design of NA-73 was undertaken, the Allison engine was the only suitable option available to them in sufficient numbers. In fact, the Rolls-Royce Merlin V-12 design that was eventually installed in the Mustang actually predated the P-51. It was first installed in British fighters, including the Hawker Hurricane and Supermarine Spitfire, in 1936. It also powered the four-engine Avro Lancaster and two-engine de Havilland Mosquito bombers.

After observing their performance at the Battle of Britain, the US government asked for rights to manufacture the Merlin engine. A battleship soon arrived from England with a sample engine and all of the drawings. Of all the industrialists called in to discuss building the engine in the United States, only the Packard Motor Car Company of Detroit accepted the challenge. The deal was sealed in September 1940, and Packard ceased the manufacture of vehicles for the duration of the war to concentrate solely on aircraft engines.

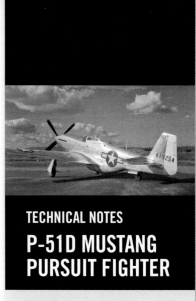

TECHNICAL NOTES
P-51D MUSTANG PURSUIT FIGHTER

ENGINE: Packard-built Rolls-Royce Merlin V-1650, 1,695 hp

WINGSPAN: 37 ft. 0 in.

LENGTH: 32 ft. 3 in.

HEIGHT: 13 ft. 8 in.

WEIGHT: 12,100 lb. maximum

CRUISING SPEED: 275 mph

MAXIMUM SPEED: 437 mph

RANGE: 1,650 miles (with external fuel tanks)

CEILING: 41,900 ft.

ARMAMENT: Six .50-cal. machine guns; ten 5-in. rockets or 2,000 lb. of bombs

NUMBER BUILT: More than 15,000 (all models)

LEFT: Three key members of the Mustang design team (left to right) were L. L. Waite, Raymond Rice, and Edgar Schmued. The elapsed time from project start to first flight was an amazing 117 days. Schmued worked around the clock and often slept at the plant.

OPPOSITE: Edgar Schmued (left) and a colleague examine a model of the Mustang in the wind tunnel.

Three hundred Packard engineers went to work on the project to assess each of the fourteen thousand parts and adapt American-built parts where needed. Engine interfaces were redesigned to accept American-built accessories. The first Rolls-Royce Merlin engines built by Packard were under fabrication in August 1941. With 1,695 horsepower at 3,000 rpm, the sheer volume of raw power available to propel something as small as a Mustang is difficult to fathom.

Ronald W. Harker, a tenacious British test pilot working for Rolls-Royce, was the first to propose installing a Merlin engine on a P-51 airframe. Work started in August 1942, with the first flight on October 13, 1942. North American emulated the work done in England and the Merlin-powered Mustang was born, shifting the airplane's performance profile from low to high altitude.

continued on page 154

ABOVE: American pilots pose with an early P-51 Mustang. Early models had a three-bladed Curtiss propeller and Allison engine while later versions had four big blades from Hamilton-Standard and a Packard-built Rolls-Royce Merlin engine.

RIGHT: Armaments specialists prepare .50-caliber Browning machine guns for installation in a P-51 Mustang. The red-ringed insignia dates the photo to the late-summer of 1943.

OPPOSITE: The P-51 Mustang was initially shunned by the military procurement bureaucracy. It took the formidable marketing skills of Dutch Kindelberger (pictured), combined with the visionary wisdom of Gen. Hap Arnold, to overcome the resistance. More than fifteen thousand were built at a 1945 cost of about $51,000 each.

continued from page 151

ABOVE: Smoke and noise are evident as all six wing-mounted .50-caliber guns in this Mustang are functionally tested. The odd-looking portable contraption trapped the bullets allowing the toxic lead rounds to be safely collected for recycling.

RIGHT: Sergeant Milton Weber hands delivery papers to ferry pilot Lieutenant Schwendeman at the 6th Ferry Group Base, Long Beach. Serial number 44-13962 was the 710th Mustang built under contract NA-109.

Thirty-one hours were expended to machine a single Merlin connecting rod compared to half an hour for an automobile connecting rod. It took 110 hours to machine a Merlin engine block as compared to 5 hours for an automobile engine block. Each completed engine was started and test run for 6 hours by Packard. It was then torn down, all parts were inspected and reassembled, and then test run another 5 hours before shipment. The last of 55,511 Merlin engines was assembled in 1950.

The improved Mustang featured a governor-controlled Hamilton-Standard four-bladed propeller, replacing the Curtiss three-blade prop. Some Mustangs received propellers built by Aeroproducts. A two-speed, two-stage supercharger, especially designed to fit the Merlin, delivered additional oxygen to the engine at any altitude, improving its top performance.

Experiments were performed to further increase Mustang performance. A small number of P-51F and P-51G model airplanes were crafted. Schmued was dispatched to England to try to obtain a more powerful 2,200-horsepower version of the Rolls-Royce Merlin engine, dubbed the 2-14 SM, while the P-51 airframe was put on a diet to shed almost 2,000 pounds. The combination of more powerful engine, lighter airframe, and a

AAF·SPEC.PROJ.NO.92752-N
U.S.ARMY P-51D-5-NA
SERIAL NO. AAF 44-13962
CREW WEIGHT 200 LBS.
SERVICE THIS AIRPLANE WITH
GRADE 130/130 FUEL. IF NOT
AVAILABLE T.O. 06-5-1 WILL BE
CONSULTED FOR EMERGENCY ACTION
TABLE FOR AROMATIC FUEL

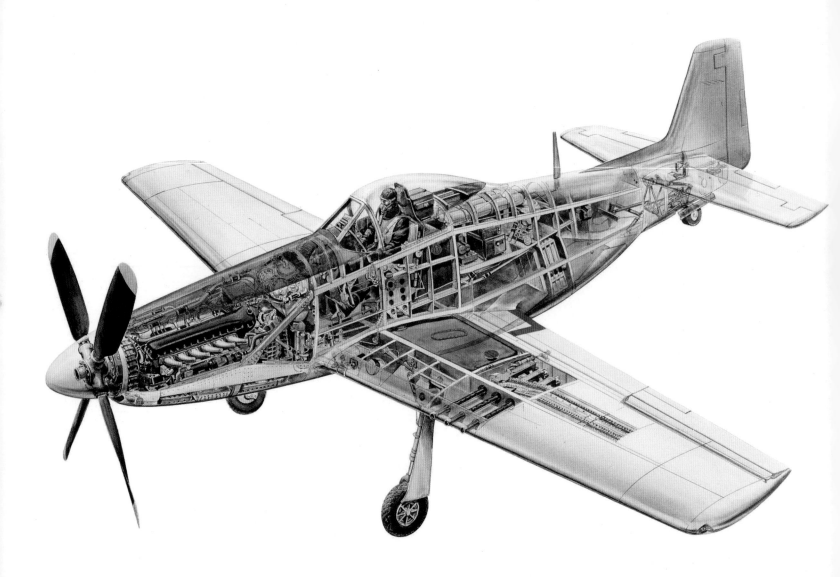

This cutaway drawing of a P-51 Mustang reveals interior details. It was not only the least expensive of the wartime pursuit planes (as measured by cost per pound) but also most frequently designated as the best of them.

five bladed propeller yielded a top speed of 498 miles per hour in level flight. However, Rolls-Royce discontinued the model 2-14 SM engine when conventional Mustangs were deemed to be "good enough" to win the war.

Automobile-style assembly line methods were brought to bear on P-51 production. At Inglewood, multiple conveyor systems were in constant motion. Fuselage interior work was accomplished on a 415-foot-long conveyor line. Employees applied the necessary protective paint; electrical, hydraulic, and fuel cell components were installed; riveting, electrical check operations and other inspections were performed; then, finally, right and left fuselage sides were mated together. To avoid time wasting distractions, any dropped fasteners were left on the floor to be swept up later.

The floor-mounted fuselage pickup lines were 1,300 feet in length. On these, more electrical and hydraulic components were added. The engine, empennage, radio, oxygen systems, canopy, and cowling were then installed all without pause of forward motion. Final assembly was accomplished on a third conveyor 600 feet long where wing and fuselage came together in a process now called wing-to-body join; more hydraulic connections were made; armor plate was added; and the pilots' seats and propellers were installed.

A 560-foot outdoor moving conveyor was designated as the engine run-up line. There, airplanes were secured wing-tip to wing-tip on a moving line. Engines were run at full power and radios were checked while the airplanes were moved sideways until it was time to be towed to a delivery spot.

Dick Schleicher recalled a gaff with the conveyor system: "[I]t happened around 1944–45 in the Inglewood plant where the P-51 conveyor line went from the production line in the building, the engine run-up area. At the end of the graveyard shift, the responsible foreman failed to switch off the conveyor electric drive motor. Result? The next morning I was called to assess the damage and prescribe fixes needed to repair the wings of seven aircraft that had telescoped at the end of the line!"

Thinner air at higher altitudes, combined with the extremely clean lines of the Mustang, yielded the longer range that allowed them to accompany heavy bomber formations all the way from England to Berlin and back. For the first time the Luftwaffe was confronted by fighter-escorted heavy bomber formations as the pitched air battles over central Europe played out. The Mustang pilots were called upon to not only protect the bombers but also destroy the Luftwaffe—and they succeeded.

In an era before the invention of air-to-air missiles, guns were the primary means to attack enemy airplanes. The type of armaments and their placement on the P-51 were constantly being evaluated and sometimes rearranged. Locations shifted between fuselage and wings. The sizes ranged from .30- to .50-caliber and 20mm cannons. Hard points with release mechanisms were available to hang various sizes and types of ordnance.

However, the Luftwaffe still had another aerial warfare card to play. The Me 262 was the first jet fighter to see sustained aerial combat and it was 100 miles per hour faster than a Mustang; however, it arrived too late and in too small a quantity to alter the outcome of the war. It also had limited fuel supply, which forced its pilots to remain close to friendly airfields. The Mustang, with greater range yielding longer loiter times, could simply wait out the jets. The Me 262 was vulnerable to attack at the lower speeds necessary for takeoff and landing—which was where a battle-seasoned Mustang pilot could score a kill.

The German surrender in May 1945 meant that the full force of American military might, which had grown exponentially since 1941, could be brought to bear on Japan. A smaller American occupation force was slated to remain in Europe as the Russians, under Joseph Stalin, also committed to shift Soviet military forces eastward.

Lisle Shoemaker, a reporter with United Press was on hand to witness the arrival of the Mustangs on an island in the Pacific Ocean near Japan:

> Wish you could have been on Iwo Jima the day the Mustangs arrived. The P-51 was a new species to the Pacific servicemen. Being an ex-North American man, I identified the planes as they swirled and roared above Iwo for their first landing.
>
> They put on a terrific show for the Marines before they put their wheels down when they finally landed—coming in one every thirty seconds on the improvised field which was only a few hundred yards behind the bloody fighting at the front—M.P.s had to fight back the foot soldiers who wanted to get out and examine these sleek looking fighter jobs.
>
> A couple of days later, the Mustangs formally relieved the Navy carrier planes as guardians of Iwo Jima. They put in a day of practice bombing and strafing on the two little rocky islands about 500 yards off Iwo's western coast.
>
> I sat in a fox hole built into the side of one of Iwo's many pinnacles and watched them work. Mustang after Mustang peeled off and dove straight for their targets—sending up huge explosions as their tracer bullets sparkled all along the reefs.

The Mustangs were brought to the Pacific because only they had the operational range, speed, and altitude necessary to escort the ultimate airborne offensive weapon of the war,

ABOVE: An artist's conception of a P-51 taking out a Luftwaffe fighter. Other dogfights fill the sky as formations of Allied bombers approach high overhead.

OPPOSITE: A contemporary magazine advertisement informs the public of the attributes of the P-51 Mustang. It was a product uniquely suited for its era that would make any company boastful.

the newly introduced Boeing B-29 Superfortress. The forthcoming bombing raids on Japan would bring the war to an end without the dreaded ground war resulting from the planned invasion of the Japanese home islands. Japan was unable to mount an effective defense against the marauding B-29s because their military, after years of combat, lacked pilots, suitable aircraft, and the fuel to fly them.

A Packard-built Rolls-Royce Merlin V-1650-7 engine cost about $25,000. The NAA portion of the cost of a P-51 was in the $20,000 to $30,000 range but this figure did not include the expensive GFE (government-furnished equipment), consisting of the propeller, the engine, the radios, and the guns. The "design-to-build" philosophy came to pay dividends on the P-51 manufacturing program. Government figures show that the cost of a P-51 airframe was $3.59 per pound, the cost of a Republic P-47 was $5.75 per pound, and a Bell P-63 came in at $6.74 per pound. The last P-51 would not leave air force service until 1957.

As defense spending escalated starting in 1940, there was political concern that some of the funds might be mismanaged. Harry S. Truman, a Democratic Party senator

ATTENTION LUFTWAFFE! Keep away from this plane. Expect to see it on the farthest trip American bombers make. Expect to see it up high—40,000 feet—but don't expect to see it for long, because the Mustang travels at over 425 m. p. h.

And you can expect to see more and more Mustangs, too. The men and women at North American are stepping up production every month. So when you see this high fighting, far flying Mustang, look out, Luftwaffe. Get out of there quick!

North American P-51 Mustang Fighter

ATTENTION AMERICANS! BONDS bought these planes. **WASTE FATS** helped arm them. **WASTE PAPER** helped ship them. **GASOLINE** flies them. Will **YOU** help to deliver the next squadron?

FULL-VISION "TEAR-DROP" COCKPIT ENCLOSURE   DROPABLE WING GAS TANKS, FOR INCREASED RANGE   SIX .50 CALIBER MACHINE GUNS

North American Aviation *Sets the Pace*

WE MAKE PLANES THAT MAKE HEADLINES . . . *the B-25 Mitchell bomber, AT-6 Texan combat trainer, P-51 Mustang fighter (A-36 fighter-bomber), and the B-24 Liberator bomber. North American Aviation, Inc. Member, Aircraft War Production Council, Inc.*

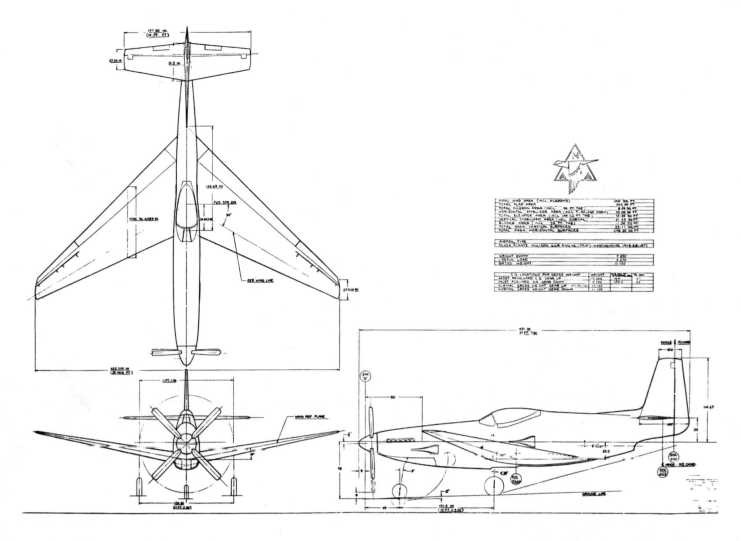

ABOVE: By 1946, engineers conceived a version of the P-51 with forward-swept wings. It was one of many concepts that never advanced beyond the drawing boards.

RIGHT: The V-12 Packard-built Rolls-Royce engine gave the P-51 Mustang its speed and excellent high-altitude performance. This is a cutaway version for instructional purposes.

from Missouri with a reputation as a straight-shooting pragmatist, headed up a Special Committee of the US Senate that investigated such matters. It was eventually estimated to have saved the US taxpayers the huge sum of $10 to $15 billion. Many companies dreaded a committee visit; however, in 1943 they declared the P-51 as "the most aerodynamically perfect pursuit plane in existence." The Mustang was a remarkable achievement that served the nation and its allies well in wartime and beyond.

Early-model P-51 Mustangs and B-25 Mitchells clutter the ramp as workers file out of the Inglewood plant at the end of first shift.

CHAPTER 9

B-25 ON STEROIDS: THE SHORT LIFE OF NA-98X

The responsibility for inducing the strain which caused the accident *must rest upon the pilot*. The Investigating Committee has no way of determining what cause or causes may have brought about his action when he pulled the airplane into an abrupt climb . . . the installation of R-2800 engines in this airplane had no bearing upon the accident. . . .

—Official accident investigation report, April 1944

(italics added by the author for emphasis)

The radial engines have cooling fins like the small engine on a rotary lawn mower or gasoline-powered chain saw. The broad diameter is necessary for cooling but increases drag.

RIGHT: NA-98X was the one and only B-25 ever to be equipped with the more powerful R-2800 engine and its lifetime was twenty-five days. The unmistakable visual clue is the large, conical spinner at the center of the propeller. All work on the promising variant was stopped and never restarted after it crashed on April 24, 1944.

OPPOSITE: All other B-25s were built with the Wright R-2600 engine rated at 1,700 horsepower. A 30-gallon oil tank embedded in each wing kept them lubricated.

In common with other aircraft operators of the era, North American was beset by a series of aircraft crashes between 1935 and 1950. Not all were survivable. One such tragic event took the life of 1st Lt. Winton Wey, the twenty-four-year-old second of three sons who grew up in tiny Eldorado, Oklahoma, where his family ran a grocery-hardware-feed store before it was foreclosed during the Great Depression. As a youngster, family members recalled, Wey scratch-built bi-wing models of World War I–era aircraft and then attached .22-caliber bullets to the wings to represent bombs. However, as an interview with his descendants revealed, his family was never told the truth about his death. The unsettling story was hidden away as a government secret, and it remained a suppressed but painful memory for the North American people involved.

By late 1943, one thousand B-25H models were being produced at Inglewood under general order NA-98. NAA engineers were continually searching for new and improved

Joe Barton, on the left, first flew NA-98X on March 31, 1944. Ed Virgin was the chief test pilot at North American Inglewood and he flew it twice.

products. Airplane number 302 of the batch was chosen for major modifications that would hopefully yield a much-improved war plane. However, serial number 43-4406 was the one and only Mitchell to be thusly reworked. It was given the company designation of NA-98X ("NA" for North American, "98" for contract number, and "X" for experimental). It was not given a military designation because it was a company-sponsored initiative and was not in response to any US Army Air Force published requirement. Military records simply refer to it as a B-25H.

Project NA-98X had two goals: The first was to demonstrate that an enhanced B-25 offered a less-expensive alternative to the Douglas A-26 Invader. There were concerns that the A-26, which was then believed to be much needed, was seriously behind schedule and possibly would not be available until after the war. The second was to restore the airplane's performance that had eroded as the design of the B-25 evolved. The earlier B-25B model had a top speed of 328 miles per hour. Maximum velocity had fallen to 272 miles per hour because of the increase in drag caused by more guns combined with the increase in weight resulting from crew-protecting armor and other engineering changes.

There was plenty of production capacity since B-25s were being produced not only at Inglewood but also at a new and modern government-owned factory in Kansas City. About three hundred Mitchells per month were rolling off the assembly line there as production finally hit its stride by early 1944.

The primary enhancement was a major performance boost resulting from upgrade to a pair of Ford-built Pratt & Whitney R-2800-51 "Double Wasp" air-cooled radial engines, capable of a hefty 2,000 horsepower each. They had not been previously available in sufficient quantity for installation on B-25s. NAA engineers were already familiar with the Double Wasps from their installation on the recently completed XB-28 prototypes.

Bigger engines would surely be the salvation needed to keep the venerable but rapidly aging B-25 design in production. A low-drag cowling, borrowed from the Douglas A-26 project, encased each engine, which drove a three-bladed propeller with large bullet-shaped spinner. Other improvements included a squared-off wing tip, allowing the ailerons—the movable control surfaces at the outboard rear of each wingtip—to be slightly enlarged, extended outboard for better roll control, a low-drag turret, and a "computing" gun sight.

By the time the modifications were completed, NA-98X became a "hot rod" version of the venerable B-25 family. It could best be described as a B-25 on steroids. Larger engines with more horsepower could propel it faster than any other B-25. Consistent with previous B-25s, two versions were envisioned: a gunship known as the "super strafer," and a medium bomber. Options for the strafer included up to eighteen Browning .50-caliber machine guns mounted forward, aft, side, and top. As a medium bomber, the solid nose was replaced by a transparent compartment containing the bombardier's crew station plus a forward-facing flexible defensive gun.

LEFT: USAAF test pilot Perry Ritchie (pointing) was an aeronautical engineer who is seen conducting a discussion of a technical concept called "power curve." *USAAF photo via the Museum of the Air Force*

RIGHT: First Lieutenant Winton R. Wey perished in the crash of NA-98X on April 24, 1944. *Photo courtesy of the Wey family*

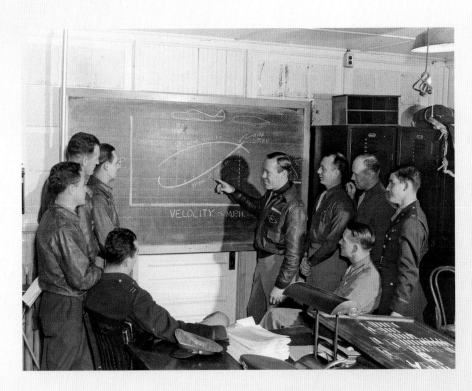

Chief pilot Ed Virgin (left) discusses P-82 flight testing with (left to right) George "Wheaties" Welch, Jim Nissen, and George Krebs. The one-piece flight suit has been adopted. Krebs later died in the crash of a B-45 jet bomber on March 17, 1947; Welch would die in the crash of an F-100 fighter on October 12, 1954.

NAA was aware it faced two challenges if the modified version of the airplane was to go beyond test and into production. Could the army air corps people be won over to the concept? NA-98X was the underdog. The competing Douglas A-26 had not yet flown but was held in high esteem.

Could the updated wing design cope with increased stress brought on by higher performance? Bigger engines would drive the need for a stronger wing. The engineers fretted about the 1,500 pounds of increased weight that would result from the combination of heavier engines plus more wing structure to support them.

The first flight, of one hour duration, took place on March 31, 1944, with company pilot Joe Barton at the controls. Climb performance was improved compared to other B-25s. At a gross weight of 29,000 pounds, no buffeting or instability occurred in a 350-mile-per-hour dive with cowl flaps open. A takeoff run of only 1,470 feet was necessary to clear a 50-foot obstacle. Since it was recognized that the increased engine power combined with balanced ailerons might make it possible to over-stress the wings, during flight testing, company pilots agreed to limit speed to 340 miles per hour and turns were not to exceed 2.67 g (expressing the load factor as the force of gravity). North American pilots working with army air force pilots assigned to Inglewood conducted fifteen more flights before turning NA-98X over to a delegation of officers from Dayton's Wright Field.

Materiel Command at Wright Field was the army air forces' nerve center for managing the design of newer, bigger, faster, and better airplanes as well as their flight testing and procurement. It was a huge bureaucracy, with seventeen thousand people in four divisions: Engineering, Production, Procurement, and Price Adjustment. Charles E. Branshaw moved from the West Coast branch office in Santa Monica, California, in April 1943 to assume responsibility for Materiel Command. The legend of his deft handling of the North American wildcat strike of 1941 grew with each retelling and helped Branshaw to rise from lieutenant colonel to the brevet rank of major general in a mere two years. He enjoyed close ties with Donald Douglas and was held in high regard within the aircraft procurement community.

Their star performer was Maj. Perry J. Ritchie, an experienced, well-known, and respected twenty-eight-year-old test pilot. Born in 1915, Ritchie grew up near Dayton, Ohio, and graduated from the University of Cincinnati with a degree in Aeronautical Engineering in 1939, with additional collegiate credentials as a member of the swimming and gymnastics teams, and president of the Aero Society for a year. From 1934 to 1939 he was a cooperative student at Wright Field—a form of internship to gain work experience—laboring as a civilian final assembly mechanic, and as a draftsman in the propeller laboratory, as well as performing tasks in the vibration-testing unit.

Ritchie enlisted on December 10, 1940, at Fort Thomas, Newport, Kentucky, and became an aviation cadet at Randolph and Brooks Fields in Texas. He earned his pilot's wings plus a commission in May 1941. After a brief stint in California, he found his way back to a home-town posting as an experimental test pilot at Wright Field.

Like other fearless and dashing test pilots of the era, Ritchie survived some difficult scrapes. The first was an engine failure in a Bell P-39 Airacobra that led to a dead-stick landing in rural New York in 1942. That was followed by a nose landing gear collapse at Wright Field attributed to a bad weld and improper design on an experimental trainer plane.

The third situation, on July 3, 1943, was far more serious. Ritchie was flying a Republic P-47C Thunderbolt, and was wrapping up a series of twenty "terminal-velocity dives"—some from altitudes in excess of 38,000 feet—to gather technical aeronautical research data on drag, compression, and Mach number. On the twentieth and final scheduled flight, excessive heating by the turbo-supercharger severed a vital control linkage to the tail. At 32,000 feet, with no elevator control, and traveling at the relatively low speed of 250 miles per hour, he forced the canopy open and threw himself from the plane. As he made his exit, he noted the tail of the airplane was on fire. He managed to pull the ripcord but lost consciousness. The tail was found hung up in a tree about three-quarters of a mile from the balance of the wreckage. Ritchie suffered serious injuries, including a broken back and torn ligament in the right groin, but it was never determined if his back injury was caused by striking the aircraft, by excessive opening shock of the parachute, or by the impact of his landing in the field.

Doctors told him he would never fly again. For his exploits in the P-47C, Ritchie was promoted to major and awarded the Distinguished Flying Cross (DFC) by Major General Branshaw for "extraordinary achievement and outstanding heroism," at a ceremony on December 30, 1943. However, after many grueling months of treatment at various military hospitals plus a visit to the Mayo Clinic, Ritchie was deemed sufficiently recovered to return to flying status in February 1944.

Ritchie was one of three test pilots who participated in P-51B Mustang spin tests. The written report on the tests, dated April 30, 1944, states that at least sixty of the dangerous flight maneuvers were conducted. The analysis ends with a recommendation that the P-51B should neither be spun nor snap rolled because "it does a very poor snap roll and usually ends up in a spin."

A broken outer-wing panel landed so gently on the camouflage netting covering the P-51 ramp that workers using a small industrial crane were dispatched to retrieve it.

Although no complete narrative of the flight tests of NA-98X was completed at the time, it is possible to reconstruct events from NAA company records, the recollections of those present, and the official army air forces accident report.

On Friday, April 21, Major Ritchie, accompanied by his Wright Field superiors, Col. Ernest Warburton and Lt. Col. Osmond Ritland, arrived from Roach Lake together. The trio was on a ten-day tour of Southern California to evaluate various new airplane programs. They met up with flight-test engineer, First Lieutenant Wey, who had flown into Inglewood separately from Dayton and brought along a package containing instrumentation.

Test pilots earn their living by taking calculated risks. Flight testing is accomplished in accordance with a written script prepared in conjunction with other engineers. NAA's chief test pilot, Ed Virgin, explained to Ritchie that maximum weight on a normal B-25 was 26,000 pounds. In combat service, the weight could be as high as 30,000 pounds. With bigger engines, NA-98X was rated for a maximum gross weight of 35,522 pounds; however, the overweight situation imposed maneuvering limitations on the pilot. The Wright Field delegation's written plan was to load progressively more weight upon NA-98X as the flights progressed.

The next day, April 22, Major Ritchie made three flights in the NA-98X—a familiarization plus two additional flights—and expressed pleasure with the airplane. Testing ended at sundown when Ritchie overflew the field and put NA-98X into a spiraling climb. Some bystanders were alarmed by the unscripted stunt, while others were either amused or entertained.

On Sunday, April 23, Ritchie was accompanied by Squadron Leader Hartford of the RAF on four of his five flights. The participation by an RAF representative was seen as an indication of interest in NA-98X by the British. (Britain had underwritten initial development of the Mustang and the RAF was a highly valued customer.) Again, testing ended at sundown when Ritchie buzzed the field and put NA-98X into a second spiraling climb. This wasn't regulation, but it was the weekend and key people were away. Nobody in authority in either army air forces or NAA took any action.

Monday, April 24, saw Ritchie, with Lieutenant Wey as copilot, make five more flights, totaling six hours forty minutes of flying time. For test flight number 28 and beyond, the aircraft weight was increased by 2,950 pounds. Loading ballast into the airplane was the standard method to increase payload for testing purposes.

Just before the final flight (number twenty-nine), Ritchie informed crew chief Edward Johnson that he planned to end the overwater portion of flight testing by buzzing the field before landing. For the third consecutive evening, at 7:38 p.m., Ritchie contacted the control tower operator by radio and asked permission for a low altitude over-flight. The request was granted. He then brought NA-98X to wave-top altitude and began the eastbound downwind dash towards Los Angeles Municipal Airport. A coastal defense anti-aircraft gun crew halted their evening baseball game briefly to watch the daily air show as Ritchie climbed just enough to clear the Playa del Rey sand dunes.

Disaster intervened when the high-speed, low-altitude dash down the runway ended with a spiraling ascent, which from the rear appeared to be vertical. The tower operator reported the altitude above the runway to be 100 feet and other witnesses estimated the speed at up to 400 miles per hour. At 200 feet altitude the outer wing panels and ailerons separated. They traveled aft and struck the tail, shearing it off. As these vital control surfaces and associated debris floated down like confetti, witnesses estimated the balance of the hulk continued upwards for another hundred feet before gravity overcame inertia and reversed the climb. The heavier remaining wing stubs, fuselage, engines, and landing gear hit an open field at such velocity that a significant gash in the earth and downstream debris field was created. Both engines were running at full power until impact and the impact forces were sufficient to separate the retracted main landing gear tires from their rims. Only the upside down mid-fuselage remained as a recognizable piece. One of the wing tips fell so softly onto the camouflage netting that covered the P-51 flight line area that the piece stayed suspended until retrieved by workers using a lift and crane the next day. Contrary to newspaper reports at the time, there was no fire.

It was very dark by the time the company photographer arrived to capture the first scenes of the carnage. Army troops from the nearby anti-aircraft guns, some of whom worked for NAA on a part-time basis, established a perimeter and were assigned to guard the wreckage overnight. Next day, further photographs were taken. As the wreckage was clearly visible from nearby Aviation Boulevard where it intersected with Sepulveda, some passersby stopped to gawk. The severed parts and associated debris were soon to become subject of intense official scrutiny. The result was not only fatal to the flight crew, neither of whom had any dependents, but also the project. All work on the promising B-25 variant was stopped and never restarted.

Total flight time on NA-98X in its brief twenty-five-day life was 40 hours 15 minutes. Major Ritchie accounted for half of that total in thirteen flights over the quick three days. He died with 2,100 hours of total flight time; 413 hours in B-25s; and 109 hours in the

B-25H. A greater disaster was averted because the worst of the wreck took place in an open field. Had the crash hit the flight line, offices, or factory, the damage would have been much worse.

In today's environment, military and commercial airplanes subject to extreme stress (as might be caused by severe turbulence) are thoroughly inspected for indications of cracking, bending, or other hidden damage before being released to fly again. In the written statement of the crew chief assigned to NA-98X, every critical structure he inspected prior to the final flight is listed by name. He asserted that there were no defects.

Stress engineer R. L. Schleicher prepared a lengthy and technical written review of the damaged pieces before concluding ". . . the failure of the subject airplane was caused by an abrupt pull-up at an excessive high speed which was beyond the flight and strength limitations of the airplane."

The crash of NA-98X left a visible gash in the grassy areas surrounding Los Angeles Municipal Airport.

An independent accident investigation team, consisting of three voting senior army air forces officers and a non-voting scribe, immediately went to work on the morning of Tuesday, April 25, 1944. Statements were taken, data was analyzed, conclusions were drawn, and the report was finished in time for the following weekend. Consistent with

An upside down section of mid-fuselage was about the only recognizable piece of NA-98X in the crash debris field.

other investigations, the accident report was marked as a classified military secret and it remained so for fifteen years until 1959.

Perry Ritchie, as an aeronautical engineer, should have fully understood the consequences of exceeding flight limitations. He paid for the mistake with his life. The death of Lieutenant Wey was collateral damage. He was just along for the ride and had no choice in the matter.

Three NAA employees in particular remained haunted by the crash, even into their old age: Norm Avery, Ed Virgin, and Lee Atwood. Avery, a retired NAA employee and noted historian, was present at the crash site and wrote about it in his 1993 book and again in a retiree newsletter article dated 2001. Avery corresponded with former co-workers from his retirement residence in Mount Shasta, California, as he researched NAA history. As long-time North American chief test pilot, Virgin had presided over a number of fatal crashes including the demise of his close personal colleagues Joe Barton and George "Wheaties" Welch, as well as the tragic crash of a B-25 that killed seven employees at Mesa in 1950. Atwood was credited as the co-designer of the B-25.

After consulting his flight log to confirm that he had personally piloted NA-98X on two separate occasions, Virgin, now living in Chevy Chase, Maryland, confided to Avery in a series of handwritten letters:

This airplane had sealed balanced ailerons and with the power (R-2800s) and the light aileron forces, the urge was to rock it around like a fighter—which Ritchie did.

His father came to see me a couple of years after the accident to discuss the tragedy. As I remember, [Major Ritchie] reported his position (5-7-10,000') over Santa Monica Bay and that he was finished with his test and coming in for a landing. Minutes later he streaked across the field downwind (normally—ocean toward shore) going like a bat out of hell at several hundred feet altitude. He made a pull-up and shed the wings in a typical B-25 wing failure when over-stressed. So I don't think q alone was responsible but a combination of

Celebrities invited to inspect the Navion included motion picture actor Clark Gable (left) and the most famous of the bomber generals—Curtis LeMay (the ubiquitous cigar happens to be in his hand). Many celebrities from nearby Hollywood visited NAA Inglewood over the years.

q and g's. [Author's note: "q" is engineering shorthand used in formulas to express dynamic pressure—sometimes also called velocity pressure—while "g" is a force equal to gravity.]

Perry Ritchie was a fighter pilot. He should not have been sent to test this airplane in my opinion. He was wild.

Atwood, who became president of NAA in 1960, wrote in a handwritten letter dated October 8, 1998: "About the wings, I believe the requirement was 5.5 g for ultimate strength and with the 2800 engines and other changes the strength was likely closer to 5.0 g. This should have been okay for normal bomber combat service but Ritchie must have exceeded it in his high speed pull up. We probably would have brought the wing up to 5.5 g if any quantity had been ordered."

To date, other than photographs, nothing of substance related to the crash has been found in official North American records. Even the "eyes only" summary of significant events for the year 1944 prepared for each member of the board of directors was silent on the matter. Nor has any utterance from Dutch Kindelberger, either public or private, been discovered. It is assumed his reticence stemmed from a close relationship with, and mutual respect for Hap Arnold. Kindelberger was too savvy to publically chide a personal friend who was also NAA's biggest customer.

Excluding aerial combat, most airframe hull losses are categorized as "accidents" because they are the result of some unfortunate combination of unintended human transgression, foul weather, bad luck, design defect, or mechanical malfunction. The parallels to the loss of NA-40 on April 11, 1939, (as detailed in chapter five) are eerie. Both accidents destroyed the only example of an NAA prototype attack bomber. The low-altitude flights were wrapping up at sundown in April after a long day of flying. Both airplanes were without mechanical defect, and in the hands of experienced army test pilots. However, the 1944 crash of NA-98X was different in one important aspect: Unlike the loss of NA-40, which was the unlucky consequence of a pilot who inadvertently deviated from an obscure and mundane procedure, the wreck of NA-98X was the direct result of a premeditated, willful, and deliberate act.

Major General Branshaw was relieved of command in May 1944 and replaced by an "acting" general officer for the next two months before a permanent replacement was named. The stated reasons for Branshaw's departure were issues of deteriorating personal health, compounded by a valiant, but failed, eighteen-month quest to decentralize Materiel Command by shifting procurement authority to the regional branch offices. He retired on January 1, 1945, and died in 1949 at the age of fifty-four.

Perry Ritchie was a young man of significant accomplishment and boundless potential. He was a good person who went to church, belonged to the Masons, and was the product of a patriotic, loving family who scrimped during the Depression to provide a university education. The reason for his reckless and self-destructive actions is unknown and was declared to be outside of the scope of the official accident investigation board. It could have been ailment, personal distress—or maybe he was just a spirited, fun-loving, young man simply venting steam. Did the recent award of the DFC by Major General Branshaw create a "halo" effect around him that caused his superiors who were traveling with him to ignore the pattern of unscripted reckless flying demonstrated on the prior two evenings?

The engine enhancement provided for NA-98X did not make its way onto the production line. The 1,700-horsepower Wright R-2600 radial engines were deemed by the wise men of government, who were empowered with the allocation of scarce resources, to be "good enough" for B-25s. Ed Virgin confided in a letter dated 1976, "We were stuck with the Wright [R-2600 engine] and made the best we could of it." (The highly regarded Pratt & Whitney R-2800 engines found their way onto a variety of military and civilian airplane designs during and after the war.)

On the Friday prior to Memorial Day weekend 1944, exactly one month after the crash of NA-98X, it was announced that Mitchell production at Inglewood would end in July. Contracts with suppliers were terminated. The one thousandth (and final) Inglewood-built B-25H was given the name *Bones* and celebrated with a special send off. Each worker on the B-25 assembly line was invited to autograph the unpainted aluminum skin in felt pen. The exploits of *Bones* were subsequently reported in the plant newspaper as the aircraft made its way into combat with the 12th Bombardment Group of the Tenth Air Force in India, starting on November 30, 1944.

All raw material and leftover parts specific to the B-25 program were then shipped to Kansas City, while the factory space previously allocated to Mitchell fabrication was vacated. Other than developmental projects, the full manufacturing resources of the sprawling Inglewood plant were, for the duration of the war, devoted to Mustang production.

CHAPTER 10

EISENHOWER'S B-25

ABOVE: Work on the interior of Eisenhower's B-25 was still underway only three days before delivery.

OPPOSITE: All B-25D and B-25J models—a total of 6,608 airplanes—were built at the North American Aviation's Kansas City plant. It took two years to achieve a sustained production rate of about three hundred airplanes per month on the automobile-style moving assembly line.

The year 1944 found Gen. Dwight D. Eisenhower as the supreme commander of the multi-national Allied military force then engaged in an epic struggle against the Nazi war machine. A frequent flyer with an eclectic mix of aircraft available to meet his every need, Eisenhower took full advantage of the mobility they provided.

In February, a brand new B-25J was randomly selected by army air forces from the NAA's Kansas City factory for Eisenhower's exclusive use. Still outfitted with machine guns and wearing camouflage paint, serial number 43-4030, one of about three hundred built that month, was ferried to NAA headquarters at Inglewood, arriving on February 29. The Field Service department immediately began extensive modifications in accordance with a freshly inked army air forces purchase contract, at the same time as their colleagues were working on the ill-fated NA-98X. In an arrangement that seems bizarre today, the modifications to Eisenhower's B-25J were carried out at the same time as the preparation of the engineering documentation relating to the work, which consisted of about a hundred drawings on 8-by-10-inch vellum.

Field Services hand-picked a small cadre of the large plant's most capable mechanics and technicians, who were then divided into two work shifts. Factory engineer Donald H.

Eisenhower's seat was like a throne. The telephone could be used for ground communication or as an interphone with the flight crew.

Kennedy was designated to oversee and document the overhaul. Scrupulous records were required since NAA wanted to be able to defend their work should the airplane ever be lost to suspected structural failure with an American icon board. Also, this meant that should additional orders be received, the modifications to the airplane could be quickly replicated. Factory records identify it as an "RB-25J(3)"—"Rebuilt" B-25 number 3. Photographs taken before and during the modifications confirm what Kennedy wrote in a letter dated 1982: "No effort was made to hide work on the special B-25 which stood in the open among others undergoing changes too late to include on the production line. Obviously, the best concealment was none at all."

The project began with removal of all paint and armaments. Kennedy held frequent consultations with a number of specialists who visited the work site. The Stress Department engineer would stop by for at least thirty minutes daily. Contributors from Heat and Vent, Fuel Systems, and an "electrical man" combined their skills to ensure project integrity. Kennedy noted: "I was impressed by the worker who accomplished the life raft installation in the tail gun compartment entirely on his own, with no drawings, so that a cable from the pilot could open the hatch and deploy the raft."

As the date for the invasion of France approached, the army became increasingly anxious for delivery. Kennedy wrote:

I had a hard time keeping up with the two shifts of workmen that modified the plane. Sometimes the day crew would curse and tear out something done by the night gang. When possible, I made sketches before the work, but there was no way one could keep ahead. The pressure was on.

Commercial [airliner] type blue wool aircraft seats were obtained from Douglas and installed. Plastic sheets were carried up the sides about halfway and blue or gray cloth the rest of the way, including headliner. The installation was not too good, as the workmen had no experience with cloth.

The modifications altered the weight and potentially the balance of Eisenhower's airplane. Here, it sits on scales for final weighing before delivery.

The airplane was configured to seat ten people comfortably, including the pilots and other flight crew. An older worker, experienced in woodworking, proudly crafted a walnut cabinet with compartments for food and "one for dry ice to keep the booze cold. A coffee thermos with spigot was on the side." The airplane may have been built with on-board liquor service but Eisenhower confidants later wrote that he was never known to consume more than a single drink per day and had a phobia about the Russians' prodigious consumption of vodka.

The top of the bomb bay was lowered so it could be used as a bunk; a bulletproof auxiliary fuel tank occupied what remained of the bomb bay; a folding map table extended the full width of the narrow passenger compartment; the lavatory was relocated further aft

Eisenhower's unmarked B-25 takes to the air at Inglewood on the day of its departure to Eighth Air Force in England. There were intermediate stops along the way.

and enclosed; a telephone was installed for contact with the pilot or ground stations; the rear entry door was reworked for easier access; the aircraft was shorn of turret and all other armaments; the nose was customized; and extra windows were installed in the aft fuselage.

The airplane, now bearing the military designation VB-25J, was test flown, photographed, and accepted by army air forces for flyaway on May 12, 1944. After stops in Long Beach, California; Luke Field, Arizona; Pittsburg, Pennsylvania; and Manchester, New Hampshire, it reached the Eighth Air Force base in England. After receiving confirmation of its safe arrival, the builder received no further updates on its fate.

Hoping for any shred of information about "his" airplane, Kennedy followed the war news closely. A War Department dispatch dated July 29, 1944, disclosed that General Eisenhower, in "air conditioned comfort," had visited the front twice in a secretly constructed fast medium bomber with blue cloth upholstered armchairs, folding work table, and a telephone to observe allied armies just after the breakout at St. Lô in Normandy. The dispatch identified the flight crew as Maj. Laurence J. Hansen, pilot; Capt. Richard F. Underwood, co-pilot; Capt. H. C. Nixon, navigator; Master Sgt. V. J. Romgosa, engineer; and Tech. Sgt. E. J. Behrous, radio operator. (The dispatch contained a bit of puffery since the B-25 had no air conditioning.)

The dearth of additional information led Kennedy and other aviation historians to incorrectly speculate that Eisenhower seldom utilized it. However, recent research has turned up solid evidence that he used the B-25 frequently, but not exclusively, during the twelve months following the D-Day invasion of France, which began on June 6, 1944.

The pilot, Laurence J. "Larry" Hansen, was born in Cleveland, Ohio, in 1917, and, endowed with an innate love for things mechanical, spent his teen years first dabbling in model airplanes, before flipping two dozen damaged motorcycles for profit after repairing

Laurence J. Hansen of Cleveland was Eisenhower's primary pilot from 1942 to 1946. He wrote a book in 1983 entitled *What It Was Like Flying for "Ike."*

them. His parents owned a manufacturing company that specialized in hydraulic hose connectors of his father's own invention. The Depression years were tough for the family-owned business. Young Larry aspired to be a pilot and saved for flying lessons from his own meager earnings.

Hansen was eager for military service. The year 1942 found the twenty-three-year-old first lieutenant piloting Boeing B-17s on combat missions from England to France. In November, he received temporary orders to proceed to North Africa. It was at Algiers where Hansen first met General Eisenhower. The two men subsequently established mutual trust and forged a lifelong friendship.

Hansen's bombing days were over. For the next four years his new role would be as a VIP transport pilot, at first in B-17s, with other aircraft types to follow.

Eisenhower was flown over enemy positions during the Normandy invasion of 1944 in a special two-seat Mustang by Ninth Air Force commander, Maj. Gen. Elwood Quesada, and there is a famous photograph that documents their safe return to Eisenhower's headquarters, then still in England. It is suspected the message conveyed by the much publicized photograph was a ruse directed towards the Germans to further conceal Eisenhower's more frequent travels aboard the B-25.

The external modifications gave this Mitchell a unique appearance. It was probably the only B-25 in Europe during 1944 with this distinctive profile and would have made a much sought-after prize for Luftwaffe pilots if they had known about it. The airplane was operated devoid of nose art, crests, stars, or any other special external markings.

After the killing of a Japanese admiral, Isoroku Yamamoto, when his transport plane was ambushed by American P-38s on April 18, 1943, it is suspected that army censors severely restricted or even banned photography of Eisenhower with the B-25. Photographs of 43-4030 in wartime service or with Eisenhower are scarce. Fortunately, a single photograph of Eisenhower with the Mitchell was located. The serial number on the tail is not visible; however, the unique side windows in the aft fuselage combined with special sheet metal modifications to cover the tail gun mounts make it evident that the aircraft is indeed B-25J serial number 43-4030.

In his autobiography about his time with Eisenhower, Hansen wrote about the arrival of a new B-25 airplane, which was to be used for fast, escorted flights back and forth across the English Channel. After a beachhead in France was established, they began to use the B-25 quite frequently, and often there would be as many as eighteen Mustang and Spitfire escorts for cross-channel protection. The Mitchell cruised more leisurely than the faster escorts and the pilots of the hot single-seat fighters sometimes groused to Hansen about the slow pace—by mid-1944, the prewar B-25 design was starting to show its age as aviation technology was quickly advancing.

Kay Summersby was assigned as Eisenhower's British motorcar driver when he arrived in England in 1942. Eisenhower also bonded with her, and by late 1944, she had advanced from civilian chauffer to trusted aide with a commission as an officer in the US Army. In her memoir, *Eisenhower Was My Boss*, Summersby wrote: "On July 29 I flew with [General Eisenhower] in a B-25 escorted by fighters. We landed at a muddy airstrip known simply as 'A-9.' It was my first visit to Normandy and my first step on liberated Europe. I saw no civilians, no dead Germans, no bomb damage. In fact, it was no different from an Army area in rural England. The only point of interest was a cow, fat and healthy, in sharp contrast to the scene in Italy where the Germans shot all cattle. We stayed only a few hours and then returned to England." Airfield "A-9" was an austere and temporary P-51 and P-38 forward operating base near the Normandy town of Le Molay, in operation from July 2, 1944, for 95 days. The single runway of steel mesh was 4,000 feet in length.

Eisenhower was constantly on the move. As Allied battle lines advanced, a favorite activity was surprise visits to the troops on the front. He genuinely enjoyed the banter with

the GIs and the visits ensured he had an unfiltered grasp of the situation on the ground. Eisenhower made one or two of these ad hoc and informal inspections per fortnight in between many scheduled meetings with Allied military and civilian leaders.

The usual B-25 channel crossing was between Portsmouth, England, and the Cherbourg Peninsula, which was some sixty miles of open water. Several weeks after the invasion, the general moved his temporary headquarters to Granville in Lower Normandy, where Summersby and the other personal staff took up residence in a small, but cozy, oceanside villa near the French town. Eisenhower operated from there with the B-25 until American troops were several miles beyond Paris, when his headquarters was relocated forward to the Paris suburb of Versailles.

As expected, the Mitchell was durable and reliable. There was space for up to four aides or guests, plus their luggage, and the aircraft was compact enough to get into and out of the smaller, sometimes sodden, airfields close to rapidly advancing Allied ground forces. But, as the dramatic events of September 2, 1944, were to demonstrate, even a sturdy B-25 could be damaged, resulting in a sequence of events that not only disrupted the general's travel plans but also put his safety at risk.

Eisenhower's calm and diplomatic external demeanor was key to his success contending with the egos of the leadership of the Allied nations, as well as those of his own

The small L-5 airplane displays the four stars of a general officer. Ike sometimes went for brief evening flights simply to clear his mind. The airplanes at Eisenhower's disposal included this standard L-5 and a customized B-17, C-47, P-51, and B-25. The choice of airplane depended on the day's mission. In May 1954, all were replaced with a pair of C-54s named "Sunflower." *Army photograph via the Eisenhower Presidential Library and Museum*

generals. However, in private he sometimes demonstrated anger. As Summersby related, "I'm going up and give (Lieutenant General George S.) Patton hell,' [Eisenhower] said, worrying because the Third Army's spectacular advance stretched supply lines to the snapping point."

The supreme commander departed in the B-25 early on the morning of September 2 for a planned face-to-face discussion with Gens. Omar Bradley and Hoyt Vandenberg. Eisenhower's luck as a frequent flyer was tested by multiple close calls, all on the same day.

As Larry Hansen recounted, "On September 2, 1944, we took off early in the morning in the B-25 to Laval, France to pick up General Hoyt Vandenberg. General Eisenhower was aboard enroute to a meeting with General Omar Bradley at Chartres, France. Upon landing at Laval, we found nothing but a mud hole and the field was very rough. I radioed to four P-47 escorts not to land because of the condition of the field. I was in a hurry to get airborne because we were holding the escorts overhead."

During the hasty departure, they found themselves on a collision course with a British Cub, which was taking off at their 90-degree position. A controller fired a flare to divert the Cub, allowing Hansen to take off. However, "I was at this point very un-maneuverable and just above the point of stall," he recalled, and although he did manage to retain control of the aircraft, the challenges of the day were just beginning.

The next stop was Chartres. The planned lengthy meeting between the generals was shortened when reports of bad weather to the west were received. ". . . We took off as quickly as possible and right after takeoff we noticed the right engine was on fire," Hansen continued. "Flames were shooting out around the engine nacelle and we immediately landed again." The plane was evacuated on the runway. The fire was the result of multiple broken exhaust stacks on one of the Wright R-2600 radial engines caused by the rough runway at Laval.

Hansen stayed with the damaged B-25 and ferried it out of Chartres later that same day. Eisenhower did not have the patience to wait for repairs. "He [had said that morning] he would be back in a couple of hours," Summersby later wrote. She and the other house-hold staff at Granville grew increasingly alarmed when daytime faded into evening and Eisenhower failed to return. They called various airfields "only to learn the great Allied army had no trace of its own Supreme Commander."

With the fire-damaged B-25 temporarily out of commission, Eisenhower, accompanied by Hansen's co-pilot, Richard "Dick" Underwood, departed Chartres with General Bradley's pilot, Major Robinson. They headed westward to Ponterson, a French coastal town just a short drive from Granville. Instead of spending the night there or finishing the journey by automobile, Eisenhower elected to make an overwater flight back to his Granville residence with Underwood piloting a small L-5 liaison-type aircraft that was kept at Ponterson as part of a small VIP fleet of various aircraft types. Eisenhower liked the L-5 and sometimes took early evening pleasure hops in them as a means to unwind.

Dick Underwood took off with Eisenhower but as the weather deteriorated, the airfield was hidden by clouds, and the remaining fuel supply was getting low. They elected to make an emergency landing on the deserted French beach, Eisenhower's second forced landing of the day. Then, Hansen noted, "[i]n order to save the plane from the incoming tide, the General and Dick pulled the airplane higher on the beach and in doing so the General wrenched his knee."

After securing the aircraft, the pair staggered nearly a mile in the darkness to a road. A soldier, driving a jeep, stopped then stared incredulously at the air force pilot and the limping army general who were both dripping wet and muddy. The GI asked no questions as he rushed them down the road to a warm and emotional reunion at the Granville villa. Eisenhower was laid up for the next three days with a stiff leg and throbbing knee. "This event was reported in the press that General Eisenhower had crashed," Hansen wrote.

"However, there was no crash and Ike suffered only the wrenched knee from tugging away at the aircraft."

Hansen persisted for decades in the defense of his co-pilot: "Dick Underwood did a wonderful job with the uneventful landing on the beach in spite of possible mines and other obstacles."

As the general's stature and entourage continued to grow, Hansen recognized the need for a bigger airplane with more range. He recommended the four-engine Douglas C-54, the military version of a DC-4 airliner, as an appropriate upgrade. Eisenhower agreed and Hansen departed for the United States to receive pilot transition training.

The first of two brand new C-54s was assigned to the general starting in May 1945. The Germans had surrendered and the skies were now safe. Unlike the unnamed and unmarked B-25 that skulked about anonymously in wartime secrecy, the new C-54s celebrated their affiliation to Eisenhower by being named "Sunflower" in honor of his home state of Kansas

Supreme Allied Commander General Dwight D. Eisenhower (second from the left) and a trusted aide, Kay Summersby, partake of a field lunch from the hood of a jeep at an airfield near Mons-en-Chaussée, France. Army Air Base A-72 was located midway between Paris and Brussels. Eisenhower is meeting with B-26 pilots and the exact date was not recorded. *Army photograph via the Eisenhower Presidential Library and Museum*

Eisenhower chats with an officer in front of a North American combat plane—likely an A-36 Apache, which was a variant of the P-51 Mustang. *Army photograph via the Eisenhower Presidential Library and Museum*

and adorned with appropriate nose art. Larry Hansen's military service ended in November 1946 when Eisenhower announced his retirement as Army Chief of Staff. He mustered out of the army air force as a decorated lieutenant colonel before rejoining the family business.

With a gap in the trail of evidence, it can be assumed that the unremarkable B-25 was then relegated to the transport of other, lesser, officers about the European theater of operations as it soldiered on without fanfare or any reminder of its former glory. In the postwar turmoil, the connection between Eisenhower and 43-4030 faded from memory and was not reestablished until 1981.

America was awash in surplus warplanes by late 1945. B-25s were cheap, abundant, and docile to fly. They filled a medium-sized transport niche in a market then devoid of suitable alternatives. A cottage industry quickly evolved turning surplus combat B-25s into corporate transports, firefighters, pilot trainers, and airborne filming platforms. Some even made their way into South America for drug-running.

Dwight David Eisenhower served as the thirty-fourth president of the United States from 1953 to 1961. Coincidently, his B-25 was also in Washington, DC, at the same time. The Mitchell had left Europe and arrived at Bolling AFB in Washington, DC, as a run-of-the-mill bomber-converted-to-transport-aircraft with the new designation of CB-25J in January, 1947. Without a large entry door, it was better suited as a VIP transport than a cargo hauler. It would spend the balance of its service life in the nation's capital with brief deployments to Eglin AFB, Florida, in 1947, and temporary duty at Sewart AFB, Tennessee, the following year.

Howard L. Naslund was an air force pilot at Bolling AFB during this time. He reported that 43-4030 was one of four B-25s assigned along with C-117s—military DC-3s factory-built with twenty-four airliner seats and no cargo door—for Special Airlift Missions, and that the B-25s were his favorite to fly. They were also very popular with the brass because they cruised faster and got better fuel economy than the C-117s. Naslund specifically commented on the factory-quality modifications. Noting that the bomb bay was skinned over by sheet metal, he wondered about the source of the modifications, but had no knowledge of its link to Eisenhower. Naslund went on to state that in 1953 the B-25s were banished by a newly arrived commander from Bolling AFB to another nearby military unit, the 1254th Air Transport Group, based across the Potomac River at National Airport. Air force records corroborate a change of status in June 1953.

Aircraft 43-4030 was reassigned to the 1001 Air Base Wing at nearby Andrews AFB in August 1958 where it briefly continued to serve as a government VIP transport for travel back and forth within the United States. In December that year, the aircraft was retired and ferried to the boneyard at Davis-Monthan AFB, in Tucson, Arizona. It was stricken from the rolls in February 1959, declared surplus, and sold for civilian use.

As the economic utility of war-surplus Mitchells faded, many were sidelined as weary, broken-down hulks at various airports. A fortunate few found new lives as restored museum pieces. There are an estimated one hundred surviving B-25s of the almost ten thousand

built, of which a surprising number (maybe twenty-five to thirty-three at this writing) remain airworthy.

Eisenhower's plane passed through several private owners, and ended up as property of the Planes of Fame Air Museum at Chino Airport, California. The museum noticed the factory quality modifications but had no idea of the heritage of the plane. Planes of Fame displayed what was subsequently determined to be 43-4030 and flew it in several air shows around California. Finally, they tracked down its origins with the help of North American (then a subsidiary of Rockwell International) and the air force. The initial restoration plan, to apply camouflage war paint and install armaments on an airplane that served without them, was wisely abandoned.

Planes of Fame put the Mitchell up for sale in mid-1981 and it was acquired by the air force for placement at the Ellsworth AFB Museum, just east of Rapid City, South Dakota. FAA records show that the civil registration of N3339G was cancelled and the airplane returned to military ownership on October 2, 1981. After an overnight journey, it touched down at Ellsworth, where local newsmen and former B-25 crewmembers were on hand to greet the historic airplane. Following welcoming ceremonies, the plane was pulled into a hangar so work could begin to restore it to its original appearance. The B-25J remains on public display at Ellsworth AFB; its final resting place, like that of its most famous owner, is now on the Great Plains.

Eisenhower's unnamed B-25J, freshly painted and wearing invasion strips, on display at South Dakota's Ellsworth AFB on June 12, 2013. The windows have been painted over. *Author photo*

CHAPTER 11

TRANSITION TO COLD WAR

First of all, the great productive capacity of the three North American Aviation plants no longer is required. The Army Air Forces has cancelled all work hitherto performed by us at Kansas City and Dallas. Those plants will be returned to the government as soon as inventory and closing-out operations can be completed.

—Dutch Kindelberger, August 1945

Mechanics service a radar-equipped P-82 night fighter. It was designed as a B-29 escort for attacks on Japan but became "a solution in search of a problem" after that mission vanished.

The P-51 Mustang had proved to be an invaluable defender of bomber formations over Germany. However, strategists anticipated that a very-long-range escort fighter would be needed to protect the Boeing B-29 Superfortresses that had been designed with the range needed to attack Japan over the vast expanses of the Pacific Ocean. The P-82 Twin Mustang was conceived to fill this niche.

Design work started out in 1943 as a simple project: join two fuselages of a P-51 with a short piece of wing in between. However, the requirement to carry sufficient fuel dictated more engineering changes than originally anticipated. The two engines each rotated a single four-bladed propeller. A gear box was needed to rotate one propeller in the opposite direction to mitigate torque at high throttle settings. In the end, only about 20 percent of parts were shared between the P-51 and P-82.

Regular Mustangs became adequate for B-29 escort missions when islands closer to Japan were captured and bulldozers operated by Navy Sea-Bees could scratch out crude but adequate runways on them. Back in California, the Twin Mustang first flew in June 1945, but was kept secret. The project was not heralded to the public until November 23, 1945. It arrived too late to see combat until the next war.

The technology of reciprocating pistons pounding in cadence achieved its apex during the waning days of World War II. The ultra-long-range P-82 became a "solution in search of a problem" after its bomber escort mission in the western Pacific evaporated.

The Twin Mustang entered postwar service in two versions and was designated F-82 when the air force was created in 1947. The long-range bombers of the early Cold War era were escorted by F-82s with two pilots. The night-fighter version had a radar-equipped bulb, which looked like a big fuel tank, attached to the wing between the twin booms. A pilot sat in one cockpit while the radar operator occupied the other. Its mission, as an interceptor, was to defend against incoming enemy bombers.

The F-82 earned a place in aviation history on February 27, 1947, when Col. Robert E. Thacker demonstrated the meaning of "very long range" by flying a Twin Mustang named *Betty Jo* nonstop and unrefueled from Honolulu to New York. The twin issues of maintenance woes combined with the arrival of the first generation of jet fighters proved to be a lethal mix for the Twin Mustang. Its service life ended when the last of the F-82s was retired from squadron service in Alaska during late 1953. It was the last piston-powered fighter to enter US military service. The future belonged to turbine-powered jets.

‡

As it became increasingly obvious that the withering Allied onslaught would ultimately yield victory, NAA weekly plant newspapers at Dallas and Kansas City published vague descriptions, some attributed directly to Kindelberger, of potential postwar follow-on work for both sites. The NAA boss knew that major production cuts would soon ensue. A project to assemble B-29s at Kansas City had been aborted in 1942. Lockheed requested that P-80 jets be built there and preliminary work started in early 1945. (That initiative ended with the immediate loss of 1,500 jobs when the Germans surrendered in May 1945.) There were hints of "classified" new opportunities for both plants. A Fairchild transport airplane, the C-82 Packet, was assembled as a "demonstration of capabilities" at the Dallas factory, but that opportunity also sputtered to a halt. In the end, there was to be no NAA-managed follow-on airplane assembly work for either city.

By early 1945, America was overproducing warplanes while the wholesale recruiting of new employees continued unabated. NAA assembled a whopping 881 Mustangs in the month of January (570 of them at Inglewood, with the balance at Dallas). Based on the experience of winding up B-25 production at Inglewood in 1944, NAA purchasing agents initiated dialogue with vendors and subcontractors early in 1945 to commence

A cutaway view of the P-82. It was redesignated as the F-82 when the US Air Force was created in 1947 and saw wartime service in Korea.

pre-termination planning. The goal was slowing of production in an orderly manner. Complications included making inventories of partly finished products, managing tools and jigs, and reducing stocks of surplus or obsolete materials. Further challenges included management of warehouse space, disposition of excess workers, potential tax issues, and controlling corporate debt.

The first hints of looming cutbacks appeared in June 1945 with the order of a 30 percent reduction in combat aircraft production. Work schedules were reduced to forty-five hours per week (five shifts of nine-hour duration) effective Monday, June 18, 1945.

The surprise of the twin atom bomb attacks on August 6 and August 9, 1945, followed by the quicker-than-expected capitulation of the Japanese military left various vast, flat, arid, and remote parts of the American landscape covered by neat rows of new or only slightly used airplanes parked wing-tip to wing-tip. Some were saved for future military need; many went to scrap; others found homes with various government agencies and allied nations; yet others were sold into private hands for a variety of purposes. The leaders of America's aircraft plants were stunned by immediate stop-work orders and the ensuing chaos.

In late August, 1945, Dutch Kindelberger provided an honest explanation to employees:

You all know by now that the victory over Japan has brought cancellations and drastic reductions in military contracts held by all plants producing materiel for the war effort.

I have been advised by the Army Air Forces as to the extent of these cancellations, as they affect North American Aviation.

First of all, the great productive capacity of the three North American Aviation plants no longer is required. The Army Air Forces has cancelled all work hitherto performed by us at Kansas City and Dallas. Those plants will be returned to the government as soon as inventory and closing-out operations can be completed.

The Army Air Forces has cancelled more than 75 percent of the production previously called for in Inglewood. As a result nearly 25 percent of the P-51H contract, together with some experimental work, remains in force at this plant.

In terms of jobs, this means that approximately 50 percent of all employees, excluding all technical engineering personnel who are not affected, will be laid off within the next few days.

With a few exceptions, the entire personnel of the Texas and Kansas plants will be laid off this week. Those exceptions include personnel transferred from Inglewood since the expansion of our operations in 1940, and personnel necessary for inventory and closing out work.

In order to establish which of our employees, based on seniority and contractual obligations, would be affected by this reduction in personnel, it was necessary to close our plants since Wednesday afternoon. You will be paid for the first eight-hour shift not worked.

. . . Supervisors in each department will have the names of employees who will be laid off.

At the Kansas City and Dallas plants, workers were politely thanked for their loyal service as they gathered their hand tools and other small items of personal property. They clocked out and departed the plant for the last time, many of them too stunned to speak. There were no "last-airplane" or any other workplace celebrations.

Every American war plant, including shipyards and airplane factories, endured drastic workforce reductions at the same time thousands of young war veterans were being mustered out of the military to resume their civilian lives. When the Kansas City production line was abruptly shut down, there were seventy-two Mitchell bombers trapped like beached whales in the Fairfax plant's final assembly area. A skeleton crew set about to rescue each of them over the next sixty days. The government accepted the bombers for delivery as "incomplete but flyable"—incomplete because they were shorn of the armaments stipulated in the contract. All of the parts remaining in the supply chain combined with aircraft tooling pulled from the now quiet factory were cut into pieces for loading as scrap aboard railroad gondola cars. By November 1945 there was only a small storefront office in downtown Kansas City, and its role was to wind up any remaining loose ends.

A longstanding military tradition is some form of after-action report to review lessons learned and write them down before people move on. An August 1945 the report on the P-51 program went on to shower North American, their products, and their executives with unmitigated praise seldom seen in an official government report. Kindelberger was described as the "spark plug and genius" of the enterprise. "The record established by North American is outstanding. Mr. Kindelberger's far-sighted vision and forceful personality kept NAA in a leading position," the report's authors wrote, adding that there was a ". . . high spirit of teamwork throughout the organization. . ." and acknowledged ". . . the long experience and past record of many of the NAA engineering and design staff who had been with Fokker Aircraft Corporation, Berliner and Joyce, and General Aviation."

The manufacturing acumen of NAA also collected kudos: "The achievement of such high levels of mass production of aircraft was truly outstanding. P-51 assembly by North America at Dallas and Inglewood was chosen for study because the acceleration of production at those plants was the fastest of all fighter plane production."

North American held a backlog of eight thousand airplane orders as of July 31, 1945; that was reduced to sixty by November 30 that year. Harold Raynor was one of the core-cadre of senior managers and specialists who gradually trickled back to Inglewood. The

NAA workforce plummeted from ninety-one thousand at peak in the fall of 1943 to only five thousand by January 1946. Demotions and downgrades were in store for those lucky few who remained on the payroll. Fortunately, the pent-up demand for consumer goods in a robust economy meant that most of the displaced workers were soon able to find new jobs. Many women permanently withdrew from the workforce and became homemakers again as a postwar baby boom ensued.

The ever-affable and gregarious Kindelberger held his employees in high regard and, over the years, hosted or attended many business-related dinners. The five thousand surviving employees included people who had taken demotions and laid away white shirts with "Foreman" emblazoned in blue letters. Kindelberger, an individual blessed with the vision to peer three years into the future, gave a dinner for the die-hards, saying "Don't throw away your foremen's shirts, boys, you're going to need them again." As usual, his words were prophetic.

Fortunately for the Kansas City economy, General Motors leased the Fairfax plant. The plant was totally emptied since virtually none of the tooling associated with airplanes could be converted to auto assembly. By June 1946 automobiles bearing the brand names of Pontiac, Oldsmobile, and Buick were rolling off newly established assembly lines in response to the worldwide-demand for new cars. The Dallas plant re-emerged as a navy facility.

✝

The core competency of North American was building military airplanes. Starting in 1944, Dutch Kindelberger and his inner circle began pondering diversification opportunities to augment the developmental projects. The medium-sized jet bomber (the B-45) and the

The desert sun, low on the horizon, casts a colorful image of the B-45 Tornado parked on desert sand at Edwards AFB.

jet fighter (the P-86) then in gestation were not enough to sustain a big company. NAA was desperate to retain more of their human capital, the experienced team of brilliant aerospace professionals, needed for the next market upswing. The team came up with four separate possibilities.

The option to build an airliner was probed; however, there were too many problems. No modern designs were on hand; developmental costs were estimated to be $10 to $40 million; and too many other companies were already at each other's throats with airliner offerings of every size and range. This option was quickly and wisely dropped from further consideration.

Consumer goods were evaluated. After all, pots and pans were made of metal, and metal fabrication was North American's forte. "Here are most of the world's consumer goods, described and priced," Kindelberger told his staff in 1944 as they thumbed the pages of a Sears Roebuck catalog. "Let's see what we might manufacture at a profit." The resulting financial figures from NAA's estimators and accountants put internal cost to produce low-end metal products at 30 percent higher than mail-order retail prices. That strategy was also abandoned.

A project to convert war-surplus B-25s into executive transports and military trainers was attempted. It was estimated that 1,500 to 2,000 suitable airframes were available for conversion. They would be sold for $100,000 each, or a fifth of the cost of a new equivalent airplane. The nose was reworked and the windshield from a Convair 240 airliner was installed on a demonstrator, which was then flown to Washington, DC, for inspection by army and navy officers. This project was abandoned when the prototype crashed on the return leg in a severe thunderstorm at Mesa, Arizona, on March 25, 1950. None of the seven NAA employees aboard survived.

However, one project did proceed: the development of a small single-engine four-place airplane suitable for civil use. It was a project that Kindelberger would come to publically rue.

The brand name of Navion was assigned to the product—the postwar public relations people at North American had a penchant for products starting with the letters "NA" (others included Navajo and NATIV)—and the four-place airplane was designed for the high end of the single-engine personal aircraft market. It was a tough marketplace in which to compete because others had already carved out their own niche and enjoyed a cost advantage. Government prognosticators had forecast demand for 450,000 private planes by the year 1950. They assumed that most every American household would aspire to own an airplane; however, demand petered out at about 100,000.

The Navion, which first flew in 1946, offered excellent visibility, retractable landing gear, 150-mile-per-hour cruising speed, stable handling characteristics, and a significant payload (1,000 pounds). The problem was profitability. NAA was saddled with the labor costs, overhead, and massive infrastructure associated with building military aircraft.

A bundle of money was sunk into the Navion's design and unit production costs were at least $10,000; however, in competition with the slicker and faster Beechcraft Bonanza, it could only be sold for $7,000. The US Air Force ordered 83 of the design and designated it L-17; however, other demand was weak and the Korean War intervened. NAA production was halted after 1,085 Navions had been assembled. In a replay of the Vega 35 transaction of 1940, the design and rights to manufacture were sold to Ryan Aeronautical Company where Navion production continued. The financial loss on Navion added up to a painful $8 million.

A B-45 refuels in flight from a KB-29. Some B-29s were modified to perform other missions, which included aerial refueling.

TECHNICAL NOTES
NAVION L-17

ENGINE: Continental
0-470-7 185 hp

WINGSPAN: 33 ft. 5 in.

LENGTH: 27 ft. 4 in.

HEIGHT: 8 ft. 7 in.

WEIGHT: 2,950 lb. loaded

MAXIMUM SPEED: 163 mph

RANGE: 700 miles

CEILING: 11,000 ft.

As is typical when companies reach beyond their core competency, none of these diversification strategies panned out. The year 1947 was the first unprofitable year for North American, and they joined other airframe-builders in relying upon tax carry-back credits from the profitable war years to remain afloat. Fortunately, a foray into Nazi-pioneered technological concepts was to expand the NAA research and development business, and yield them a place in forthcoming aerospace history.

Captured enemy airplanes were always of interest, and provided an opportunity for engineers to glean new ideas for better products. Novel airplanes like the innovative Japanese Zero were scrutinized early in the war; however, further significant aviation breakthroughs stalled in Japan as the war progressed.

The Messerschmitt Bf 109 (Me 109 in NAA records) was a formidable Nazi fighter airplane and nemesis of Allied bomber formations. A captured example was brought to Inglewood earlier in the war for disassembly and reverse engineering. The airplane and its components were reduced to very small pieces in the quest for secrets. The photographic record, with dozens of images, remains in NAA files. Interest in the latest German technology later intensified because of their stunning advances in not only jet- and rocket-powered airplanes but also the unmanned aerial weapons, the V-1 buzz bomb and V-2 rockets, both of which were used to terrorize the British.

On April 29, 1945, American infantry troops probing the German homeland discovered a new Nazi jet, under construction at the Oberammergau complex and about 80 percent complete. Work had started on Messerschmitt project 1101 in mid-1944. In a unique feature, the sweep of the wings could be set before flight at 30, 40, or 50 degrees. This was for flight testing only and not intended for the production article, which was never built. The captured prize was first taken to Wright Field near Dayton, and then turned over to Bell Aircraft. The top view of project 1101 bears a striking resemblance to the later F-86. A later photograph shows the wings from what appears to be a Me 262 jet airplane in 1947 amidst the concrete rubble from bomb shelter demolition. The German technology was surely of interest to engineers developing the first North American jet-powered aircraft, the B-45 bomber and a jet fighter, conceived as the P-86 but re-designated F-86 when the US Air Force was established.

North American played a major role in development of unmanned offensive weapons modeled after the German V-1. Postwar, the X-10 Navaho proved a versatile pilotless air-breathing jet aircraft. There were versions suitable for air-drop from a large mother-ship, or take-off and landing from a runway like any other manned airplane. Navajos sometimes crashed during testing but no serious damage was done because there was no pilot aboard and the experiments were conducted at remote desert airfields; however, no production orders were forthcoming.

Vertically launched liquid-fueled versions were modeled after the feared V-2 rockets. They were launched from Cape Canaveral and Patrick AFB on the east coast of Florida on a down-range trajectory towards the Bahamas. North American played a leading role developing and refining the technology that culminated in the NASA space program and the moon landings of 1969–1973.

‡

Dutch Kindelberger continued to receive public adulation in the postwar era. Lengthy and laudatory articles about him appeared in the popular press, including *Time* and the *Saturday Evening Post*. He received a Certificate of Merit award signed by President Harry S. Truman and dated March 22, 1948. It stated ". . . in recognition of service from September

The flying days for this captured Bf 109 (bearing the insignia of the USAAF) are over as it awaits disassembly (earlier in the war) in the quest for any secrets it might hold. It was reverse engineered into very small pieces that were then relegated to the scrap heap.

1939 to September 1945 in connection with the manufacture and mass production of military aircraft which advanced the nation's air supremacy. . . . "

Kindelberger became a victim of his hard-charging, workaholic life style when his health took a turn for the worse starting in 1947. He initially suffered from ulcers and later endured a chronic heart-related ailment that would ultimately lead to his demise. On some days he would not arrive at work until 10:00 a.m. because of failing health. His ever-stable (but aging) executive team—including Atwood, Rice, and Smithson—all soldiered on. Unlike at Boeing in 1934, there was to be no major infusion of fresh blood at North American. There was no significant rotation of the top executives until Kindelberger passed away in 1962, and only advancing age forced the others out.

It was, no doubt, becoming evident to the executive team that North American Aviation Inc. was trapped in a postwar bind. The business environment for building airplanes had shifted over the 1940s. It was neither feasible nor profitable to whip up a small batch of one-off fighter or trainer airplanes for a customer like Peru or Thailand. Ever-increasing complexity drove the developmental effort for sophisticated new models exponentially; Kindelberger contrasted the electrical system of a Mustang to that of a Sabre jet by comparing a doorbell to a television set.

Unable to downshift into the private airplane market and wisely avoiding the cutthroat airliner business, the NAA leadership must have privately concluded that their future success would rely solely upon the largess of the federal government. The laudable peacetime diversification attempts had all failed. The future business base was to become inextricably linked to Congressional appropriations as contracted for by the air force, navy, Atomic Energy Commission, and eventually NASA. Employment rebounded as orders arrived at Inglewood for other new products.

After demobilizing and basking briefly in the glow of the twin 1945 victories, the American military soon awoke to evolving new threats in Europe and Asia. Communism

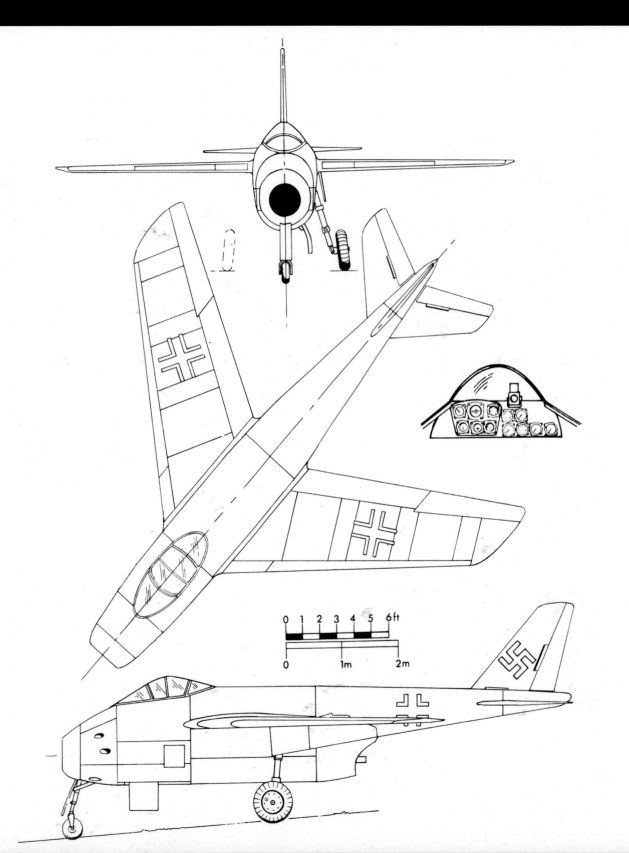

0 1 2 3 4 5 6ft

0   1m   2m

replaced fascism as the next threat to Western security. The Soviets erected an "Iron Curtain" around a large tract of Europe while the mainland Chinese were simultaneously embracing communism, making bellicose threats about Taiwan, and abetting trouble in Korea. Accordingly, the American military scrambled to regain a technological edge in competition with the Soviets. The sun again began to shine on Inglewood as Congress reopened the money spigot with defense spending increases starting in 1948. A cold war was underway as both sides sought to capitalize on the military innovations pioneered by the Nazis: faster jet-powered airplanes with swept wings, and liquid-fueled missiles in the tradition of the V-2.

The navy coveted a role augmenting the air force heavy bombers in the Pentagon's post-war nuclear delivery arsenal. A medium bomber called the AJ-1 Savage was developed by North American for this mission. It had two propellers powered by R-2800 radial engines and a jet engine tucked away on the centerline of the aft lower fuselage in an arrange-ment sometimes called "two turning and one burning." Designed to carry a 10,000-pound weapon, it was too heavy for use on some older aircraft carriers still in service.

Five companies vied for the lucrative contract for a first-generation jet-powered medium bomber. Douglas was the first entrant into the competition with the XB-42 medium bomber. Jet engines arrived to replace the two piston engines of the

ABOVE: This postwar photograph was to document removal of the Inglewood plant bomb shelters; however, the severed wings of what appears to have been a Me 262 intrude into the scene.

OPPOSITE: American infantry troops discovered the Messerschmitt P.1101 at the Oberammergau Complex on April 29, 1945. It was about eighty percent complete. The top view bears an uncanny resemblance to an F 86.

German-inspired V-1 technology was carried forward into the Navajo project yielding significant technical strides but no production contracts.

original design and it was re-designated XB-43. However, it soon became evident that simply replacing piston engines with jets did not yield an optimum airplane. (An example of the XB-43 awaits restoration at the Smithsonian Institution in Washington, DC.)

Convair of San Diego, formed from the merger between Vultee Aircraft Division and Consolidated Aircraft Corporation, had the XB-46. Only one example of this four-engine sleek but underpowered aircraft was assembled; however, the bomb bay was too narrow to haul a nuclear weapon and it was fraught with other design and performance problems.

North American at Inglewood had their XB-45, while Martin of Baltimore's entrant was the XB-48, which bore a faint resemblance to a B-26 Marauder. Two examples of this six-engine homely beast were tested as an alternative to Boeing of Seattle's B-47, which was a late entrant into the competition—but emerged as the grand-prize winner.

Design on the B-45 Tornado started in 1944, before George Schairer of Boeing discovered the concept of swept wings combined with jet-powered airplanes in previously secret German files, when he was invited to inspect Nazi technology in 1945. Although this information was immediately shared with all American airplane builders, NAA was already well along and committed to the straight wing B-45 design with four jet engines buried deeply within wing-wrapping cowls. The airplane entered squadron service and the reconnaissance version enjoyed a bit more success.

The now mostly forgotten North American B-45 Tornado did accomplish significant aviation milestones. It was the first American four-engine jet bomber to fly, the first jet bomber anywhere capable of carrying an atomic bomb, and the first multi-jet reconnaissance aircraft to refuel in mid-air.

The Boeing B-47 Stratojet was first to deliver the game-changing performance of a swept wing combined with six jet engines innovatively mounted in under-wing pods. The pods provided an important safety margin between the wing and the jet engine in the unlikely event of fire or catastrophic engine failure. The combination of swept-wing and under-wing jet engines redefined the large airplane configuration paradigm.

Boeing's Wichita plant was re-tooled and production did not stop until 2,063 Stratojets were assembled. The mission intended for the B-45 Tornado was instead shouldered by the B-47 medium bomber.

‡

The P-51 was redesignated the F-51 Mustang when the US Air Force (USAF) was created in 1947. Robert "Bob" Hutton (1921–2015), whose experiences as an instructor pilot during World War II can be found in chapter four, went on to become an F-51 pilot with a hundred combat missions in Korea (although he consistently referred to his aircraft as a P-51, and never once called it an F-51).

The postwar transition to jets remained a busy time for those who specialized in cleaning up wreckage. Fortunately, nobody was injured because the Navajo was an unmanned drone.

One of the last of the "incomplete but flyable" B-25s is prepared for departure from Kansas City's Fairfax Airport in mid-October 1945. It has been shorn of the armaments stipulated in the contract. Nobody from the military is present.

A postwar stint in the family-owned construction business was unfulfilling to Hutton's still-youthful desire for adventure. Three months after he wrote a letter to the air force requesting reinstatement, he was summoned to Hamilton AFB, near San Francisco. Within sixty days, Capt. Bob Hutton, still a junior officer in the USAF, came to enjoy card games and comradeship aboard a troop transport ship underway to Japan. Consistent with his lingering long-term goal from the earlier war, this time he was destined for a posting to a Mustang-equipped fighter squadron and the anticipation made him tingle with excitement.

Hutton arrived before the outbreak of hostilities in Korea but soon found himself and his Mustang embroiled in a serious shooting war in a small country previously unheard of by most Americans. The Japanese had ruled and occupied the South Korea peninsula until their surrender in August 1945 while North Korea fell within the Russian sphere of influence. Lacking a viable agreement to reunify the split nation, an arbitrary boundary line was drawn at the 38th Parallel. At 0400 hours (local time) on June 25, 1950, North Korean military forces stormed southward across the border and into South Korea. The first United Nations airplanes to arrive in Korea were F-51 Mustangs. The low-level work was turned over to them on July 5, 1950, as they flew from the small, muddy airfields before the airstrips, many of them dating to the Japanese occupation, were lengthened and improved to meet the more demanding requirements of the jet fighters.

The USAF Far East Air Force's (FEAF) Fifth Air Force headquarters were at Itazuke Air Base in Japan. Senior officers located there were overseeing modernization efforts to transition from the aging F-51s into modern jets as hostilities erupted. Conditions in Korea forced FEAF to return the recently retired airplanes reposing in Japan to service while requisitioning additional Mustangs from American boneyards and air national guard units.

The air force quickly rounded up 145 Mustangs and brought them to Alameda, California. They were wrapped in plastic to protect them from salt water and loaded aboard the US Navy aircraft carrier USS *Boxer*. After a fast eight-day crossing of the Pacific Ocean, the carrier pulled into Tokyo Bay for docking on July 23, 1951. Thirteen days later, the Mustangs were fully prepared for combat and ready for deployment to the war zone. To minimize crew fatigue, three pilots were allocated for each airplane deployed to the frontlines.

Hostilities became more heated as the Russians provided the North Koreans with airplanes, aircrews, and other modern weaponry and Communist China poured ground troops into the hostilities. For weeks the Mustangs worked over the enemy with rockets, machine guns, and napalm. Hutton flew his full quota of one hundred dangerous combat missions in the World War II–vintage propeller-driven planes before the ultimate jet aircraft of the era, the F-86 Sabre and MiG-15, burst onto the scene.

Hutton's primary combat mission was to search for targets for others to destroy. The workaday combat reconnaissance sorties were performed at high speeds and low altitudes (500 to 1,500 feet) in search of worthwhile ground targets for aerial attack—especially enemy encampments, fuel or ammo dumps, armored vehicles, or troop concentrations. Soviet built T-34 tanks were of special interest.

The airplanes flew fast and clean, with neither auxiliary fuel tanks nor external ordinance to slow them down on their aerial hunt. Success relied upon the visual acuity of the human eye and quick reporting by two-way radio. Even though a photo reconnaissance version of the Mustang (the F-6) was developed during World War II, only one F-51 in the unit had a camera installed.

Although Hutton made no mention of the dangers when interviewed, other sources make it clear that flying an F-51 in the low-level air-to-ground combat air support missions could instantly turn into a life-threatening situation. Equipment could malfunction: The radios were built on the vacuum tube technology of the era, which was always failure-prone, but especially so when constantly jarred by the very bumpy Korean runways during the frequent landings and take-offs necessary to rearm. The insidious dust in the air during the dry season could foul the spark plugs if the air filters were not carefully monitored, while water in the fuel during the rainy season was believed to be the cause of engine stalls that brought down two Mustangs. Dry rot and vibrations sometimes caused gasoline leakage where rubber hoses connected metal fuel lines.

Low-level flight over enemy forces invited small arms fire, and bullet holes were commonly found in the F-51s upon their return to base. The holes were routinely patched with scraps of sheet metal secured by rivets. However, if a single .30-caliber bullet ripped into a radiator or other cooling system component, the engine would immediately overheat and

A proud aviator poses with a P-51 before the tough slog of the Korean War wore the luster off not only the airplanes but also the pilots. The Mustang was a unique combination of speed, simplicity, and durability. Each was initially sent to Korea accompanied by three pilots so the aircraft could remain in the fight as the pilots rotated in and out of the cockpit.

The Mustang could carry a variety of munitions to include guns, bombs, and rockets. Here, rockets are fired in flight.

then seize within about two minutes, at which point the pilot might have to bail out. That could be a problem in itself: although pilots wore parachutes, there was no ejection seat to ensure rapid egress and provide sufficient altitude for the parachute canopy to reliably open—the canopy of a contemporary air force emergency parachute was 28 feet in diameter and fabricated of ripstop nylon.

Once Hutton and his colleagues had spotted the targets, normally other nearby F-51s, fully armed with a lethal mix of guns, rockets, bombs, and napalm, were called upon to eliminate them. Napalm, an incendiary form of jellied gasoline, was a standard weapon because it was effective against not only troops but also tanks and other vehicles. The Soviet T-34 tanks were a serious challenge. Hastily aimed munitions could bounce off the armor plating. A strategy evolved to first immobilize the beast by attacking the tracks before carefully aimed rockets, with shaped explosive charges, could penetrate the armor.

On two occasions, when others were unavailable, Hutton was authorized to mount an attack using his wing-mounted Browning machine guns, the only weapons at his disposal. On two other instances, he was ordered to break away from the hunt for lucrative targets to provide Rescue Search Combat Air Patrol (RESCAP) for another, downed pilot. The goal of RESCAP was to guide rescue forces to the site while employing well-aimed .50-caliber bursts from the F-51's six machine guns to defend the downed pilot from hostile ground forces.

With United Nations sanction, the countries of South Korea, South Africa, and Australia also provided Mustang-equipped squadrons to the war effort. The last Republic of Korea F-51 was not retired until 1957. Of 62,607 American-flown F-51 sorties during the Korean War only 474 Mustangs were reported to be lost.

Aviators earned a rest and recuperation (R&R) leave after every thirty or so missions. Hutton would then depart for Japan in a tired Mustang much in need of maintenance and, after a well-earned break from combat, would catch a hop back to Korea in a transport plane. Hutton and his unit were fortunate. He could only recall the loss of a single F-51 from his unit and it happened while he was absent on R&R in Japan.

After returning from Korea, Hutton decided to remain in uniform and was first assigned to an F-51 unit at Portland (Oregon) International Airport. It was from there that he deployed on temporary duty to Arizona. Yuma became the next assignment for Hutton, his bride, and their young family over the next several years when the Air Defense Gunnery School was established in the early 1950s. The mission grew until four squadrons of North American Mustangs were utilized to tow target sleeves. As the tactics and technology of air defense evolved, the towing role for the F-51 was phased out after a year. Hutton remained at Yuma as an operations officer and flight instrument instructor on Mustangs. After service on Okinawa, his last assignment was at Truax Field, Madison, Wisconsin as Base Operations officer. It was there that he retired as a lieutenant colonel in 1966, when the active duty unit was shut down.

‡

The Korean War resulted in a surge of orders at North American for urgently needed warplanes. The postwar doldrums were over. Full-throttle hiring resumed and the plants were again buzzing with activity day and night. Kindelberger hosted yet another dinner for his foremen and this time boasted: "There is nothing I like better than being up to my ass in business."

Kindelberger was always full of pithy but quotable expressions. When commended for pulling a rabbit out of his hat with the F-86 design he retorted, "You can't pull a rabbit out of a hat unless you carefully put the rabbit in the hat beforehand." The North American (i.e., Kindelberger's) retrospective view of the Korean War was written around 1960:

It was difficult to tell where the skirmishes left off and the conflict began, but the Korean War was going full blast by June of 1950. The communist encroachment was opposed in the air only by prop oldsters and junior-grade jets. North American aircraft by nature of their exceptional longevity were fielded early in the war and served well. The P-82s outgrew their enginitis and succeeded in downing the first enemy aircraft. The P-51 was the standard operational fighter for United Nations forces and was an excellent vehicle for low level bombing and strafing. They changed the designation to F-82 and F-51, but the old warhorses were little more than World War II products. Even the steadfast AT-6 trainer was mustered for ground spotting.

Then came MIG-15s barreling in and clearing the skies with their superior performance and fire power. "There is nothing sadder than a second-rate plane at least to the boy who is flying it," Dutch mentioned. Saddest of all were the U.N. pilots manning the dozen or so types of Brand X jets of the time. These British and US jets were little more than trainers and were totally incapable of contesting the MIG-15. The state of Russian technology was convincingly demonstrated. Dutch said later "Our conception of the Russian is crazy. We thought of him as a peasant with a cow, and his wife out pulling the plow—stopping only now and then to scratch. But Russia is building up and improving her industries all the time."

TECHNICAL NOTES
B-45 TORNADO

ENGINES: Four General Electric J47s 6,000 lb. thrust each

WINGSPAN: 89 ft. 0 in.

LENGTH: 75 ft. 4 in.

HEIGHT: 25 ft. 2 in.

WEIGHT: 110,000 lb. maximum

MAXIMUM SPEED: 570 mph

RANGE: 1,000 miles

CEILING: 37,550 ft.

ARMAMENT: Two .50-cal. machine guns, 22,000 lb. of bombs

NUMBER BUILT: 99, including 33 B-45C long-range versions and 10 RB-45C high-altitude versions

It takes a jet to stop a jet. The wizardry of engineering and manufacturing of North American had a jet in production to do the stopping. The F-86E's and F's were rushed from flight test to Korea [and the kill ratio shifted decisively in favor of the Americans].

In contrast to the lackluster B-45, the swept-wing F-86 Sabre Jet of the same era earned aerial-combat fame as a dogfighter in the war-ravaged skies over Korea at a place called "MiG Alley." American forces, enforcing a United Nations mandate, found themselves facing a formidable weapon. MiG-15s, also influenced by German technology of swept wings and jet power, tore into B-29 bomber formations with devastating effect. Only the NAA F-86 could equal the MiG-15 in a dogfight, and then only if strict attention was paid to tactics. A competent and well-trained pilot needed to understand the strengths and weaknesses of the flight envelope of each aircraft.

It was at this point the title of the "world's finest fighter" passed from the Mustang to the F-86 Sabre. The ongoing goal of American airpower is to ensure domination of the skies over any battlefield where US military forces are engaged and, accordingly, the Mustang, the last major vestige of North American-built piston-powered combatant, was ordered to stand down in deference to newer, faster, and more-advanced jet fighters.

Under the leadership of Dutch Kindelberger and Lee Atwood, NAA adroitly avoided the stumbles that wounded (sometimes fatally) other aerospace firms in the immediate postwar era. The F-86 Sabre and F-100 Super Sabre series of air superiority jet fighters, as well as a portfolio of other exciting projects, put NAA at the top of its game as the decade of the 1940s gave way to the 1950s. Atwood became president of NAA in 1960, with Kindelberger acting as chairman, a post he held until his death in 1962 when he was succeeded by Atwood. In 1967, following the tragic fire on Apollo 1 for which NAA was ascribed some responsibility, NAA merged with Rockwell-Standard. Lee Atwood died in March 1999, aged ninety-four.

American combat pilots head for their airplanes during the Korean War.

Nothing, other than the real estate, remains of either the Inglewood or Kansas City plants. Inglewood was torn down in 1980 and General Motors replaced the Fairfax plant with a new and modern automobile factory in 1987. Of their product, a few fine examples of the warbirds are preserved, including the T-6 trainer, B-25 bomber, and P-51 escort fighter. These are occasionally flown by the individuals and institutions with the means to muster sufficient expertise and other necessary resources. The airplanes are tributes not only to North American Aviation but also the individuals of the "Greatest Generation"— the designers, assemblers, and brave airmen who took them into battle. They provide an opportunity for their descendants and other admirers to witness a demonstration flight, hear the throaty roar of an unmuffled reciprocating engine, and maybe even get a whiff of the pungent exhaust.

A montage of the North American product line as the decade of the 1950s approached.

APPENDIX A
NORTH AMERICAN AIRCRAFT DELIVERED 1941 TO 1945

	AIRCRAFT DELIVERED (Units)				AIRFRAME WEIGHT DELIVERED (Thousands of Pounds)			
Calendar Year	Total	Company	Percentage Represented By Company Production	Position of Company in the Industry	Total	Company	Percentage Represented By Company Production	Position of Company in the Industry
1941	19,433	2,552	13.1	3rd	90,572	9,302	10.3	5th
1942	47,836	6,033	12.6	2nd	314,799	36,785	11.7	5th
1943	85,898	9,106	10.6	3rd	758,814	66,149	8.7	5th
1944	96,318	14,858	15.4	1st	1,101,032	124,043	11.3	4th
1945	47,714	8,219	17.2	1st	599,609	57,136	9.5	3rd
1941-1945	297,199	40,768	13.7	1st	2,864,826	293,415	10.2	4th

The table includes civil transport planes of 12 places or more, but excludes experimental production. Airframe weight is defined as the weight of the empty airplane, less the weight of certain items consisting generally of the major portion of the Government furnished equipment. Airframe weight as used in the table includes the weight of spare parts delivered.

APPENDIX B
NORTH AMERICAN FINANCIAL PERFORMANCE 1937 TO 1947

	Net Sales	Other Income Less Interest and Other Income Deductions	Cost of Sales and Other Costs Excluding Federal Taxes on Income	Net Income Before Provision for Federal Taxes on Income	Provision for Federal Income and Excess Profits Taxes (See Note 4)	Net Income
YEAR ENDED DECEMBER 31:						
1937	$ 3,469,102	$ 357,119#	$ 3,110,118	$ 716,103	$ 220,000	$ 496,103
1938	10,062,346	108,104#	7,859,335	2,311,115	407,029	1,904,086
1939	27,608,651	73,722	19,093,281	8,589,092	1,501,000	7,088,092
1940	36,862,514	117,474	26,897,652	10,082,336	2,992,000	7,090,336
NINE MONTHS ENDED SEPTEMBER 30, 1941	60,865,687	49,756	44,156,766	16,758,677	9,932,723	6,825,954
YEAR ENDED SEPTEMBER 30:						
1942	235,026,119	288,515	204,526,127	30,788,507	21,887,666	8,900,841
1943	463,483,954	351,669	426,630,332	37,205,291	25,414,968	11,790,323
1944	680,049,499	1,067,535*	629,980,361	49,001,603	34,813,084	14,188,519
1945	376,273,731	1,014,052*	348,393,964	26,865,715	19,114,147	7,751,568
1946	52,414,239	344,717	49,572,460	3,186,496	1,189,213	1,997,283
1947	19,855,321	621,409	32,204,989	11,728,259*	11,700,000*	28,259*
SIX MONTHS ENDED MARCH 31, 1948	19,323,720	169,614	18,251,895	1,241,439	488,000	753,439

\# Includes airline transportation revenues of $4,779,742 in 1937 and $1,503,591 in 1938, less related expenses of $4,506,319 and $1,384,884, respectively.

* Denotes red figures.

APPENDIX C
NORTH AMERICAN HEADCOUNT 1938 TO 1948

EMPLOYEE RELATIONS

The following table contains certain information relating to employees of the Company and its subsidiaries:

Date	Number of Employees
December 31, 1938	2,700
December 31, 1939	4,600
December 31, 1940	8,200
September 30, 1941	16,600
September 30, 1942	48,100
September 30, 1943	87,800
September 30, 1944	64,000
September 30, 1945	10,600
September 30, 1946	8,500
September 30, 1947	16,300
March 31, 1948	20,600

Employment reached a wartime peak in 1943 of approximately 91,000 at all plants, including approximately 25,000 at the California plant. In the period following V-J Day contract terminations, employment at the California plant reached a low of approximately 5,000 in January 1946.

The average hourly rate for direct factory labor has approximately doubled since 1939.

APPENDIX D
NOTICE TO ACCOMPANY EXECUTIVE ORDER NO. 8773

1. By executive order dated today, the President of the United States has directed that the Secretary of War immediately take possession of the Inglewood plant of North American Aviation, Inc. at Los Angeles through such person as he may designate.

2. In accordance with the directive of the President the Secretary of War has this day directed me to take immediate possession of the Inglewood plant of North American Aviation, Inc.

3. Pursuant to these orders, possession of the plant has been taken by the United States.

Signed: Charles E. Branshaw, Lt. Colonel, Air Corps
June 9, 1941

EXECUTIVE ORDER NO. 8773

WHEREAS, on the 27th day of 1941, a Presidential proclamation was issued, declaring an unlimited national defense emergency and calling upon all loyal citizens in production for defense to give precedence to the needs of the Nation to the end that a system of government which makes private enterprise possible may survive; and calling upon all our loyal workmen as well as employers to merge their lesser differences in the larger effort to insure the survival of the only kind of government which recognizes the rights of labor or of capital, and calling upon all loyal citizens to place the Nation's needs first in mind and in action to the end that we may mobilize and have ready for instant defensive use, all of the physical powers, all of the moral strength and all of the material resources of the Nation; and

WHEREAS North American Aviation, Inc., at its Inglewood plant in the City of Los Angeles, State of California, has contracts with the United States for the manufacture of military aircraft and other material and articles vital to the defense of the United States; and the United States owns aircraft in the course of production, raw material, machinery, and other property situated in the said Company's plant, and

WHEREAS a controversy arose at said plant over terms and conditions of employment between the company and the workers which they have been unable to adjust by collective bargaining; and whereas the controversy was duly certified to the National Defense Mediation Board, established by the Executive Order of March 19, 1941; and whereas before the negotiations had been concluded before the said Board, and in violation of an agreement between the bargaining representatives of the company and the workers authorized to appear before the Board and conduct the negotiations, production at said plant of said aircraft and other articles and materials vital to the defense of the United States was interrupted by a strike which still continues, and

WHEREAS the objectives of said proclamation of May 27, 1941 are jeopardized and the ability of the United States to obtain aircraft essential to its armed forces and to the national defense is seriously impaired by said cessation of production, and

WHEREAS for the time being and under the circumstances hereinabove set forth it is essential in order that such operations be assured and safeguarded that the plant be operated by the United States;

Now, therefore, I, Franklin D. Roosevelt, pursuant to the powers vested in me by the Constitution and laws of the United States, as President of the United States of America and Commander in Chief of the Army and Navy of the United States, hereby authorize and direct that the Secretary of War immediately take possession of and operate the said plant of North American Aviation, Inc., through such person or persons as he may designate, to produce the aircraft and other articles and material called for by its contracts with the United States or otherwise, and to do all things necessary or incidental thereto. Such necessary or appropriate adjustments shall be made with respect to existing and future contracts and with respect to compensation to the company, as further orders hereafter issued by the Secretary of War shall provide. The Secretary of War shall employ or authorize the employment of such employees, including a competent civilian advisor on industrial relations, as are necessary to carry out the provisions of this order. And I hereby direct the Secretary of War to take such measures as may be necessary to protect workers returning to the plant.

Possession and operation hereunder shall be terminated by the President as soon as he determines that the plant will be privately operated in a manner consistent with the needs of the national defense.

Franklin D. Roosevelt

FRANKLIN D. ROOSEVELT
THE WHITE HOUSE
June 9, 1941, 10:40 a.m., E.S.T.

APPENDIX F

This warm letter from Gen. Henry "Hap" Arnold was one of many received from public and private dignitaries who could not attend a gala celebration of Kindelberger's twenty-five years in aviation manufacturing held in Los Angeles on December 28, 1943.

WAR DEPARTMENT

HEADQUARTERS OF THE ARMY AIR FORCES

WASHINGTON

December 22, 1943

Mr. J. H. Kindelberger, President
North American Aviation, Inc.
Inglewood, California

Dear Dutch:

It gives me great pleasure to send you my heartiest congratulations upon the occasion of your 25th anniversary in the Aircraft Industry. During the past quarter of a century the Industry has grown from an infant to a full man-sized organization and nobody knows better than I the part you have played in its progress. The time, effort, and energy you have devoted to this gigantic job speaks for itself, and the results are apparent in the production which we are getting today.

In the years to come may we continue to have your wholehearted support and the benefit of your wide knowledge and experience.

With Season's Greetings and every good wish, I am

Sincerely,

H. H. ARNOLD
General, U.S. Army
Commanding General, Army Air Forces

FOR VICTORY BUY UNITED STATES WAR BONDS AND STAMPS

DEC 28 RECD

APPENDIX G

The Mustang was conceived to meet the needs of the British and French. As such, the prototype (designated NA-73X) flew as a civilian (rather than military) aircraft. Each civil aircraft is required to carry and prominently display a government-issued Registration-Airworthiness Certificate. It is an essential document, somewhat analogous to a motor vehicle registration form. The actual Airworthiness Certificate (pictured above) from the P-51 prototype, NA-73X, was found safely tucked away in North American files on December 9, 2014. This small, but important, scrap of paper was carried aboard it during the entire flight-test program—including when pilot Paul Balfour crashlanded the airplane in a freshly plowed bean field, thus bringing its fifth flight to an inglorious ending on November 20, 1940.

The story of its preservation is noteworthy. The document was found stapled to an undated note. (The staples are visible at the top of the form.) Long-time North American employee, Arlie Staigh, wrote that he had been involved in dismantling the prototype Mustang in either late 1941 or early 1942. He removed the registration form and kept it for about twenty years, without mention of whether it was retained at work, home, or elsewhere. While as working on the Sabreliner program, which first flew in 1958 and entered service in 1962, he decided to return the historic document to officials.

The registration was issued in October 1940, immediately prior to the first flight of NA-73X at the hands of test pilot Vance Breese on October 26. Lacking any other guidance, it is presumed an unknown office administrator decided to file it along with other, mostly insignificant, general company correspondence dating from 1940—where it remained until discovered.

THIS CERTIFICATE MUST BE PROMINENTLY DISPLAYED IN THE AIRCRAFT

UNITED STATES OF AMERICA
DEPARTMENT OF COMMERCE
ADMINISTRATOR OF CIVIL AERONAUTICS
REGISTRATION-AIRWORTHINESS CERTIFICATE

THIS AIRCRAFT MAY BE FLOWN ONLY BY U. S. CERTIFICATED PILOTS

EXPERIMENTAL   IDENTIFICATION MARK NX19998   Serial No. 75-3097

Passengers (less crew) NONE   Engine ALLISON V1710-39 1000 HP

Model NORTH AMERICAN X73 1 PC-CLM   A. T. C. --

ONLY BONA FIDE MEMBERS OF THE CREW MAY BE CARRIED

Weight empty as equipped (See equipment reverse side) -- lb. Gross weight (Not to be exceeded) -- lb.

Maximum pay load is -- lb. with fuel of -- gal.

Maximum pay load is -- lb. with full fuel tanks 137 gal.

Cargo spaces: Location and capacity—OPERATIONS RESTRICTED TO MANUFACTURER'S FLIGHT TESTS IN THE VICINITY OF FACTORY WITH LANDINGS AT MINES FIELD & WITHIN THE CONTINENTAL LIMITS OF U S NO FLIGHTS OVER AIR SPACE RESERVATIONS NO PHOTOGRAPHIC MISSIONS

THIS CERTIFIES, that the aircraft described above is a civil aircraft of the United States of America and has been found to be in condition for safe operation.

REGISTERED OWNER: NORTH AMERICAN AVIATION INC

5701 IMPERIAL HIGHWAY INGLEWOOD CALIFORNIA

Unless sooner suspended or revoked, this certificate expires JULY 15 1941

BY DIRECTION OF THE ADMINISTRATOR:

Chief, Certificate Section.

ANY ALTERATION OF THIS CERTIFICATE IS PUNISHABLE BY A FINE OF NOT EXCEEDING $1,000 OR IMPRISONMENT NOT EXCEEDING 3 YEARS, OR BOTH 10-40 (OVER)

Form ACA-8—Rev. 7-10-40   16—16255

Sold to   Sold by   Date of sale

CHAPTER NOTES

Research for *Warbird Factory* was accomplished mostly between May and November 2014, which was also when information was gathered from various web-based sources.

CHAPTER 1: THE GENESIS OF NORTH AMERICAN AVIATION

Quotation from Ernest R. Breech: monthly company magazine, *General Motors World*, July 1933 edition, pp. 14–17.

Incorporation of NAA in 1928 by Clement Melville Keys: NAA corporate records.

Anthony Fokker Tri-motor flying stunt: speech by John J. Sloan to the Historical Branch of the Los Angeles Section of the Institute of Aeronautical Sciences, November 28, 1952.

History of Anthony Fokker, Fokker-America, and the crash of TWA flight 599: Herbert M. Friedman, "The Legacy of the Rockne Crash," *Aeroplane* magazine, May 2001.

Transcontinental & Western Air: T&WA evolved into Trans World Airlines (TWA) and its history ran from 1925 to 2001, when it was merged into American Airlines.

The fascinating story of William Knudsen: best told by Arthur Herman, *Freedom's Forge*, Random House, 2012.

General Motors 1929 investment in Fokker and Bendix: Alfred P. Sloan Jr., *My Years with General Motors*, p. 362 (GM paid a mere $592,000 to purchase Allison Engineering outright in 1929).

Ford Tri-motor details: "History of the Ford Tri-Motor," www.eaa.org.

William Boeing at the Senator Hugo Black hearings: Harold Mansfield, *Vision: A Saga of the Sky*, Madison Pub., 1986.

Testimony of William E. Boeing: transcript of "Senate Investigation of Air Mail and Ocean Mail Contracts," January 23, 1934 to February 7, 1934, Part 5, starts on p. 2,247.

History and impacts of the Air Mail Act of 1934: "The Air Mail 'Scandal'—America by Air," www.airandspace.si.edu.

History of General Aviation, recruitment of Kindelberger by Breech: Security & Exchange Commission Form S-1, Common Stock Registration Statement, May 11, 1948.

CHAPTER 2: DUTCH

Pioneers of aviation: PBS Video Series *Pioneers of Aviation*, Bill Winship, 2009.

Wright brothers' expectation of aviation: "When my brother and I built and flew the first man-carrying flying machine, we thought we were introducing into the world an invention which would make further wars practically impossible. That we were not alone in this thought is evidenced by the fact that the French Peace Society presented us with medals on account of our invention. . . ." Orville Wright letter, June 21, 1917.

Number of airplanes built for World War I: Daniel Yergin, "The First War to Run on Oil", *Wall Street Journal*, August 16, 2014, C3.

Biographical information on James H. Kindelberger:

• Report: "P-51 Construction and Production Analysis," prepared by Industrial Planning Section, Air Materiel Command, August 1945.

• Article in company newspaper, *North American Log*, "J. H. Kindelberger", pp. 6–7.

• NAA history prepared by Columbus Division, NAA, circa 1960.

• "The Cats of MiG Alley," *Time* magazine, June 29, 1953, p. 84.

Number of O-47 aircraft built and delivered: The exact number of various types of aircraft built varies even within NAA records. Contributing factors, including airplanes crashed during flight testing, create variances between "built" and "delivered" statistics. Some airframes were consigned to destructive static test procedures, and aircraft builders were sometimes awarded "equivalent" airframe credit for spare parts produced.

Moving from Dundalk to Inglewood:

• NAA history prepared by Columbus Division, NAA, circa 1960.

• Oral histories gathered by the NAA retiree group "The Bald Eagles."

Unwritten strategy of NAA and personality attributes of Kindelberger and Atwood: adapted from John W. Casey with Jon Boyd, *North American Aviation: The Rise and Fall of an Aerospace Giant*, Amethyst Moon Pub., March 2011.

Background on Ernst Udet:

• Sherman, Stephen, "Ernst Udet: German Ace," www.acepilots.com/ww1/ger_udet.html, updated April 15, 2012.

• O'Brien Browne, "Ernst Udet: The Rise and Fall of a German World War I Ace," *Aviation History*, November 1999.

Farm of 300 acres near San Diego: letter by James H. Kindelberger to G. B. A. Baker Reyant of the British Defense Ministry, regarding Mustang status items, October 28, 1941.

Biographical information on Donald Douglas and James McDonnell: www.boeing.com/history/pioneers.

Biographical information on Glenn L. Martin and the Glenn L. Martin Company: www.mdairmuseum.org/history-research.html.

Evolution of "design for production": Stan Smithson, *Skyline* magazine, Vol. 7, No. 1, February 1949.

Kindelberger's comments on auto companies building airplanes: "Dutch vs. Charlie," *New York Times*, August 14, 1942.

General Motors East Coast airplane factories: Robert L. Caleo, "From Autos to Aircraft: General Motors' WWII Conversion from Wildcats to Avengers," *Naval Aviation News*, July–August 1995.

Kindelberger's house, piloting skills, some of his quotations, and 1938 trip to Europe: Wesley Price, "Merchants of Speed," *Saturday Evening Post*, February 19, 1949.

Attributes of a good organization by Lee Atwood: "Procedures Manual" of NAA, July 1, 1943.

CHAPTER 3: WAR AT HAND

The story of William Knudsen: best told by Arthur Herman, *Freedom's Forge*, Random House, 2012.

The story of the massive B-24 project at Willow Run: best told by A. J. Baime, *The Arsenal of Democracy: FDR, Detroit, and an Epic Quest to Arm America*, Houghton Mifflin Harcourt, 2014.

Sharing of inventions, plus text of Kindelberger speech at Carnegie Institute, November 30, 1941: internal document "Brief History of North American Aviation, Inc. 1928–1944."

Corporate structure of NAA and links to General Motors:

• "Procedures Manual" of NAA, July 1, 1943.

• Security & Exchange Commission Form S-1, Common Stock Registration Statement, May 11, 1948.

Assistance from General Motors to NAA & construction of new plants at Dallas and Kansas City: report entitled "P-51 Construction and Production Analysis," prepared by Industrial Planning Section, Air Materiel Command, August 1945.

Staffing of new Dallas and Kansas City plants: weekly plant newspapers *North Ameri-Kansan* and *Takeoff*, May 12, 1941.

Kindelberger's statement after the Pearl Harbor attack: Dallas plant weekly newspaper *Takeoff*, December 11, 1941, p. 1.

Kindelberger's early wartime industry leadership role and industry challenges:

• NAA history prepared by Columbus Division, NAA, circa 1960.

• Correspondence between NAA and the Truman Commission dated 1943 regarding specific problems at the Dallas plant.

Alfred P. Sloan's description of Kindelberger: Alfred P. Sloan autobiography, *My Years with General Motors*, Doubleday 1963.

New airplane factory innovations and contracting issues: Irving Brinton Holley Jr., *Buying Aircraft: Materiel Procurement for the Army Air Forces*, Center for Military History, United States Army, 1989, pp. 30–31, 415.

Biographical information of Harold Raynor:

• *Skyline* magazine, August 17, 1951.

• Encyclopedia Astronautica website, www.astronautix.com.

Crewing *Whiskey Express*: wartime field reports of John "Jack" Fox, NAA field services representative.

"Component breakdown" method of production: *Skyline* magazine.

CHAPTER 4: TRAINERS AND TRAINING

Arrival at Dundalk, the start of the trainer project, and praise for the AT-6: NAA history prepared by Columbus Division, NAA, circa 1960.

Zap Flap: the patent-protected invention of the Zap Flap Development Corporation, Edward F. Zap (Zaparka), proprietor. Flaps are movable panels on the underside and rear of the wing. Zap's version was first tested in 1932.

Recollections of Dick Schleicher, NA-16 design attributes, and dinner meeting between Kindelberger and Arnold at Mayflower Hotel: oral histories gathered by the NAA retiree group "The Bald Eagles," 1960s through 1980s.

Elmer Bruhn (mentioned by Schleicher): Bruhn's *Analysis and Design of Flight Vehicle Structures* remains a highly regarded source within the stress-analysis field.

Working overtime off the clock: one version of this anecdote (from The Bald Eagles' oral histories) places this event late on a weekday evening (11:00 p.m.); however, plant manager Bob McCulloch stated it was on a Saturday.

Travels of Edmond T. "Eddie" Allen:

• H. C. Tafe memo, May 29, 1936: remitted a check in the amount of $500 to Eddie Allen at an address in New York City.

• H. C. Tafe memo, January 26, 1938: "Eddie Allen was in the other day. He said he was in Buenos Aires. . . ."

• Serious engine-cooling problems were encountered on the early B-29 flight-test program. Allen was the pilot in command of a Superfortress that suffered an in-flight fire over Seattle on February 18, 1943. All aboard, plus people on the ground, were killed in the resulting fiery crash.

Development and descriptions of the NAA trainers:

• Dan Hagedorn, *North American's T-6: A Definitive History of the World's Most Famous Trainer*, Specialty Pr., 2009.

• Peter C. Smith, *North American T-6: SNJ, Harvard and Wirraway*, The Crowood Pr., 2000.

Dundalk "gang" was a term of pride for the people who had migrated from Dundalk to Inglewood in November 1935. Periodic reunions and recognition dinners were held over the subsequent decades.

AT-6 Technical notes: USAF Museum, Hill AFB, Utah, www
.hill.af.mil/library/museum.

Pilot-training process: Jeff Skiles, "Bomber School," *EAA Sport
Aviation* magazine, June 2014.

Training pilot interview: face-to-face discussion followed by
multiple telephone calls with retired USAF Lt. Col. Bob Hutton
at his residence in Madison, Wisconsin, May–June, 2014.

Frank Priebe reference: Priebe was a family friend when the
author was growing up in Wisconsin. He died in the tragic
crash of a PBY amphibian at the Rhinelander, Wisconsin,
airport on October 15, 1970.

RAF instructor pilot observation: NAA document "Brief History of
North American Aviation, Inc. 1928–1945," quote for *New York
Sun* newspaper report.

Comments of Brig. Gen. George Stratemeyer: "Training Pilots and
Combat Crews," *Skyline* magazine, Vol. 3, No. 1, January 1942,
pp. 2–5.

Letters from Mr. Meadowbrook and Air Ministry Group Captain
Pirie and description of export fighter airplanes NA-50 (to
Peru) and NA-68 (to Thailand): official records of NAA.

Chuck Yeager reference: Chuck Yeager, *Yeager: An Autobiography*,
Bantam Books, 1985.

3716 Army Air Forces Base Unit (airplane mechanics' training
provided by NAA):

• Wartime brochure, Boeing Historical Archives.

• "The Army's Mechanics are Tops," *Skyline* magazine, Vol. 3,
No. 3, July 1942.

CHAPTER 5: B-25 MITCHELL MEDIUM BOMBER

Comments on the B-25C: Lt. Gen. Henry "Hap" Arnold quoted in
Skyline magazine, Vol. 3, No. 1, January 1942, p. 15.

History of the Martin B-10 and the NAA XB-21: National Museum
of the USAF, www.nationalmuseum.af.mil.

XB-21 lessons learned: John Casey with Jon Boyd, *North American
Aviation: The Rise and Fall of an Aerospace Giant*, Amethyst Moon
Pub., 2011.

History of the Douglas B-18 Bolo, B-23 Dragon, B-25 development,
and General Billy Mitchell: National Museum of the USAF,
www.national museum.af.mil.

Crash of NA-40: NAA company records, Kindelberger's written
report to the board of directors.

Kindelberger's bi-wing accident: "The Cats of MiG Alley," *Time*,
June 29, 1953, p. 84.

B-25 technical notes: National Museum of the USAF,
www.nationalmuseum.af.mil.

Ed Virgin's description of the B-25: Norm Avery, *B-25 Mitchell:
Magnificent Medium*, Phalanx Pr., 1993, p. 94.

Insignia history: Department of the Navy, Navy History &
Heritage, and other websites.

Bore sighting: aiming of fixed guns was accomplished by
sighting down the rifled bore to a fixed point and securing
the weapon to ensure the line of fire was along the centerline
of the airplane.

Rejecting of the A-26 for Pacific operations late in World War II:
General George C. Kenney, *General Kenney Reports: A Personal
History of the Pacific War, 2nd Ed. (USAF Warrior Studies)*, Office of
Air Force History, USAF, 1987, p. 532.

Renaming of Douglas A-26 to B-26: Warbird Alley,
www.warbirdally.com/a26.htm.

XB-28 Dragon information:

• Technical notes: National Museum of the USAF,
www.nationalmuseum.af.mil.

• NAA records.

Circular Error of Probability, bomb-damage assessments, and Law
of Armed Conflict: author's military experience augmented by
additional readings.

Norden bombsight quote: book review of *Double Agent* by Peter
Duffy; reviewed by Henrick Bering, *Wall Street Journal*, July 26,
2014, C7.

CHAPTER 6: STRIKE

History of NAA Inglewood 1941 strike: John H. Ohly, edited
by Clayton Laurie, *Industrialists in Olive Drab: The Emergency
Operation of Private Industries During World War II*, Center of
Military History, US Army, 1999, Chapter 2.

Biographical information on Charles E. Branshaw: official
USAF website.

History of National Labor Relations (Wagner) Act: National
Labor Relations Board, www.nlrb.gov/resources/
national-labor-relations-act.

US Army units mobilized to break the strike: *Los Angeles Times*,
June 1941.

Union perspective on the strike:

• www.nextnewdeal.net, Next New Deal—The Blog of the
Roosevelt Institute, David B. Woolner, "FDR's Championing
of Labor Unions Key to Prosperous Post-War Economy,"
July 22, 2011.

• Art Preis, *Labor's Giant Step*, Pathfinder Pr., 1964.

Friendship between Donald Douglas and Charles E. Branshaw:
Bill Yenne, *Hap Arnold: The General Who Invented the US Air Force*,
Regenery Pub., 2013.

Role of Henry "Hap" Arnold on P-51 procurement:

• *Skyline* magazine, Vol. 8, No. 4, November 1950.

- Paul A. Ludwig, *P-51 Mustang: Development of the Long-Range Escort Fighter*, Ian Allan Pub., 2003.

Strike consequences:

- Report: "P-51 Construction and Production Analysis," prepared by Industrial Planning Section, Air Materiel Command, August 1945, p. 90.

- NAA internal document "A Brief History of North American Aviation, Inc. 1928–1945"

Executive Order 8773: Appendix D: www.wikisource.org.

Notice to Accompany Executive Order 8773: Appendix E: transcribed from photographs of it being posted at the plant on June 9, 1941.

CHAPTER 7: WORKING ON THE SUNSHINE ASSEMBLY LINE

New employee sign-up process and NAA training steps: *Skyline* magazine, Vol. 3, No. 2, March 1942.

Women Airforce Service Pilots (WASPs): www.wingsacrossamerica.us/wasp.

List of company provided employee services: report "P-51 Construction and Production Analysis," Industrial Planning Section, Air Materiel Command, August 1945, p. 92.

Evacuating airplanes to Phoenix: oral history of NAA test pilot Robert Chilton, as well as working papers of Field Service Representative Jack Fox, who was dispatched to an intermediate stop, the small airport at Palm Springs.

Anti-aircraft fire on February 25, 1942: letters to the editor on the fiftieth anniversary of World War II, *South Bay Daily Breeze*, February 23, 1992.

Responsibilities of a stress engineer: interview with a practicing aircraft stress engineer.

CHAPTER 8: THE P-51 MUSTANG

Comparison of the P-51 to fighter aircraft of other nations: A. D. Harvey, "German Aircraft Design during the Third Reich," *Air Power History* magazine, Vol. 61, No. 2, Summer 2014, pp. 28–35.

NA-35 statistics: NAA records and www.avistar.org/air/usa/lok_vega35.php.

Sale of NA-35 design to Vega: minutes of the board of directors meeting of July 12, 1940, stating, "The President [Kindelberger] reported that because of the large amount of business on hand and in prospect, it is not advisable to pursue further the development and sale of the newly designed primary trainer, in view of which he has accepted an offer of $100,000 cash from the Vega Aircraft Company for this design."

Work and personal history of Edgar Schmued:

- Dallas plant newspaper *Takeoff* article about Schmued and Ken Bowen.

- Copyrighted but unpublished autobiography written by Schmued in 1985 found in NAA records.

XP-51 serial number 41-038: the number-four Mustang of the first British production batch and the first delivered to the Army Air Corps for evaluation in 1941. It was obtained by the Experimental Aircraft Association (EAA) in 1976 for restoration. It last flew in 1982 and is proudly preserved and displayed at their Oshkosh, Wisconsin, museum.

First flights of the NA-73 prototype: NAA internal document "Chronological Record of Events Related to the NA-73 airplane" to R. S. Johnson from E. V. Sedgwick, September 7, 1944. Source cited as Villepique.

Guggeheim nomination: letter from Kindelberger to Dr. Alexander Klemin, Secretary, The Daniel Guggenheim Medal Board. Award recipients during that era were:

- 1939: Donald W. Douglas, transport airplanes

- 1940: Glenn L. Martin, high-performance fighter airplanes

- 1941: Juan T. Trippe, oceanic air transport

- 1942: James H. Doolittle, notable achievement

Design of P-51, attributes of P-51F & P-51G, and certain improvements: Edgar Schmued, unpublished paper dated 1985, "Design of the P-51 Mustang."

Role of Maj. Gen. Oliver Echols in opposing the P-51: Paul A. Ludwig, *P-51 Mustang: Development of the Long-Range Escort Fighter*, Ian Allan Pub., 2003, p. 70.

Muir Fairchild letter dated 8/31/42: ibid, p. 75.

Role of Benjamin Kelsey: letter dated July 28, 1981, from Lee Atwood to *Air Force* magazine related to the design history of the P-51.

Telegram from Materiel Command dated July 5, 1943 and following internal memo dated August 25, 1943: P-51 correspondence files in NAA records. The chronology is undated and not credited.

Raid on Regensburg and Schweinfurt of August 17, 1943: Bill Yenne, *Hap Arnold: The General Who Invented the US Air Force*, Regenery Pub., 2013.

Most aerodynamically perfect pursuit plane in existence: Security & Exchange Commission Form S-1, Common Stock Registration Statement, May 11, 1948.

P-51 technical notes: National Museum of the USAF, www.nationalmuseum.af.mil.

Production cost comparison: report: "P-51 Construction and Production Analysis," prepared by Industrial Planning Section, Air Materiel Command, August 1945.

P-51 enhancements (Rolls-Royce Merlin engine): *Skyline*, September–October 1944.

History of the Packard Motor Car Company: History Channel, www.history.com/this-day-in-history/last-packard-produced.

Arrival of Mustangs at Iwo Jima: *Skywriter*, May 4, 1945.

CHAPTER 9: B-25 ON STEROIDS: THE SHORT LIFE OF NA-98X

Overview of the crash: Norm Avery, *B-25 Mitchell: Magnificent Medium*, Phalanx Pr., 1993, p. 62.

Virgin's lament about the Wright R-2600 engine: handwritten letter from Ed Virgin to Norm Avery, November 1, 1976.

Design attributes of NA-98X: www.joebauger.com.

Official Army accident investigation reports with Perry J. Ritchie as the pilot in command:

- P-39M at Bell in New York
- XAT-13 at Wright Field, Ohio
- P-47C at Greenville, Ohio
- B-25H at Inglewood, California

Roach Lake: Peter W. Merlin and Tony Moore, *X-Plane Crashes*, Specialty Pr., 2009, pp. 20–23. Relates an incident at Roach Lake during the visit by the Wright Field team to the Northrop flying wing (N-9M) project. They state that on April 19, 1944, the army pilots were quarreling about who would fly the airplane. Maj. Perry J. Ritchie settled the dispute by climbing into the airplane and taking off. He failed to lower the landing gear and bellied-in the airplane upon landing, walked away, and then returned to defiantly lower the landing gear handle. The airplane was repaired.

Biographical information on Ritchie:

- Dayton, Ohio, newspaper stories, April 1944.
- Genealogic research into the Ritchie family tree using census records of 1920 and 1930 plus military enlistment records.

Death certificates of Wey and Ritchie: Los Angeles County public records.

National Advisory Committee for Aeronautics (NACA) Wartime Report L5G31: Ralph P. Beilat, Langley Field, "A Simple Method for Estimating Terminal Velocity Including Compressibility on Drag", August 1945 (p. 11 mentions Ritchie by name).

Type of mission, dates, durations, and persons aboard NA-98X: Official flight log of aircraft 43-4406.

Travel and instrumentation brought from Wright Field by Lt. Wey: a copy of Wey's travel orders was part of the official accident report. He was authorized travel by military air and the order provided for excess baggage consisting of a 75-pound parcel.

Travel arrangements for Ritchie, Warburton, and Ritland: a copy of their shared travel order was part of the accident investigation report. Each was endorsed "By Order of Major General Branshaw," which was likely a boilerplate on all orders issued by his headquarters.

Maximum gross takeoff weight for NA-98X: article by Norm Avery, *NAA Retirees Bulletin*, Summer 2001, p. 5. The article also stated, "Although [Ritchie] was emphatically cautioned by NAA structures engineers and company test pilots, he chose to ignore their warnings to stay within red-line parameters."

Organization of Materiel Command: Irving Brinton Holley Jr., *Buying Aircraft: Materiel Procurement for the Army Air Forces*, Center for Military History, United States Army, 1989.

List of commanders of Materiel Command: Lawrence R. Benson, "Acquisition Management in the US Air Forces and Its Predecessors," Air Force History and Museum Program, 1997, p. 51.

Various letters from Ed Virgin dated 1975–1976 and discussing a variety of issues: Norm Avery was first hired at NAA in 1940 as a draftsman on the B-25 program. He was at the plant the night of April 24, 1944, and army soldiers guarding the crash site allowed him entrance. Avery devoted the remainder of his life to documenting the history of NAA and its products. The letter from Virgin is handwritten and it is difficult to discern if the term is "rock it around" or "nock it around like a fighter." Either phrasing yields the same meaning.

Letter from Lee Atwood, October 8, 1988: letters from Virgin, Atwood, and others are found in Norm Avery's working papers related to the B-25 program.

Wey family history: provided by telephone interview with his surviving nephew, March 24, 2012.

Ritchie at college: Cincinnati University yearbook, 1939.

History of Branshaw as commander of Materiel Command: Irving Brinton Holley Jr., *Buying Aircraft: Materiel Procurement for the Army Air Forces*, Center for Military History, United States Army, 1989, p. 509.

The death of Ed Virgin at age 96 in 2002: reported in *NAA Retirees Bulletin*, Summer 2002.

CHAPTER 10: EISENHOWER'S B-25

Two important members of Eisenhower's inner circle wrote books about their experiences with him and there is considerable overlap in the events recounted (to include hitching a ride with the soldier driving a jeep):

- Laurence J. Hansen, *What It Was Like Flying for "Ike"*, Aero-Medical Consultants, 1983.
- Kay Summersby, *Eisenhower Was My Boss*, Prentice-Hall, 1948.

Description of factory modifications: a letter dated September 16, 1982, from Donald H. Kennedy was found in the working papers of NAA historian Norm Avery. There was also a photocopy of a magazine article written by Kennedy regarding details of the conversion of 43-4030, but without source or date.

Shootdown of Admiral Yamamoto's airplane: Donald Holloway, "Death by P-38," *Aviation History* magazine, May 2013.

Delivery flight routing from Inglewood to England: US Air Force Historical Research Agency, Maxwell AFB, Alabama.

Location of European wartime airfields: www.skylighters.org/ETOfields.

Story of Eisenhower's trip in a P-51: *Skywriter* weekly newspaper, August 1, 1947, p. 1 (Elwood Quesada was visiting Inglewood and making a presentation).

Comments of retired USAF Lt. Col. Howard L. Naslund: typed letter dated August 31, 1977, from Naslund to Norm Avery in response to a magazine article authored by Avery.

Assignment history of 43-4030 from February 1944 to February 1959: email from US Air Force Historical Research Archive, Maxwell AFB, Alabama, dated April 16, 2014. No entries are dated between May 1944 and January 1947, during which time it was assigned to the European Theater of Operations.

Options to restore B-25J serial number 43-4030: there is correspondence in the working papers of Avery suggesting that consideration was being given to altering it from a transport into a combat configuration. Avery stated that the nose was custom-built and unique. He successfully argued for its "as is" preservation.

History of 43-4030 at Planes of Fame Museum, Chino Airport, and arrival at Ellsworth AFB, South Dakota: John W. Thomas, "Ike's Own Bird," *Aerospace Historian* magazine, Vol. 30, No. 2, June 1983, pp. 128–130.

Caption to accompany photo of Eisenhower with the B-25: Kathy Struss of the Dwight D. Eisenhower Presidential Library & Museum, Abilene, Kansas. Email to the author dated January 14, 2014.

Cancellation of FAA registration: Federal Aviation Agency, registry.faa.gov/aircraftinquiry.

Final note: The story of Eisenhower's B-25 appeared in *Air Force* magazine, December 2014. It was condensed from this chapter.

CHAPTER 11: TRANSITION TO COLD WAR

P-82 history: NAA records and National Museum of the USAF, www.nationalmuseum.af.mil.

Expectations of postwar aircraft projects at Dallas and Kansas City NAA plants: various reports, articles, and news items in plant weekly newspapers.

Strength of Army Air Forces on January 4, 1944: a large file of 3x5 cards found in NAA records with events organized by date from 1925 to 1960.

January 1945 production figures: *Skywriter*, February 7, 1945, p. 1.

Production cutbacks: *Skywriter*, June 1, 1945, p. 1.

Contract Cancellations: *Skywriter*, August 20, 1945, p. 1.

Messerschmitt Project 1101:

- Three-view drawing: NAA records.

- Narrative: Luft46 website: www.luft46.com/mess/mep1101.html.

Backlog of orders and layoffs at the end of the war: Security and Exchange Commission Form S-1, Common Stock Registration Statement, May 11, 1948.

Shutdown of the Fairfax Plant: John Fredrickson and John Roper, *Kansas City B-25 Factory*, Arcadia Pub., 2014, Ch. 9.

Design history of the P-51: report: "P-51 Construction and Production Analysis," prepared by Industrial Planning Section, Air Materiel Command, August 1945.

Postwar diversification strategies—consumer goods and Kindelberger quotes: Wesley Price, "Merchants of Speed," *Saturday Evening Post*, February 19, 1949. The quote in *Saturday Evening Post* was "There is nothing I like better than being up to my tail in business." Given Kindelberger's reputation for salty language, it is likely he actually used the term "ass."

B-25 rework project:

- "Modified B-25 Pushed as Trainer," *Aviation Week*, March 27, 1950.

- Number of available airframes was found in NAA internal documents.

Kindelberger's health problems starting in 1947: the 1998 interview with Lee Atwood was found on the NAA history website provided by their retired employee group.

George Schairer's visit to Germany: Harold Mansfield, *Vision: A Saga of the Sky*, Madison Pub. Associates, 1986, pp. 258–261.

Technical Notes P-82, L-17, and B-45: National Museum of the USAF, www.nationalmuseum.af.mil.

Role of F-51s during the Korean War:

- "One Year of Aerial Combat in Korea," *Skyline* magazine, Vol. 9, No. 4, November 1951.

- Multiple interviews (phone and face-to-face) with USAF Lt. Col. Robert Hutton, Ret., June 2014.

- USS *Boxer* transporting Mustangs: Robert F. Futrell, *The USAF in Korea 1950–1953*, Duell, Sloan and Pearce, 1961.

- Writings of Edgar Schmued dated 1985 described the air-to-ground role of the F-51 in Korea as a "suicide mission" because of the cooling system's vulnerability to ground fire.

- Other: David R. McLaren, *Mustangs over Korea*, Schiffer Pub., 1999.

NAA view of the Korean War: NAA history prepared by Columbus Division, NAA, circa 1960.

SOURCES

Avery, Norm L. *B-25 Mitchell: The Magnificent Medium*. St. Paul, MN: Phalanx Pub., 1992.

———. Working papers as housed at Boeing Historical Archives.

Baime, A. J. *The Arsenal of Democracy: FDR, Detroit, and an Epic Quest to Arm America*. New York: Houghton Mifflin Harcourt, 2014.

Busha, James P. *The Fight in the Clouds: The Extraordinary Combat Experience of P-51 Mustang Pilots During World War II*. Minneapolis, MN: Zenith Press, 2014.

Casey, John W. and Jon Boyd. *North American Aviation: The Rise and Fall of an Aerospace Giant*. Tucson, AZ: Amethyst Moon Pub., 2011.

Fletcher, Eugene. *The Lucky Bastard Club: A B-17 Pilot in Training and in Combat, 1943–1945*. Seattle, WA: Univ. of Washington Pr., 1988.

Futrell, Robert Frank. *The United States Air Force in Korea, 1950–1953*. New York: Duell, Sloan and Pearce, 1961.

Graham, Jim (descendant of James Howard Kindelberger). Email and telephone interviews, November 2014.

Hagedorn, Dan. *North American's T-6: A Definitive History of the World's Most Famous Trainer*. North Branch, MN: Specialty Pr., 2009.

Hanson, Laurence J. *What It Was Like Flying for "Ike"*. Largo, FL: Aero-Medical Consultants, 1983.

Herman, Arthur. *Freedom's Forge: How American Business Produced Victory in World War II*. New York: Random House, 2012.

Holley, Irving Brinton, Jr. *Buying Aircraft: Materiel Procurement for the Army Air Forces*. Washington, DC: US Army Center for Military History, 1989.

Hutton, Robert "Bob". In-person and telephone interviews, May–June 2014.

Kenny, General George Churchill. *General Kenney Reports: A Personal History of the Pacific War, 2nd Ed. (USAF Warrior Studies)*. Washington, DC: Office of Air Force History, USAF, 1987.

Ludwig, Paul A. *P-51 Mustang: Development of the Long-Range Escort Fighter*. London: Ian Allan Pub., 2003.

Macias, Richard. "We All Had a Cause: Kansas City's Bomber Plant, 1940–1945," *Kansas History* magazine. Topeka, KS: Winter 2005–2006.

Mansfield, Harold. *Vision: A Saga of the Sky*. New York: Madison Pub. Associates, 1986.

McLaren, David R. *Mustangs over Korea: The North American F-51 at War, 1950-1953*. Atglen, PA: Schiffer Pub., 1999.

Merlin, Peter W., and Tony Moore. *X-plane Crashes*. North Branch, MN: Specialty Pr., 2008.

Murray, Russ. *Biography: J. H. Kindelberger*. Inglewood, CA: North American Rockwell Management Assoc., 1972.

North American Aviation Inc. Official records as housed at Boeing Historical Archives.

Ohly, John H. and Clayton D. Laurie, ed. *Industrialists in Olive Drab: The Emergency Operations of Private Industries During World War II*. Washington, DC: US Army Center for Military History, 1999.

O'Leary, Michael. *Building the P-51 Mustang: The Story of Manufacturing North American's Legendary World War II Fighter in Original Photos*. North Branch, MN: Specialty Pr., 2010.

Smith, Peter C. *North American T-6: SNJ, Harvard and Wirraway*. Marlborough, UK: The Crowood Pr., 2000.

Summersby, Kay, *Eisenhower Was My Boss*. New York: Prentice-Hall, 1948.

Yeager, Chuck. *Yeager: An Autobiography*. New York: Bantam Books, 1985.

Yenne, Bill. *Hap Arnold: The General Who Invented the US Air Force*. Washington, DC: Regenery Pub., 2013)

INDEX

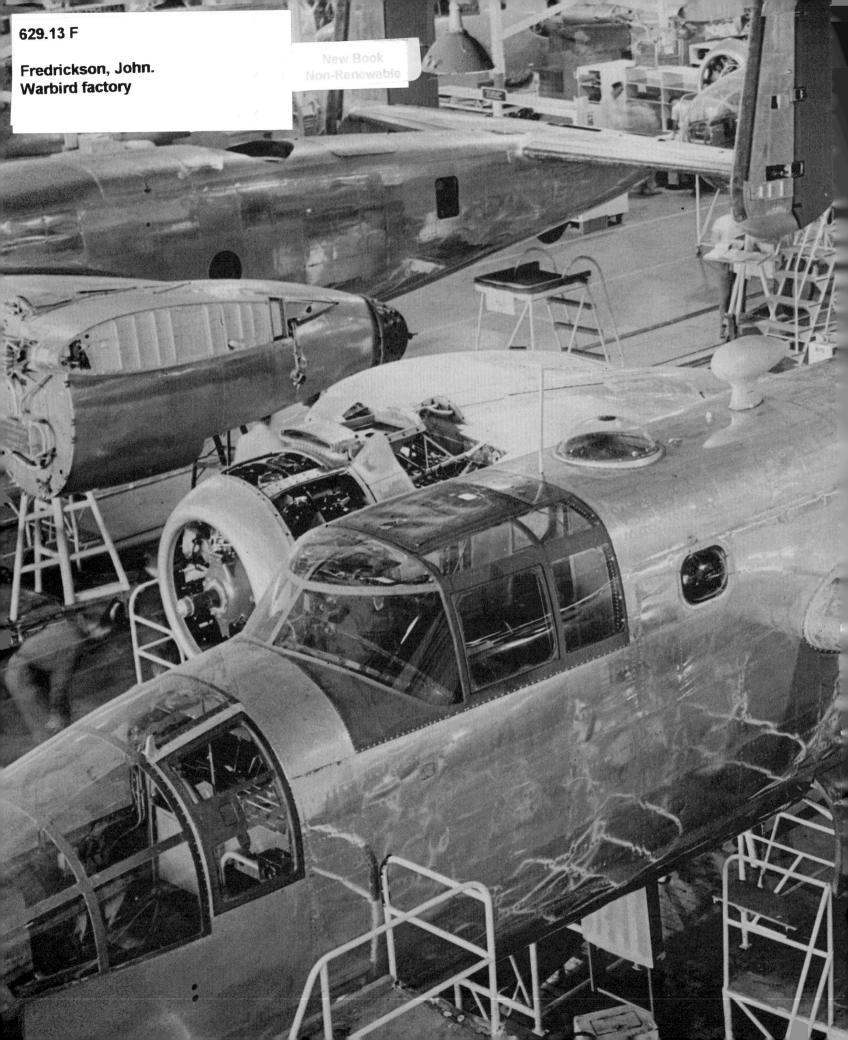